W9-BWR-082

ISRAEL'S PROPHETS

An Introduction for Christians and Jews

by

David J. Zucker

PAULIST PRESS
New York / Mahwah, N.J.

ACKNOWLEDGMENTS

The Publisher gratefully acknowledges use of the following material: excerpts from the four volumes of the *Interpreter's Dictionary of the Bible*, 4 Volumes and Supplement, Tennessee: Abingdon Press, copyright renewal © 1990 by Abingdon Press; *Interpreter's Dictionary of the Bible*, Supplementary Volume, copyright © 1976 by Abingdon.

The Scripture quotations contained herein are from the New Revised Standard Version of the Bible, copyrighted, 1989 by the Division of Christian Education of the National Council of the Churches of Christ in the United States of America. All rights reserved.

Copyright © 1994 by David J. Zucker

All rights reserved. No part of this book may be reproduced or transmitted in any form or by any means, electronic or mechanical, including photocopying, recording or by any information storage and retrieval system without permission in writing from the Publisher.

Library of Congress Cataloging-in-Publication Data

Zucker, David J., 1942–
    Israel's prophets : an introduction / by David J. Zucker.
      p. cm.
    Includes bibliographical references.
    ISBN 0-8091-3494-2 (paper)
    1. Bible. O.T. Prophets (Nevi'im)—Criticism, interpretation, etc. 2. Prophets. 3. Prophets in rabbinical literature. 4. Midrash—History and criticism. 5. Prophets in the New Testament. 6. Bible. N.T.—Criticism, interpretation, etc. I. Title.
BS1286.Z83   1994
224'.061—dc20   94-10626
                                                                CIP

Published by Paulist Press
997 Macarthur Boulevard
Mahwah, New Jersey 07430

Printed and bound in the
United States of America

CONTENTS

To Donna with love and joy,
and to our children Jeremy Daniel,
Joshua Seth, and Ian Michael
with joy and love

Acknowledgments

Thanks are due to some wonderful people who helped to bring about this book. To Hyman Lotven of Springfield, Missouri. Hyman in his own special way served as friend, mentor, confidant, and a man of unlimited wisdom and insight. Hyman is the Amos of the Springfield Jewish community. Darlene Keith, also of Springfield, a truly committed Christian, a Southern Baptist, a woman whose heart is as large as her spirit, who taught me about her love for Christianity, Judaism and dialogue. She is a true woman of faithfulness. Rev. Dr. Jack Hart, Emeritus Senior Minister, First and Calvary Presbyterian Church, Springfield, and professor at McCormick Theological Seminary, Chicago. Jack is a good friend. He read this manuscript in an earlier form, and his voice of encouragement and excitement sped this work on to publication. Thanks to Ann B. Christensen, of Aurora, Colorado, a good friend and neighbor who is studying for the ministry at the Iliff School of Theology, Denver. Ann carefully and closely proofread the (almost) final text and made many valuable suggestions. Finally, grateful thanks to Marvin R. Wilson, Professor of Biblical and Theological Studies at Gordon College, who read through the text, offered perceptive insights, and also agreed to write the Foreword for this book.

ABBREVIATIONS

The following abbreviations are used in this work.

Jewish Scriptures, Hebrew Bible

Gen	Genesis
Ex	Exodus
Lev	Leviticus
Num	Numbers
Deut	Deuteronomy
Jos	Joshua
Jgs	Judges
Sam	Samuel
Kgs	Kings
Is	Isaiah
Jer	Jeremiah
Ez	Ezekiel
Hos	Hosea
Jl	Joel
Am	Amos
Ob	Obadiah
Jon	Jonah
Mic	Micah
Nah	Nahum
Hab	Habakkuk
Zeph	Zephaniah
Hag	Haggai
Zech	Zechariah
Mal	Malachi
Ps	Psalms
Prov	Proverbs
Job	Job
Song	Song of Songs
Ruth	Ruth
Lam	Lamentations
Eccl	Ecclesiastes
Est	Esther
Dan	Daniel
Ezr	Ezra
Neh	Nehemiah
Chr	Chronicles

Christian Scriptures, Christian Bible

Mt	Matthew
Mk	Mark
Lk	Luke
Jn	John
Acts	Acts of the Apostles
Rom	Romans
Cor	Corinthians
Gal	Galatians
Eph	Ephesians
Phil	Philippians
Col	Colossians
Thes	Thessalonians
Tim	Timothy
Tit	Titus
Phlm	Philemon
Heb	Hebrews
Jas	James
Pet	Peter
Rev	Revelation

Other abbreviations

BCE	Before the Common Era
CE	Common Era
c.	circa (about)
cf.	confer (compare)
EJ	Encyclopedia Judaica
H	Hebrew
IB	Interpreter's Bible
IDB	Interpreter's Dictionary of the Bible
IDBS	Interpreter's Dictionary of the Bible Supplement
OT	Old Testament
NT	New Testament
NEB	New English Bible
NIV	New International Version
NRSV	New Revised Standard Version
R	Rabbi
RSV	Revised Standard Version
TANAKH	Torah-Nevi'im-Ketuvim (the New Jewish Publication Society translation of the Jewish Scriptures)

INTRODUCTION

The Hebrew prophets were the true moral and religious leaders of their generation. They were men and women imbued with God's spirit. By today's standards some were sophisticated statesmen who interacted with the power-brokers of their day. Others were more formal religious leaders whose voice was heard, even when their message was one of chastisement. Still others reflected their origins in the countryside, and their message was striking with its pastoral imagery.

The Hebrew Bible contains fifteen books which are formally designated as the writings of the prophets. They begin with the three longest books: Isaiah, Jeremiah and Ezekiel. These are then followed by Hosea, Joel, Amos, Obadiah, Jonah, Micah, Nahum, Habakkuk, Zephaniah, Haggai, Zechariah and Malachi. This last dozen are often designated as the "twelve minor prophets." *Minor* in this case means that their books are shorter in length, not that they are less important in what they have to say.

These prophets, and by extension their messages, have been described as ranging from the relatively primitive to the relatively sophisticated, from the highly visionary to the concretely ethical, from the seemingly objective perspective to the intensely participatory.

The Bible uses several terms for prophet, and we are not entirely sure how people in biblical times understood the distinction between these words, nor are there clear-cut differences in the function of the *ro'eh*, the *hozeh*, and the *navi*. Furthermore, there is a suggestion in the Bible itself that even then there was some confusion as to the proper use of the terms. Consider a line from the book of Samuel, situated some three thousand years ago, about 1050 Before the Common Era (BCE). There we read (in 1 Samuel 9:9):

1

> Formerly in Israel, anyone who went to inquire of God would say, "Come let us go to the seer" [ro'eh]; for the one who is now called a prophet [navi] was formerly called a seer [ro'eh].

Yet apparently the variant terms continued in use, for in the book of Chronicles there is the memorable line (1 Chron 29:29), "... the records of the seer [ro'eh] Samuel, and in the records of the prophet [navi] Nathan, and in the records of the seer [hozeh] Gad..."

The classic period of the prophets was for about two centuries, roughly 750–550 BCE. This preceded the fall of the northern kingdom (722/721) and followed the fall of the southern (586). Among the names who prophesied in this period are Amos, Hosea, Micah, Isaiah, Jeremiah and Ezekiel.

The prophets were powerful leaders in their day. They were men and women who were understood by their contemporaries to speak the voice of God — they were filled with the divine spirit.

The prophets spoke to their contemporaries, but in the traditions of Judaism and Christianity (and Islam) they also spoke to those who followed them as well.

In the years following the end of the period of the Hebrew Bible, about 250–200 BCE, Judaism continued to develop. Rabbinic or Talmudic Judaism was one part of that ongoing history. The early years of the first century of the Common Era (CE) brought about another development, the rise of the Christian Church. Christianity grew out of the soil of Judaism, and its earliest leaders were Jews. Jesus of Nazareth was born, lived, and died a Jew. Jesus was schooled in Judaism and the teachings of the prophets as he indicates time and again in his speeches and parables.

As Marvin R. Wilson reminds us, "Both Jesus and the apostles granted full authority and inspiration to the Old Testament writings (Mt 5:17–18; Jn 10:35; 2 Tim. 3:14–17; 2 Pet 1:20–21). Only one document was normative for them; they lived their lives 'according to the Scripture.' ... The Old Testament was the primary source used for teaching" (*Our Father Abraham: Jewish Roots of the Christian Faith*, 112). For Christianity, the Hebrew Bible pointed the way to the figure of Jesus-as-Messiah. In a similar fashion, the rabbis of the Talmudic period quoted the prophets (and other parts of the Hebrew Bible) to support their vision of the world. At times both the rabbis and the early Church quoted the same verses but saw different messages.

This book is intended to accomplish several goals. First and foremost it is an introduction to the lives, writings and literary style of the Hebrew prophets. Throughout the book there are suggested biblical readings indicated by italic type [*Suggested reading*]. Yet in addition, it is structured to consciously address a need for both Jews and non-Jews to study the prophets in such a way as to see how these sacred texts were understood by the religious leaders of the early centuries of the Common Era. In the case of Jewish writers this means primarily the midrashic literature of the Talmud, and various collections of midrash. All of the midrashim (plural of midrash) appear in English translation. Technically some of these collections were edited after several hundred years into the Common Era, but they may well reflect earlier traditions. Very broadly, the various collections follow a similar range of interpretive thought. In the case of the Christian writers, a conscious effort was made to focus on the Christian Scriptures themselves.

The translations used for this book come from *The New Revised Standard Version* (NRSV) of the *New Oxford Annotated Bible* (New York: Oxford University Press, 1991). This Bible was chosen because it presents both a modern translation and inclusive, gender-neutral language whenever possible. On occasion reference will be made to differences in versification as reflected in the Masoretic tradition of the Hebrew Scriptures. The NRSV translation will then be followed by the Hebrew tradition in brackets and marked with an "H" for Hebrew (for example: Mal 4:6 [3:24 H]). Aside from the differences in inclusive language, on some occasions there will be notable variations in the rendering into English between the NRSV and the newest standard Jewish translation. In those cases, the discrepancy will be noted and the Jewish translation will follow the *TANAKH: THE HOLY SCRIPTURES* published by the Jewish Publication Society (Philadelphia, 1985).

I have also tried to formulate my writing in gender-neutral language. If, for example, Israel is referred to as an erring "wife" either I have sought to present this image as an erring "spouse," or at least I have drawn attention to the fact that the concern of the prophet is "faithlessness," not specifically *female* faithlessness. God is above and beyond sexuality and "... while, admittedly, ... God is often described in masculine-acting terms with masculine pronouns, feminine imagery is also used in the Bible" to describe God and God's relationship with the people of Israel. (See Brenda Forster, "The Biblical 'Omen and Evidence for the Nurturance of Children by Hebrew Males," 321 ff.)

A few words on the order of these chapters. I begin with a description of the prophets in their various roles (Chapter 1: What Is a Prophet?). Then (in Chapter 2: The Former Prophets) I consider six of the most important of the early prophets: Samuel, Nathan, Ahijah, Elijah, Micaiah ben Imlah, and Elisha. Chapter 3 (The Latter Prophets) is an overview of the messages of the Classical or Literary Prophets: Isaiah, Jeremiah,

Ezekiel, and the Twelve (Hosea, Joel, Amos, Obadiah, Jonah . . .). The prophet known as First Isaiah, the author of Isaiah 1–39, is considered in Chapter 4. This is followed immediately by Chapters 5 and 6, devoted to Jeremiah and Ezekiel respectively. So far this has followed both a general historical order and the order in which the prophets appear in the Bible. The author(s) known as Second and Third Isaiah whose words and prophecies are found in Isaiah 40–66 flourished in the sixth century BCE, sometime after Ezekiel. These prophecies have been received as part of the book of Isaiah so I placed my explanation of their work after Ezekiel (Chapter 7: Second and Third Isaiah).

The twelve minor prophets are presented in their own historical order as I understand it. This means that they are not presented in the traditional literary order as found in either the Jewish or Christian Bibles. Chapter 8 features Amos, Hosea, and Micah; Chapter 9 deals with Zephaniah, Nahum, Habakkuk and Obadiah; the prophecies of Haggai, First Zechariah (chapters 1–8) and Malachi comprise Chapter 10; and Chapter 11 is devoted to the prophecies of Joel and Second and Third Zechariah (chapters 9–14). Finally I conclude with Chapter 12: Jonah. This prophet is a great personal favorite, and in my mind his story is in a class by itself.

A Glossary and Bibliography are found at the conclusion of this volume.

Judaism and Christianity have a great deal to learn from and to teach one another. Indeed, Judaism, Christianity and Islam have a great deal to learn from and to teach one another. A book contrasting all three traditions and their views of Scripture, and more specifically the prophets, would be in order, but it is not the task of this present volume.

As I have written elsewhere in this book, "To properly read, study and most importantly to understand the prophets of the past, we have to be aware of *their* mind-set and how *they* thought and understood events in *their* own time." We begin with the past, and as we study together, we build bridges for understanding that will strengthen our own lives as we work for a time that the knowledge of the Lord will cover the earth, as the waters cover the sea.

THE HEBREW PROPHETS:
SEEKING A PROPER PERSPECTIVE

Some of the most difficult problems facing serious students of the Hebrew prophets is how to place those ancient orators within proper perspectives. That there are several "perspectives" is abundantly clear. Who were these men and women? What was their relation to society? Are the words we have received their actual words that they spoke, or are these edited versions of their best "sermons"? How did they see themselves, and how were they seen? How did they understand themselves and how were they understood? If they were so clearly and unambiguously speaking "the word of the Lord" why were they frequently ignored, or at least not taken more seriously? Is there not a very good chance that hundreds of years after the fact *we* are guilty of indulging in a blanket condemnation of ancient Israel, confusing those who were the limited few (the actual objects of the prophets' denunciations) with the many innocent who were also a part of that society?

It is easy to read a Zephaniah or a Joel or Jeremiah or Hosea and to assume that the whole of their world was riddled with corruption. This surely would be a misreading of the text and a misrepresentation of the facts. In our own society there are leaders in business, academia, politics and religion whose morality is nearly non-existent: They exploit the helpless, cheat the poor, and are liars and swindlers. Yet in our day, surely they are the exceptions, not the rule. The issue for the prophets was "not that Israel *was unjust*, but that [some in] Israel *had acted* unjustly" (Samuel Sandmel, *The Enjoyment of Scripture*, 240). Furthermore we need to bear in mind that our present-day theology is radically different from that of the Hebrew prophets. We have been influenced by the events and thinkers of the intervening years. We are a product of our times as

5

they were of theirs. They saw God's hand directly at work in history. The threat of an Assyrian invasion was not only a real event for the eighth century BCE prophet Micah, it was but an extension of God's role in history. War, political alliances, economic hardships: these were not human-made events based on economic motives or national territorial interests. Pestilence, drought and famine: these were not "merely" the result of the natural world; all of them were expressions of the divine will. In addition we should bear in mind that the prophets were speaking to a *contemporary audience* that readily understood their allusions and references. The prophets fully expected that God's role in shaping history would be realized in the near future, perhaps a decade of years if not even earlier. If they thought in much longer periods of time, as occasionally did an Isaiah, Jeremiah or Ezekiel, they would specifically make mention of it (Is 7:8; 23:15; Jer 25:11–12; Ez 4:4–6). Punishment, and latterly repentance and salvation, were *near* events, not events set hundreds of years, much less thousands of years in the future. This is particularly difficult to appreciate for a Christian reader (explains Leslie C. Allen in *The Books of Joel, Obadiah, Jonah and Micah*, 291–292), for "Christianity with its center of gravity pushed forward into a posthistorical day of reckoning has tended to pay less attention to this belief" (that God worked so directly — and swiftly — in history).

Brevard S. Childs, Professor of Old Testament at the Yale Divinity School, has commented that the "early church was not able to hear the Old Testament on its own terms, but increasingly the canonical text was subjected to the dominance of ecclesiastical tradition." He goes on to suggest that the "'plain sense' of the Old Testament text was drowned out by traditional interpretation which assumed that the New Testament had superseded the Old" (*Introduction to the Old Testament as Scripture*, 42).

Our task is to study these men and women so filled with God's spirit. We want to learn what they said, and the circumstances in which they prophesied. Only then do we want to see how they were understood in a secondary sense in the Christian Scriptures and the midrashim of the rabbis.

To properly read, study and most importantly to understand the prophets of the past, we have to be aware of *their* mind-set and how *they* thought and understood events in *their* own time.

Chapter 1

WHAT IS A PROPHET?

1. Opening Remarks

There is so much to be said, so much to be learned. The question is where to begin. The prophet is the spokesperson of God. As Samuel Sandmel wrote, a prophet was "someone deemed close to the Deity," a person who through some form of special knowledge or revelation was "able to predict" what would be (*The Hebrew Scriptures*, 48). The prophet's role is to comment on life, to chastise, moralize, advise, speak of the present and of the future. Abraham Joshua Heschel in his momentous work, *The Prophets*, described the message and witness of the prophets. "The prophet's eye is directed to the contemporary scene; the society and its conduct are the main theme of his speeches. Yet his ear is inclined to God" (1.21). The phrase "Thus says the Lord" is the hallmark of the prophet. Yet the prophet is much more than the person who conveys God's message. Again Heschel provides an important insight for us when he notes that the "prophet is not a mouthpiece, but a person; not an instrument, but a partner, an associate of God" (1.25).

Without doubt a central problem is the distance in time between our present day and the period of the prophets of Israel. They lived within a given context and held a worldview, a time and thought very different from this time. In addition, students of the past recognize that the period under question covers many years and varying circumstances. How do we recognize that while these men and women were individuals in their own right, they were also part of a larger society and a wider pattern? Furthermore, given the fact that in some cases the Bible presents a great deal of their statements, such as with Isaiah, Jeremiah and Ezekiel, and in some cases very little actual "prophecy," as with Nathan, Elisha, and Jonah, how can one know these prophets? In addition, we need to consider the value of the material. Is it all equal or are some speeches or prophecies more important than others? Do generalizations about a period tell us about individual personalities? Alternately, by focusing only on the individual, can the wider context be seen? Among the men and women labeled prophets in the Bible are Moses, Miriam, Micaiah, and Malachi, Hosea, Hananiah, Hulda, Habakkuk, and Haggai. Their lives vary from major leaders to obscure voices. Most of the ancient prophets were men, but certainly not all. Reference is also made to women prophets or to women prophesying (Ex 15:20; Jgs 4:4ff; Is 8:3; Ez 13:17; Neh 6:14), and notable among them Hulda (2 Kgs 22:14; 2 Chr 34:22). We have her prophecy recorded, but we do not know a great deal more about her.

The lives of the prophets as we shall see span a time period of eight or nine hundred years, even if the major voices fall into a period of about two hundred years.

Let us begin with an example. To highlight the fact that our subject covers a wide period of time with diverse personalities, some more important than others, consider this analogy:

Imagine studying the history of the United States with a focus on the United States presidency. To contrast past and present, three periods could be considered. First, the first four presidents: George Washington, John Adams, Thomas Jefferson, and James Madison. They presided from 1789–1817, some twenty-eight years. Next one might consider the sixteenth through nineteenth presidents: Abraham Lincoln, Andrew Johnson, Ulysses S. Grant, and Rutherford B. Hayes. They presided twenty years from 1861–1881. Finally consider the last four presidents, or roughly speaking the past twenty-five years. What differences we see in personalities, in their political world, and most of all in the power that is at their fingertips! Some were great leaders, others more mediocre. In some administrations there were events of major consequence, in others considerably less happened. One can generalize about these three periods and those dozen or so individuals, or we could focus on specific personalities. To get a fair picture of the history of the United States and the role of the presidency, I submit we would need to present some broad strokes and likewise to consider some aspects or personalities in greater detail. A similar methodology will be used to discuss prophecy in ancient Israel.

2. Some Terms and Terms of Reference

A. *BCE and CE*

When referring to the passage of time, more and more people are now using the terminology "Before the Common Era" (BCE) and "Common Era" (CE) where in previous generations people used the more restrictive and exclusionary terms "Before Christ" (BC) and "Anno Domini" (AD — literally "In the year of our Lord"). While there are millions of Christians worldwide, the clear majority of humankind on this planet are non-Christians: Muslims, Indian religions, Buddhists, Jews, Shintoists, Daoists [Taoists], Zoroastrians, nature-worshipers and the like. The terms "Christ" — messiah or savior — and "In the year of our Lord" are certainly appropriate for Christians, but the more neutral and inclusive terms coming to popularity now referring *to exactly the same periods* are Before the Common Era (BCE) in place of Before Christ, and Common Era (CE) in place of Anno Domini (AD). Thus 150 BCE is the same period of time as 150 BC, and 1999 or 2005 CE is exactly the same point as 1999 or 2005 AD.

B. Hebrew Scriptures, "Old Testament," TANAKH

When Christians pick up a standard Bible they understand that it has two parts, what is frequently called the Old Testament, and then, beginning with the gospels, the New Testament. For Christians, "Old" and "New" are more than merely synonyms for "former" and "latter." There are values associated to the terms Old and New Testaments. Broadly speaking Christians understand the "Old Testament" to be God's original words to the Jews, and then the "New Testament" to be the new promise, an updated covenant, a revised contract. Old and New therefore take on a "value." For Jews the Jewish Bible, or, as it is frequently called in scholarly circles, the Hebrew Scriptures (as opposed to the Christian Scriptures), continues to be the ongoing covenant with God. Jews recognize that for Christians there is another, additional Scripture. Jews understand that Christians regard their later Scriptures as holy, and as a record of God's continuing relationship. Jews appreciate that for Christians the Christian Scriptures (the New Testament) is God's new promise, but Jews continue to believe that for Jews the original contract is still in place. This in fact is recognized in the Christian Scriptures in Romans 9:2ff and 11:1ff, where it is clear that God's covenant with the Jewish people is unbroken.

The terms Hebrew Scriptures, Jewish Scriptures, and Jewish Bible are all synonyms. The term Hebrew Bible is also a synonym, but probably would refer to a Bible written in Hebrew.

The Hebrew Scriptures are often referred to as the TANAKH. TANAKH is an acronym; the letters T, N, and Kh [K] refer to words (just as, for example, the acronym NASA refers to the National Aeronautics and Space Administration). The three words are Torah (Teaching), Nevi'im (Prophets) and Ketuvim (Writings). The order of the books of the Hebrew Scriptures (TANAKH) is different from that of a Protestant or Roman Catholic Bible.

C. A Comparison of Canons

The canon or canonized version of the Bible is the officially recognized text by the specific religion. The Jewish canon was fixed between the years 90–100 CE.

THE BOOKS OF THE HEBREW SCRIPTURES
(THE TANAKH)

Torah (Pentateuch) "Teaching" (sometimes translated as the "Law")

1. Genesis   (*Bereshit*) "When [God] began to [create]"/
                              "In the beginning"
2. Exodus   (*Shmot*)   "[These are] the names"
3. Leviticus   (*Vayikra*)   "[The Lord] called"
4. Numbers   (*Bamidbar*) "...in the wilderness [of Sinai]"
5. Deuteronomy (*Devarim*)   "[These are] the words"

Nevi'im "Prophets"

"The Former Prophets"
6. Joshua
7. Judges
8. 1, 2 Samuel   (8, 9)
9. 1, 2 Kings   (10, 11)

"The Latter Prophets"
10. Isaiah   (12)
11. Jeremiah   (13)
12. Ezekiel   (14)
13. The Twelve
    Hosea   (15)
    Joel   (16)
    Amos   (17)
    Obadiah   (18)
    Jonah   (19)
    Micah   (20)
    Nahum   (21)
    Habakkuk   (22)
    Zephaniah   (23)
    Haggai   (24)
    Zechariah   (25)
    Malachi   (26)

Ketuvim "Writings"

14. Psalms   (27)
15. Proverbs   (28)
16. Job   (29)
17. Song of Solomon
    [Song of Songs]   (30)
18. Ruth   (31)
19. Lamentations   (32)
20. Ecclesiastes   (33)
21. Esther   (34)
22. Daniel   (35)
23. Ezra–Nehemiah   (36, 37)
24. 1, 2 Chronicles   (38, 39)

Protestant Canon	*Roman Catholic and Orthodox Canon*
(Pentateuch)	(Pentateuch)
1. Genesis	1. Genesis
2. Exodus	2. Exodus
3. Leviticus	3. Leviticus
4. Numbers	4. Numbers
5. Deuteronomy	5. Deuteronomy
(Historical Books)	(Historical Books)
6. Joshua	6. Joshua
7. Judges	7. Judges
8. Ruth	8. Ruth
9–10. 1, 2 Samuel	9–10. 1, 2 Samuel
11–12. 1, 2 Kings	11–12. 1, 2 Kings
13–14. 1, 2 Chronicles	13–14. 1, 2 Chronicles
15. Ezra	15. Ezra
16. Nehemiah	16. Nehemiah
	17. Tobit*
	18. Judith*
17. Esther	19. Esther**
	20–21. 1, 2 Maccabees*
(Poetical and Wisdom Books)	(Poetical and Wisdom Books)
18. Job	22. Job
19. Psalms	23. Psalms

20. Proverbs
21. Ecclesiastes
22. Song of Solomon

24. Proverbs
25. Ecclesiastes
26. Song of Songs
(Song of Solomon)
27. Wisdom of Solomon*
28. Ecclesiasticus
(Wisdom of Ben Sirach)*

(Prophetic Books)

(Prophetic Books)

23. Isaiah
24. Jeremiah
25. Lamentations

26. Ezekiel
27. Daniel
28. Hosea
29. Joel
30. Amos
31. Obadiah
32. Jonah
33. Micah
34. Nahum
35. Habakkuk
36. Zephaniah
37. Haggai
38. Zechariah
39. Malachi

29. Isaiah
30. Jeremiah
31. Lamentations
32. Baruch#
33. Ezekiel
34. Daniel**
35. Hosea
36. Joel
37. Amos
38. Obadiah
39. Jonah
40. Micah
41. Nahum
42. Habakkuk
43. Zephaniah
44. Haggai
45. Zechariah
46. Malachi

* Deuterocanonical (Apocryphal) book — canonical in Roman Catholic and Orthodox canons.

**Book includes materials in the Roman Catholic and Orthodox canons which are featured in the Protestant Apocrypha as additions to Esther and additions to Daniel (The Prayer of Azariah and The Song of the Three Jews, the Story of Bel and the Dragon and the Story of Susanna).

Book canonical (Deuterocanon) in Roman Catholic canon only.

In the Roman Catholic canon, Ezra and Nehemiah are sometimes labeled as 1, 2 Esdras.

The Prayer of Manasseh, a book found in the Apocrypha, is not included in the Roman Catholic canon, but is considered Deuterocanonical by the Eastern Orthodox community.

D. Variant Terms

In different works dealing with the prophets, writers will use variant terms when referring to the same material. The terms Hebrew prophet or Israelite prophet are synonyms. Likewise, the term "former" prophets is the same as the pre-literary or pre-classical prophets. The "latter" prophets are the same people as the literary or classical prophets. The term "literary" means here that these books are listed by the prophet's name, i.e. Isaiah, Jeremiah . . . Malachi.

E. The Christian Scriptures

Though there will be regular references to Christian Scriptures (the New Testament) and its understanding of Hebrew prophecy, our primary purpose is to see the Hebrew prophets *in their own context* and to study their meaning *as they intended it*, not as reinterpreted through later religious leaders. Nonetheless, some brief remarks about the use of the word "prophet" in the Christian Scriptures will be helpful.

The term "prophet" appears in the Christian Scriptures in different contexts. One is where reference is made to those prophets of the Hebrew Scriptures such as in Matthew 8:17 where there is specific mention of "Isaiah the prophet" (see also Mt 12:17; Mk 7:6; Lk 4:17ff; Jn 12:38ff). Another context is where Jesus or others are referred to as prophets or people speak prophecy. Predominantly this is in the books of Matthew, Luke, and Acts. In answer to the question "Who is this?" in Matthew 21:11, the crowds answer "This is the prophet Jesus from Nazareth in Galilee" (see Mt 13:57; Mk 8:28; Lk 7:16, 39, etc.). In the fourth gospel John refers to Jesus as "the prophet," and it is a virtual synonym for the term messiah (Jn 1:21; 6:14; 7:40). In the Christian Scriptures, John the Baptist is called a prophet (Mt 11:7ff), and Judas and Silas are also called prophets in Acts (15:32). Furthermore, the author of 1 Corinthians suggests that speaking prophecy has great value for the community (see 1 Cor 14: 1, 5, 39).

> The NT prophet is in essential function like that of the OT: he conveys to them who will believe the divinely imparted meaning of history (cf. Acts 21:10). (B. D. Napier, "Prophets, Prophetism," in *Interpreter's Dictionary of the Bible* [henceforth *IDB*], 896)

The Christian Church, broadly speaking, understands the predictive prophecies of the Jewish Bible not as complete in themselves, but as the word of God's promise, as a hope which will be fulfilled through Jesus. Bruce M. Metzger addressed this in one of his introductions to the Christian Scriptures: "All four evangelists quote Old Testament prophecies which they regard as fulfilled in the person and work of Jesus, but Matthew includes . . . additional such prophetic proof-texts. . . . Matthew's emphasis upon Old Testament prophecies is designed to show that the mission of Jesus was neither haphazard nor capricious, but as part of a well-ordered and divinely pre-arranged whole" (*The New Testament*, 90).

Our concern will be otherwise, to see the prophets *as they were*, not as "signs of longing for the future and predictions of things to come . . . as God's word of promise . . . [in] Jesus Christ" (A. N. Ramsey, "The Authority of the Bible," in *Peake's Commentary on the Bible*, 2).

In his book *A Guide to the Prophets*, Stephen Winward remarks that there are those who study the prophetical books as a manual for divining the future. The fact is, however, that the "prophets were primarily concerned with the declaration of the word of God to their contemporaries, and not with the prediction of future events" which would take place hundreds, much less thousands, of years after them (27). The prophets were concerned with future salvation, but it was in terms of the ancient tradition. The prophets' sense of "the future" will be dealt with later in this chapter (Section 7.C).

F. Midrash

Whenever the Bible was not explicit or specific, the early interpreters of the post-biblical world (i.e. the rabbinic period, and their successors as well) sought to provide new insights as to what might be meant in a given context. Consequently there developed alongside the Bible a supplement, an additional way to understand what God desired of humankind. The generic term for this exegesis or interpretation is "midrash" (plural: "midrashim"). The Hebrew for sermon, "*derasha*," is based on the word "midrash." Through midrash "a Scriptural passage yielded far more than could be discerned on the surface. The sacred words became an inexhaustible mine . . . of religious and ethical teaching" (A. Cohen, *Everyman's Talmud*, xviii). As the Babylonian Talmud, *Sanhedrin* 34a suggests, "one biblical statement may carry many meanings." Tales and allegories, ethical reflections, epigrams and legends, all were different ways in which midrash might be expressed. In this book "midrash" is understood as a *generic* term for midrash/aggadah. For a more detailed description of midrash and its relationship to aggadah, see the article by Joseph Heinemann in the Bibliography.

Midrash was always clearly linked to the biblical text. As Gary G. Porton has clearly noted:

> Midrash is "a type of literature, oral or written, which has its starting point in a fixed, canonical text, considered the revealed word of God by the Midrashist and his audience, and in which this original verse is explicitly cited or clearly alluded to." ... For something to be considered Midrash it must have a clear relationship to the accepted canonical text of Revelation. Midrash is a term given to a Jewish activity which finds its locus in the religious life of the Jewish community. While others exegete their revelatory canons and while Jews exegete other texts, only Jews who explicitly tie their comments to the Bible engage in Midrash (55).

3. Three Words for Prophet

The most common term used for the word prophet in the Bible is *navi* (Nun-Bet-Aleph) (sometimes *nabi*) and the plural is *nevi'im* (*nebi'im*). It is found in many books and applied to a broad range of people, from Genesis (referring to Abraham — Gen 20:7) to the book of Malachi (referring to Elijah — Mal 4:5 [3:23 H]).

> [The term prophet refers] to surprisingly disparate personalities from an Aaron (Exod. 7:1) to an Elijah (I Kings 17–19; 21), from the "true" to the "false" (e.g. 1 Kings 22), from the relatively primitive (e.g. I Sam. 10), to the relatively sophisticated (the Isaiahs, e.g.), from the highly visionary (see Ezek 1–2) to the concretely ethical (Amos; or Nathan in II Sam. 12; or Elijah in 1 Kings 21), from the seemingly objective perspective (of an Amos, e.g.) to the intensely participatory attitude (of a Jeremiah) (Napier, 896).

While "navi" is the most common term and used over three hundred times in various contexts, there are two other words which are also found in the Hebrew Scriptures, the words *ro'eh* (Resh-Aleph-Hey) and *hozeh* (Het-Zayin-Hey). Both of these terms have been translated as the word "seer," that is one who *sees* into the future or who possesses some sense of clairvoyance. To differentiate between the two, a felicitous translation suggested by Samuel Sandmel may help. While the *ro'eh* is a "seer," the *hozeh* might in some instances be translated as "gazer" (*The Hebrew Scriptures*, 49).

The Bible poses more problems than answers when it uses these terms. We really are not entirely sure how people in biblical times understood the distinction between these words, nor are there clear-cut differences in the function of the *ro'eh*, and the *hozeh*, and the *navi*. Furthermore, there is a suggestion in the Bible itself that even then there was some confusion as to the proper use of the terms. Consider a line from the book of Samuel, situated some three thousand years ago, about 1050 BCE. There we read (in 1 Samuel 9:9):

> Formerly in Israel, anyone who went to inquire of God would say "Come let us go to the seer" [*ro'eh*]; for the one who is now called a prophet [*navi*] was formerly called a seer [*ro'eh*].

The simple sense of this comment is that the term *ro'eh* is no longer in use; the seer now is called a *navi*. Yet turning to Isaiah (30:10) who lived about three hundred years after Samuel (c. 750 BCE) we read:

> ... who say to the seers [*ro'im*], "Do not see" [*lo tir'u*]; and to the prophets [*hozim*], "Do not prophesy [*lo tehezu*] to us what is right; speak to us smooth things, prophesy [*hazu*] illusions. ...

In this passage, following Sandmel, the term *hozim* could read "gazer" and therefore be translated "to the gazers, do not use your clairvoyance for truth ... use clairvoyance for illusions."

Clearly at the time of Isaiah, in the eighth century, the terms *ro'eh* and *hozeh* are still in use, as is *navi* which is found frequently in the book (see 37:2; 38:1).

Indeed the ongoing use of the terms is attested to in the book of Chronicles where in a memorable line all three are used (1 Chr 29:29), "... the records of the seer [*ro'eh*] Samuel, and in the records of the prophet [*navi*] Nathan, and the records of the gazer [or seer — *hozeh*] Gad" [my translation].

"Since the term *hozeh* (and not *ro'eh* or *navi*) is found when reference is made to a king (*hozeh ha-melekh*), it most probably indicates that the seers who bore this title were officially attached to the court, the so-called prophets" (Shalom M. Paul, "Prophets and Prophecy," *Encyclopedia Judaica*, 1155).

For all these references to seer or gazer, those actual terms are in a great minority when compared to the more popular term *navi*. Together *hozeh* and *ro'eh* appear in one form or another less than thirty times, less than one-tenth of the times *navi* appears. Further, *neither the term ro'eh nor hozeh appears before the book of Samuel!*

Perhaps the clearest demonstration of the *ro'eh* in action is the narrative where Saul meets Samuel in 1 Samuel 9–10. Here Samuel, among other roles, is featured as a clairvoyant. Indeed Samuel identifies himself as a seer (*ro'eh*) in 9:19.

The term *navi* as a designation for prophet comes into its own in the monarchical period, and its earlier usage is somewhat suspect. It is so infrequent prior to the middle eleventh century BCE that the references probably reflect a later editor's hand suggesting that Abraham, Moses, Aaron, Miriam, and Deborah acted as *spokespersons* for God, and in this way demonstrated *navi*-like behavior. James Newsome notes, "However, it is clear that both 'seer' and 'prophet' (or similar terms) were used in the ancient Near East at a very early date, and thus there is no fundamental reason why the words should be denied to Abraham, Moses and Aaron" (*The Hebrew Prophets*, 5 n. 3). Newsome's argument notwithstanding, there is another reason why the term *navi* probably is anachronistic when applied before the eleventh century.

The term *navi*, or its use as a verb, is found with more frequency in the book of Samuel. It is used not as a mark of honor, however, but in a much more pejorative way, as a word to dismiss someone's wildly erratic or more likely ecstatic behavior.

In 1 Samuel 10:5ff, Saul is told by Samuel that he is going to meet a band of prophets (*hevel nevi'im*) and that they will be prophesying (*mitnab'im*). Saul does meet them and he does prophesy. On that occasion and later in 1 Samuel 19:23f he appears to be in a trance and people come to make fun of him using the phrase "Is Saul also among the prophets [*nevi'im*]?" The clear sense is: "Is Saul associated with those strangely acting people?" In time, perhaps over a period of two hundred years, the word *navi* would become an honorable one, but it was not always so.

The fact that *navi* is used so sparingly before the period of the monarchy, and comes into its own in the period of the classical prophets (c. 750–550 BCE), is a compelling argument. Arguments from silence are no less real for their absences — the term *navi* simply was not used before a certain time (see Napier, 905).

4. A Prophetic Succession

A. *From Moses to Elijah to Isaiah*

That the term *navi* takes on popular usage fairly late in the history of Israel does not mean to suggest that the great prophets of the classical period were without predecessors or precedent. A strong case can be made that there is a continuous line of prophetic-like activity that reaches from Moses, through Elijah, into the period of Isaiah, his contemporaries and successors.

Early on in this chapter I suggested that the prophet is the spokesperson of God, and that the prophetic role is to comment on life, to chastise, moralize, advise, to address the present and future. In broad perspective, Moses fulfills all of these roles. Indeed the very "prophetic" phrase "Thus says the Lord" can be found on his lips in the book of Exodus, but Moses' *primary* function is to lead the people, to guide them, to mold them into a nation, to *teach* them what it means to be in covenant with God. It is not by accident that in Jewish tradition Moses is known as *Moshe Rabbenu*, "Moses our Teacher."

To revere Moses as teacher is to recognize that this was indeed his primary function. Moses is the dominant human figure of the *Torah*, which should properly be translated as "Instruction" or "Teaching," and not as Law, for "Law" lacks the dynamics and vitality of the words "instruction" or "teaching." How then does one square the view of Moses-as-teacher with the claim in the Torah that Moses was in fact a *prophet*? This problem is relatively easy to solve. The key sentence is found in the closing words of Deuteronomy:

> Never since has there arisen a prophet [*navi*] in Israel like Moses, whom the Lord knew face to face. He was unequaled for all the signs and wonders that the Lord sent him to perform … against Pharaoh and … in the sight of all Israel (Deut 34:10–12).

The book of Deuteronomy, many scholars tell us, was probably written in the seventh century, well into the period of the classical prophets (this idea shall be discussed further, below). Moses in the Torah is portrayed as a participator. He speaks with God face to face (Num 12:7–8); Moses has seen God on Mount Sinai, and this is unique. "In the Deuteronomic perspective, Moses is the model, the ideal, prophet" (Napier, 906). Yet nowhere, *not once* in the Torah is there the phrase "Moses the prophet," as one finds frequently the phrase Isaiah (ben Amotz) the prophet, Jeremiah the prophet, Haggai the prophet, and the like.

Moses acts prophet-like. "Prophetism is to confront man with God-in-history — it is timelessly the bringing of Israel, always now, up from Egypt into existence under God!" (Napier, 906). It is in this sense that one can say that Moses is a prophet.

We can explain the term prophet in association with Aaron, Miriam, Deborah, and earlier with Abraham in the same way. These all were special leaders who had a unique relationship with God in the minds of the ancients. Yet the label prophet really is anachronistic when applied to them. To suggest an analogy, the president of the United States in the period following the Second World War has become a figure of worldwide importance. Some have been more statesman-like, of greater stature than others. Yet to read that power into the past would likewise be anachronistic. George Washington, Thomas Jefferson, Abraham Lincoln, and other presidents in the past were great leaders — *in our country* — but they were not "world statesmen" of "international stature."

There is a linkage from Moses to Elijah to Isaiah, but unlike the monarchs of Judah and Israel there is neither a direct blood line nor a series of dynasties. These early prophets will arise in the eleventh, tenth, and ninth centuries. Prominent among them will be the names Samuel, Nathan, and Ahijah in the eleventh/tenth century. These leaders in turn, will be an influence on their successors the classical prophets, but this shall be considered in greater detail below.

B. Former Prophets and Latter Prophets

As explained earlier, the Jewish Bible (the Hebrew Scriptures) is divided into three sections: *Torah* (Teaching), *Nevi'im* (Prophets), and *Ketuvim* (Writings). Within the section *Nevi'im* there is a further subdivision into *Nevi'im Rishonim* (earlier or former prophets), and *Nevi'im Akharonim* (later or latter prophets). Since this division is somewhat different from Protestant and Roman Catholic Bibles, it bears repeating.

The books of the former prophets cover the period from c. 1200–c. 550 BCE, from Joshua to the captivity in Babylonia. In order they are Joshua, Judges, 1 and 2 Samuel and 1 and 2 Kings. The books of the latter prophets cover from the mid-eighth century, and move down to the fourth or third centuries BCE.

Not only does the period of the former and the latter prophets overlap, there is an overlapping of time within the books of the latter prophets themselves. The latter prophets constitute the major books of Isaiah, Jeremiah, and Ezekiel, plus the minor or smaller books of Hosea, Joel, Amos, Obadiah, Jonah, Micah, Nahum, Habakkuk, Zephaniah, Haggai, Zachariah, and Malachi.

Some points should be highlighted. First, though in traditional Christian writings Daniel and Lamentations are considered part of the books of prophecy, they are not part of the Hebrew canon's *Nevi'im*.

Second, in a Protestant Bible Joshua and Judges are followed by *Ruth*, and then by Samuel and Kings, which in turn are followed by Chronicles, Ezra and Nehemiah, Esther, Job, Psalms, Proverbs, Ecclesiastes, Song of Solomon, and finally *Isaiah*. Likewise Jeremiah is followed by *Lamentations* and then Ezekiel and *Daniel*, until one finally gets to the twelve minor prophets. The twelve are in the same order in both canons. The order in a Roman Catholic Bible is essentially the same, though there are the additions of books which in Judaism and in the Protestant tradition are considered as part of the Apocrypha (see above, Section 2.C — A Comparison of Canons).

C. Writers, Orators, and Biographers

Earlier we mentioned that the latter prophets are also known as the literary prophets. They are called literary because these books bear their names. "The phrase is misleading, however, if it conveys the impression that the great prophets were literary figures. They were preachers, not writers; heralds of God, not authors of books. They declared the word of God to individuals who came to enquire of them, or to whom they themselves were sent. Most of their messages, however, were delivered to the public" (Winward, 23).

In time they were set down as written words. Stephen Winward suggests four stages of transmission from the oral to the written word.

In some cases "*the prophets themselves* put some of their messages into writing — whether by the manual act of writing, or by dictating to a scribe. Isaiah, Jeremiah, Ezekiel, and Habakkuk are all said to have done this (Isaiah 8:16; 30:8; Jeremiah 30:2; 36:4 Ezekiel 43:11; Habakkuk 2:2)" (Winward, 25). Amos may have recorded his own visions, since they appear in the first person (Am 7:1-9).

A second possibility was where *disciples* of the prophets set down their words. Isaiah was accompanied by a band of disciples, and in his book, as in Jeremiah, we find biographical stories told about the prophet or by him (Is 6-7).

Collectors of the prophetic words set down an orally transmitted tradition in later years. They arranged their collections according to chronology or topic. Consequently what might be thought to be a continuous flow of thought may really be a series of related incidents.

Finally, "the redactors and editors who followed the collectors, added dates and additional historical material, reinterpreted some oracles to fit the changed conditions of their own time, and included later messages of consolation and hope to counterbalance the earlier words of judgment and doom. They helped to make a collection of collections into a unified whole — to give it the form of a book" (Winward, 26).

5. An Historical Overview

The Hebrew prophets were real men and women living within a specific place and time. It is necessary to see the context of their prophecy to understand the content of the words. Furthermore the prophets were very conscious not only of time and place, but also of history. They knew their past and saw the past as converging into the present, just as the present would merge into the future.

In terms of Hebrew prophecy, there are three discernible phases: the early history which provided the antecedents for the former prophets, the period of these early *Nevi'im*, and then the great days of the latter prophets.

A. Antecedents c. 1750–1050 BCE

The first seven hundred years of biblical "history" directly relevant to our study spans the time from Abraham to the end of the period of the judges. Abraham receives his "call" while living in Mesopotamia, not far from the Persian Gulf. Go forth from your land, the place of your birth, to a place where I shall show you, says God. I will give you descendants numerous as grains of sand on the shore, as stars in the skies. The Abraham clan, his children and grandchildren, settle in the new land. A hundred and fifty years pass. There are adventures and misadventures, intrigues and exiles, but by the period of the fourth generation leading into the fifth, the Abraham clan, now known as the Jacobsons or the Israelsons, have been forced to relocate temporarily to Egypt to the south. It is about 1600 +/– BCE.

For a long while the Jacobson-Israelson clan prospers, but eventually difficulties arise. According to Exodus 1:8 "Now a new king arose over Egypt who did not know Joseph," the scion of the family. In short order their fortunes falter and fail and their former successes are forgotten. Then they are enslaved by the Egyptians. The period of bondage is not short. Literally dozens, perhaps hundreds of years pass. Finally a leader arises who is called by God, selected to lead the people from servitude to serving God.

Moses had been reared in the Egyptian court, but had spent many of his adult years in the deserts of Midian in the area of Sinai/Horeb.

After triumph and tragedy, Moses, aided by his brother Aaron and sister Miriam, leads the people from Egypt. The Egyptian experience, perhaps some four hundred years in "exile" from the land, would impress itself on the minds of the people and even more so on the minds of the prophets. Egypt and the physical exodus both would become powerful symbols in Jewish history.

For forty years the people were in transition. Most of those years they were stationed at Kadesh Barnea in the Sinai Peninsula, but then finally Moses is told that the time is ready for a new stage of development. He will take them to the land, but he himself, though he will see it from afar, will not enter.

For a number of years there is a unified effort to conquer and settle the land. This takes place under the leadership of Moses' successor, Joshua. Then for about a hundred and fifty years c. 1200–1050 (or perhaps 1020) BCE there is the age of the judges. This is a time of periodic conflict, a cycle of allegiance to God, followed by failure to follow the covenant, idolatry, punishment, and a return to allegiance to God and God's demands. This chaotic time features charismatic figures, the judges. They assume leadership, but neither is their guidance and authority well organized nor is it ongoing. The final verse in the book of Judges sums up the period: "In those days there was no king in Israel; all the people did what was right in their own eyes" (Jgs 21:25).

B. The Former Prophets c. 1200–750 BCE

The last of the judges, Samuel, was truly "a man for all seasons." He was one of the pivotal characters of the eleventh century, figuratively a mover and shaker, and literally a king-maker and king-breaker. Samuel was a judge, a priest, a prophet, a seer, a politician, and an advisor to monarchs.

Samuel was to appoint both Saul and David as rulers of the new state. The Davidic dynasty was to last for eighteen generations, reaching from the eleventh to the sixth centuries, but there would be strong kings and weak, blasphemers and godly rulers alike. The unified monarchy solidified by David would not succeed past his son Solomon, for David's grandson Rehoboam was far from an able ruler. Under Jeroboam the northern kingdom seceded, and in the two hundred years from 920–721 Israel would be ruled by nine different families. The most famous was the Omride dynasty of Omri-Ahab-Ahaziah which lasted about four decades, c. 882–842 BCE, and it was during this period that, among others, Elijah and Micaiah prophesied.

A hundred years would pass before the period of the first classical prophet, Amos, but the memory of Elijah as a leader who would stand up to authority was strong and no doubt influenced Amos.

While internal political developments concerned the prophets, they were likewise aware of the wider geopolitical configurations of their day. This is even more true of the latter prophets, but the former prophets were cognizant of the rise and fall of nations and empires.

The early period of the former prophets, c. 1200–750 +/– BCE, coincides generally with a decline in the traditional great empires of the ancient Near East: Egypt, Babylon, and the Hittites. Aside from an Assyrian raid about 1100 BCE there is relative quiet for about three hundred years, time enough to allow, in our context, the rise of first the united and then the divided kingdoms. During this time Syria (sometimes called the Arameans) also becomes a local power, as do the Phoenicians in Tyre and Sidon in present-day Lebanon. Hiram of Tyre was an ally of David and Solomon and provided materials — at a steep price — for the temple. Later a Tyrian king would marry his daughter Jezebel to King Ahab of Israel (c. 875 BCE).

Toward the middle of the early period of the former prophets, c. 900 BCE, Assyria, which was located inland along the northwestern end of the Tigris west of Babylon (modern northwest Iraq), assumed a role of military might. For over a hundred years beginning about 885 BCE with Ashurnisirapal the Assyrian rulers had a conscious foreign policy of featuring torture, mutilation, and massacre of their conquered enemies as part of their military tactics. The Assyrians boasted of this fact in their inscriptions and reliefs (C.E. Van Sickle, *A Political and Cultural History of the Ancient World*, 126). Theirs was a foreign policy of "calculated frightfulness." Though Ahab in the ninth century joined a coalition to head off an Assyrian invasion, it was only a matter of time before the end would come. Under Tiglath Pileser III (746–727 BCE) and Sargon II (722–705 BCE) Assyria ruled the whole area without a great deal of effective opposition. The states in Syria-Palestine, including Israel and Judah, paid tribute to Assyria, and when Israel tried to participate in a revolt she was crushed, and in 721 BCE the northern kingdom simply ceased to be.

C. The Latter Prophets c. 800–250 BCE

The golden years of the classical prophets are c. 750–550 BCE. These were tumultuous years: foreign alliances and intrigue, invasion from the Assyrians and Egyptians, defense and defeat. The years include the fall of the northern kingdom Israel and the isolation of the southern kingdom Judah, and its eventual defeat by the newest world empire, Neo-Babylonia.

These two hundred years, c. 750–550 BCE, meant the loss and assimilation of the ten northern tribes, and the end of the Hebrew monarchy. It was the time of the destruction of the first temple and the Babylonian exile. It is against this background that Amos, Hosea, Isaiah, Micah and later Jeremiah, Ezekiel and latterly Second Isaiah as well as others would preach and prophesy.

The period begins with the politically and morally corrupt northern kingdom still intact, and therefore the object of the prophecy of Amos. As noted, however, it was soon to fall. In Judah, King Hezekiah (716–687 BCE) worked hard to restore the pure worship of God. He tore down the idols and altars to foreign gods set up by his father King Ahaz. Hezekiah was aided in his struggle by the prophet Isaiah ben Amotz, even if Hezekiah did not always follow Isaiah's advice about foreign affairs.

Though Hezekiah strove toward reforms, his son and successor Manasseh, in a long forty-five year reign (687–642 BCE), was a terrible disappointment. He was among the most immoral of Judah's rulers. During the reign of Hezekiah's great-grandson Josiah (640–609 BCE) there would be major changes both internally in Judah and externally in the ancient Near East.

The Assyrian empire was under siege. Egypt threw off Assyrian domination, and the Scythians from southeastern Europe, a horde of barbarians, swept through Mesopotamia, along the Mediterranean coast and toward Egypt. The prophet Zephaniah (c. 630–625 BCE) saw this as the end of days. The whole first chapter and the opening verses of the second are filled with fear.

> The great day of the Lord is near, near and hastening fast, a day of wrath, a day of distress and anguish, a day of ruin and devastation, a day of darkness and gloom, a day of clouds and thick darkness, a day of trumpet blast and battle cry ... (Zeph 1:14–16).

(By way of literary contrast, consider the equally powerful description found in *TANAKH*, the Jewish Publication Society translation of this same passage:)

> Approaching most swiftly, hark the day of the Lord! ...
> A day of trouble and distress, a day of calamity and desolation
> A day of darkness and deep gloom, a day of densest clouds,
> A day of horn blasts and alarms. ...

In this period there is the call to prophecy of Jeremiah, but that event is overshadowed by the "discovery" of the "Scroll of the Teaching" (*Sefer ha-Torah*). This is not the occasion to discuss it at length, but the description in 2 Kings 22–23 makes clear that this was a major event in the king's life, and subsequently in the life of Judah. This Scroll of the Teaching is Deuteronomy, and it is validated by the female prophet Huldah (2 Kgs 22:14ff). This "find" leads to a further reform. As the Jewish historian Simon Dubnov observed, undoubtedly Jeremiah took a part in proclaiming and promoting the book that so vividly expressed his own ideas (*History of the Jews*, Vol. 1, 285).

The beloved King Josiah dies in battle at Megiddo in 609 BCE in a vain attempt to halt the northward march of Egypt's Pharaoh Neco II. His successor would be subject to Egyptian vassalage. Meantime, though Assyria had fallen to Neo-Babylonia, relief was not to come. Caught between the two competing empires for a period of twenty years, the rulers of Judah tried first one and then an opposing policy with equal disaster. An initial invasion by the Babylonian ruler Nebuchadnezzar in 597 BCE forced the deposing of King Jehoiachin and his exile along with many of the aristocrats and intellectuals. Ten years later, despite an heroic revolt, Judah finally fell and the temple was destroyed in 586 BCE. The Babylonian exile was to begin.

This period of demoralization, dejection, and devastation physically, mentally, emotionally, and spiritually was addressed by the prophetic words of Ezekiel and Second Isaiah. This is not the end, they promised. God has further purpose for you.

The Babylonian exile — as a forced exile — lasted for many years. Eventually, Babylon was overthrown by Cyrus the Persian, and those who wished to return to the land were allowed to do so.

The next three hundred years, from c. 538–c. 238 BCE, would see the restoration of the temple, though not the monarchy. It was the time of the Persian period, and latterly Hellenism under Alexander the Great and his successors. In these years one finds the prophecies of Obadiah, Haggai, Zechariah, Malachi, Joel, Second and Third Zechariah, and Jonah.

6. Parallel Prophecy in Cognate Cultures

Though the moral message and godly concerns of the prophets were a unique phenomenon in a limited period of Hebrew history, there did exist in the ancient Near East some kind of parallel prophetic figures.

There are Egyptian priests who have a primary role as interpreting the word of the deity, and one finds examples of prediction of future events, though in the latter case they are not understood as divine revelation. There were also "prophets" at Mari which is located in modern Syria.

Likewise in Anatolia in Turkey in the fourteenth century BCE there are "inspired speakers" who seem to act in a prophetic manner. Even more familiar are the references to the prophets (nevi'im) of Baal and of Asherah which are mentioned in the famous Elijah episode on Mount Carmel. Since these foreign prophets are designated as nevi'im, one can assume that for the Israelites of that day they were seen to be efficacious prophets. Certainly Elijah's reproach to the people (1 Kgs 18:21), "How long will you go limping with two different opinions? If the Lord is God, follow him; but if Baal, then follow him," would be utterly meaningless if the people did not credit the Baal prophets and the Asherah prophets as "real" and "efficacious" speakers of a divine message. If the Baal-Asherah prophets had lacked credibility there would have been no contest!

What is clear from this episode, however, is that these foreign nevi'im are ecstatics, much in the form of Israelite prophets of two hundred years earlier at the time of Samuel. (See "Is Saul among the prophets?") The Hebrew is also instructive for understanding these Baal-Asherah prophets, for their mode of prophecy seems to be a kind of wild dance accompanied by "ravings" (vs 29) and here the word has as its root the same letters as navi (Nun-Bet-Aleph).

As far as I know, to date actual Canaanite sources have yielded very little information on prophets, though according to an Egyptian source of the eleventh century called "The Journey of Wen Amon to Phoenicia" a local becomes possessed and delivers an oracle. Even earlier were the famous oracles of Balaam but he is not designated as a prophet. Yet even so one can say that at the very least the ancient Israelites felt that prophecy was not entirely unique to their experience, and that a kind of parallel activity is found in other cultures of their time and place. (See H. B. Huffmon, "Prophecy in the Ancient Near East," in Interpreter's Dictionary of the Bible Supplement [henceforth IDBS]; and for Balaam, see Nehama Leibowitz, Studies in Bamidbar, "Numbers," "Balak.")

It should be clear, however, that all the above examples are always offered with the caveat that they were "prophet-like" or "parallel" activity. The specific and more narrow understanding of a prophet's role would be limited to those men and women who were designated such as speaking the true word of the Lord. This final distinction of being a true versus a false prophet will be dealt with presently.

7. What Does a Prophet Do, How Does One Prophesy?

Up to this point we have defined the three kinds of prophets known in ancient Israel: the *ro'eh* (seer), the *hozeh* (gazer/seer), and the most popular term, the *navi* (prophet). Consideration has been given to the continuation of prophetic tradition in a broad sense from Moses through Elijah and to Isaiah and his successors. Further there has been some discussion of the historical background of ancient Israel, and parallel prophet-like activity in the ancient Near East. The role of the Hebrew prophets, their *particular* activity, now needs further delineation.

A. Hearing and Speaking

The role of the prophet was *involuntary*. Though there were bands of prophets, or prophetic guilds, one did not study to take on this role. Unlike other occupations, there were no formal classes or schools of biblical prophecy, where a person would sit at the feet of the teacher and learn this task. Amos states the case in classic fashion when he says quite starkly: "The lion has roared; who will not fear? The Lord God has spoken; who can but prophesy?" (Am 3:8; cf Jer 4:19).

The prophet is *inspired;* one does not seek out this task. Indeed to be a prophet is often an unenviable role. Jeremiah minces few words on this subject: "Cursed be the day on which I was born . . . when my mother bore me. . . . Why did I come forth from the womb to see toil and sorrow, and spend my days in shame?" (Jer 20:14, 18).

> The special gift of a prophet is his ability to experience the divine in an original way and to receive revelations from divine word. The prophet belongs entirely to God; his paramount task is to listen to and obey his God. In every respect he has given himself up to his God and stands unreservedly at His disposal (Johannes Lindblom, *Prophecy in Ancient Israel*, 1).

The prophet is one who hears the word of God and then who must transmit that revelation. Most frequently the vehicle of communication is the spoken word. The prophet, or at least the classical prophets, also were known to use symbols to convey their message. This shall be developed more fully in the subsequent section on the classical prophets. "The relationship between the Lord and the prophet was not impersonal and external, but direct and intimate" (Winward, 20). On occasion the prophet suggests that he himself is, as it were, an *ex-officio* member of the heavenly council. This image is sustained in the case of Micaiah ben Imlah (1 Kgs 22:19-23), Isaiah (6:1ff) and Jeremiah (23:21-22). Amos suggests that God reveals divine secrets or purposes to the prophet (3:7).

The prophet hearing the word of God and then being commissioned to speak it orally is part of the aforementioned scene in Isaiah 6, and a similar idea is repeated in Jeremiah (1:9): "Then the Lord put out his hand and touched my mouth; and the Lord said to me: Now I have put my words in your mouth." If Isaiah's lips require a special sign, and Jeremiah speaks of God touching his mouth, then it follows that the third major figure of the prophets would likewise record an episode that highlights his purpose for speaking. Early on in the book of Ezekiel we learn that God offers this prophet a scroll on which messages were written. God says, "O mortal,… eat this scroll, and go, speak to the house of Israel" (Ez 3:1). The message was both received and ingested before it was transmitted and spoken.

B. Ecstatics and Non-Ecstatics

One way the prophets of ancient Israel received their message was through a form of ecstasy. Reference was made earlier to the episode of Saul among the prophets (1 Sam 10:1-13). Samuel foretells that Saul will meet and temporarily join a group of ecstatics who are returning from visiting Gibeah, a noted "high place." He will join them and will speak in ecstasy (in Hebrew, v'hitnab'ita, the same root as "prophesy" — Nun-Bet-Aleph) and you will be turned into a different person (vs 6).

> The ecstatic prophet, therefore, was a person who, like the seer, was usually closely identified with the worship of God … and who, under the influence of a trance-like state of mind, uttered divine oracles. Ecstatic experiences could be either violent or calm, but they need not be thought of as occasions when all self-control was lost. Rather, they were moments when, to the frequent accompaniment of music-making, singing, dancing, or more bizarre forms of behavior, the concentration of the individual or of the group was focused upon the divine presence in such a manner that the will of God became known (Newsome, 3; see also Sandmel, *The Hebrew Scriptures* 49, and 1 Kgs 18: 28-29; 22:10-12; Ez 5:1-12).

At times the seer (ro'eh) was also an ecstatic prophet, for Samuel is at the head of a group of ecstatics at Naioth in Ramah (1 Sam 19:19-20).

To say that *some* prophets (nevi'im) were ecstatics is not to indicate that this was common fare. For the most part it appears as an early phenomenon.

> It would be contrary to the evidence to deny the importance of ecstasy in the experience of some of the canonical prophets, but it would also be an error to exaggerate it.... There are degrees of concentration and excitation, of enlightenment and exaltation, and the prophets were not always — and the evidence suggests not usually — in a state of ecstasy when they received revelation from God (Winward, 21; yet cf. Ez 1; Jer 23:9).

When a prophet spoke of being filled with the spirit or having God's spirit come upon one, it could have meant to be in a trance, but more often it is a form of speech, a synonym for "compelled" or "bursting with energy" (Mic 3:8; Is 61:1; Ez 2:2; 3:12; 36:26–27).

C. Predicting the Future

In popular usage today "prophecy" is roughly synonymous with "prediction of the future" (R. B. Y. Scott, *The Relevance of the Prophets*, 2). There were prophets who did speak words which "predicted" specific events which would happen in a future time. There also were prophets whose words have to be understood in a more generic sense of the future. Abraham Joshua Heschel explained that the "prominent theme is exhortation, not mere prediction. While it is true that foretelling is an important ingredient and may serve as a sign of the prophet's authority (Deut 18:22; Is 41:22; 43:9), his essential task is to declare the word of God to the here and now; to disclose the future in order to illumine what is involved in the present" (1.12). Future history and the *meaning* of that history will be discussed further when we review the messages of the classical prophets. In the meanwhile, however, it is important to note that not all prophetic predictions did come true! For example, Amos declares that Israel shall be decimated (literally but ten percent left), but his words need to be understood as figurative, not literal.

> The city that marched out a thousand shall have a hundred left, and that which marched out a hundred shall have ten left (Am 5:3).

Likewise Ezekiel predicts that a valley of dry bones shall be physically resurrected (37:1–14). This is poetic, not literal language. (Isaiah

17:1 predicts the total ruin of Damascus, but clearly this did not take place, Damascus still exists. Ezekiel 26:7–14 speaks of Tyre's destruction by Nebuchadnezzar, and yet this did not take place (see Ezek 29:17–19). Much predictive prophecy about the nations is conditional on the response of those who hear (see Jer 18:5–10, Jonah 3:4–10).

There are, naturally, examples of prophets predicting *real events within a short period of time,* which do come about. Nathan explains that David and Bathsheba's first son shall die, and he does (2 Sam 12:13–19). Micaiah ben Imlah predicts the death of King Ahab who then is killed in battle (1 Kgs 22:23, 28, 37). Isaiah prophesies that the siege of Jerusalem will be lifted, and it is (Is 37:33–38).

Certainly a broad characterization of Hebrew prophecy is that it deals with future events, but it thinks of trends rather than a particular and specific time frame.

New conditions might quite legitimately bring about a different course of events. When something predicted did not happen, this was not regarded *ipso facto* as an example of false prophecy (Huffmon, 695). Likewise some prophecies such as Haggai 2:20–23 and Zechariah 6:11ff were set into so vague a future that one could rationalize that they might still be fulfilled.

D. Clairvoyance

As noted above, in addition to the prophet-as-*navi* there was also the seer (*ro'eh* or *hozeh*). Despite the statement that they are synonymous (1 Sam 9:9), the *ro'eh* seemed to have a particular role as clairvoyant.

Certainly Samuel's "seeing" the encounter that Saul would have with the ecstatics is one example; the blind prophet Ahijah "seeing" King Jeroboam's wife and his foretelling the death of their son is another (1 Kgs 14). Ahab's death is foretold by Elijah (1 Kgs 21:19ff); Elisha "sees" an enemy ambush and latterly asks that the Lord grant special sight (!) to one of his servants (2 Kgs 6:8–10, 17). Whether these are examples of prediction or clairvoyance may only be a matter of semantics.

E. False Prophets

The book of Deuteronomy spells out clearly what is the mark of a false prophet. It is a pragmatic test: Does it come about? (Deut 18:20ff). Furthermore, even if it were to come about and the prophet wanted to worship idols or perform ungodly acts, this is another criterion for false prophecy (Deut 18:18ff; see also 13:1ff [13:2ff H]).

At times prophets offered contradictory words. Who was right? One way was to wait to see what would happen (see Micaiah ben Imlah; 1 Kgs 22). Further Ezekiel noted that God can choose to deceive a prophet (14:9).

There were other criteria. Jeremiah (6:14) suggests that a true prophet does not give comfort when there is no basis for it, "saying, 'Peace, peace' when there is no peace." (*TANAKH* offers this translation of the same verse: "Saying 'all is well, all is well,' when nothing is well" (in Hebrew: *shalom, shalom, v'eyn shalom*). In a similar manner, a true prophet is moral. Prophets cannot be adulterers or godless (Jer 23:9–11). A true prophet predicts judgment and disaster! Taking on his own contemporary prophets, Jeremiah calls them purveyors of false hopes:

> The prophets who preceded before you and me from ancient times prophesied war, famine, and pestilence against many countries and great kingdoms. As for the prophet who prophesies peace, when the word of that prophet comes true, then it will be known that the Lord has truly sent the prophet (28:8–9; see Deut 18:20ff).

Jeremiah's younger contemporary Ezekiel is just as harsh on the false prophets. They prophesy out of their imagination; the Lord did not send them, explains Ezekiel. They mislead the people and have given them false hope (Ez 13:1–16). Ezekiel explains that God will deal with these liars.

> My hand will be against the prophets who see false visions and utter lying divinations; they shall not be in the council of my people, nor be enrolled in the register of the house of Israel, nor shall they enter the land of Israel; and you shall know that I am the Lord God (13:9).

The false prophets are to be cut off forever; they will be banished, exiled, never to return.

F. Institutions and Individuals

Another way to characterize Hebrew prophets and prophecy is to speak of a division between institutionalized prophecy and individual action. These rubrics, however, are not hard and fast, for while some ancients prophesied as non-institutionalized independent prophets, they did so in a group, and other prophets were associated with an institution but certainly had an independent voice. (See Nathan's denunciation of King David.)

i. Institutional Prophecy

There are basically two kinds of institution-related, or, perhaps better, *institution-supported* prophets, those of the *cult* and those of the *court.* The *cult-prophet* did exist, and there are examples where a prophet also acted in a priestly manner (Samuel) or was well aware of the traditions of the cult (Isaiah, Ezekiel, Malachi, Joel — see Is 6; Ez 40–48; Mal 2:1ff; Jl 1:9ff). Certainly in the pre-classical period there were close associations between priest and prophet.

> Samuel and his prophetic guild were closely attached to the sanctuary at Shiloh until its decline or destruction at the hands of the Philistines. Then Samuel seems to have transferred his activities to the shrines at Mizpeh and Naioth, while other members of the guild moved to Nob (1 Sam. 19, 21, 22) (Newsome, 7).

Elijah has strong cult-associations as is demonstrated in the Baal prophets' encounter, and at Shunem there is the expectation that Elisha will visit regularly, either at the new moon or the sabbath (2 Kgs 4:9, 23).

There were also *court-prophets*, the first of whom probably is Nathan, and his contemporary Gad, the seer (*hozeh*). David certainly had these men as part of his entourage (1 Chr 29:29 et al.).

King Ahab of Israel has four hundred court prophets and he seeks their advice before a military campaign (1 Kgs 22:5-6).

In Jeremiah's day, he attacks as "false prophets" a number of his prophetic contemporaries (Jer 23) who seem to be associated with the court, and possibly the cult as well (Jer 28; see the prophet Hananiah).

ii. Independents

Most of the Hebrew prophets acted independently and were loners. The often quoted line of Amos that he stands by himself ("I am no prophet, nor a prophet's son; but I am a herdsman, and a dresser of sycamore trees" — Am 7:14) is no less important for its familiarity. (When Amos claims he is "no prophet," he means he is not a "professional" prophet, and by "prophet's son," though the literal translation is "son," the probable meaning is a prophet's "disciple." Not only is Amos' properly self-righteous answer of note, but the priest Amaziah's (albeit incorrect) assumption that Amos was a professional prophet also underscores that there were bands of prophets who would roam about speaking.

Even if at times the great prophets had followers, they spoke as individuals, and as individuals they suffered at the hands of those they castigated. Certainly they received their messages as individuals and not as a group effort.

The diverse call of many of the prophets also underscores their individuality. Amos was out in the countryside working (Am 7:15), Elisha was plowing (1 Kgs 19:19ff), and Jeremiah was a priest before becoming a prophet (Jer 1:1–8).

To be independent of court and cult, however, does not deny that there were bands of prophets. They appear in the episode of Saul with Samuel, accompanied (appropriately enough for a band) by musical instruments: lyre, timbrels, flutes and harps. Likewise Elijah and Elisha appear in company. "From the narratives about Elijah and Elisha, it may be inferred that the 'sons of the prophets' were united in guilds or associations. They had a leader, shared meals, and lived together (II Kings 2:1–8; 4:38–41)" (Winward, 17).

To be part of a group or to be in association was neither inherently "good" nor "bad." What was at question was whether you prophesied honestly or with a lying spirit.

8. Priest–Prophet–Wisdom: No Strict Divisions

In the late nineteenth–early twentieth century it was in mode to suggest deep divisions between the various sections of the Hebrew Scriptures. Priest, prophet, and wisdom writer were seen as people apart if not actually antagonistic to each other. Isaiah's opening chapter was often quoted, or perhaps quoted out of context.

> What to me is the multitude of your sacrifices? [demands God] I have had enough of burnt offerings of rams.... I do not delight in ... lambs, or ... goats.... I cannot endure solemn assemblies with iniquity ... learn to do good; seek justice ..." (Is 1:11, 13, 17; see also Am 5:21–24).

The key is not that God disapproves of ritual. As discussed above, a number of the classical as well as the pre-classical prophets were associated with priestly or cult-related activities. The key is that God wants righteousness *and* ritual. It is the *iniquitous* assemblies that God cannot abide. Ritual is not a substitute for righteousness, nor presumably would righteousness be a substitute for ritual. Prophets and "prophetism almost certainly remained in close rapport with the cultus. The relationship, indeed, was one of mutual indebtedness ... the prophets were familiar with the ritual and meaning of the cultus ... sometimes spoke in language borrowed from it ... they even quoted directly from its rituals, prayers and liturgies" (Napier, 902).

Scholarship now realizes that wisdom, priesthood, and prophetic utterances could well be combined in the life and words of one person. These were not necessarily pure forms. One often learned from or was influenced by another. "Prophecy is distinct but not separate from the rest of Israelite existence" (M. J. Buss, "Prophecy in Ancient Israel," *IDBS*, 694). Indeed they were often understood as being in close cooperation, as attested (negatively) in Jeremiah 18:18. Israelite society was a dynamic enterprise, as today in modern society a person may play many roles, depending on time, circumstance, and place.

9. Do the Prophets Predict the Coming of a Messiah?

Do the prophets, do any of the prophets of the Hebrew Bible, predict the coming of the messiah? The term "messianic" refers to the idea of a messiah, a savior, a redeemer. These are all good Jewish words, as are the terms salvation, redemption and resurrection. They are, naturally, good Christian words as well! Judaism clearly has concepts about messianism, as does Christianity. The actual "word Messiah derives from the Hebrew *mashiah*, anointed.... The Messiah of the future, the one who will bring peace and glory to Israel, will be the anointed one, the chosen descendant from the house of David" (Marc Angel, "Messiah — Jewish View," 130). In other words, according "to the Hebrew Scriptures God will establish, through a descendant of David, called the Anointed or 'Messiah,' his everlasting reign on earth. This will be characterized by perfection in the material and moral realms" (Andre Lacocque, "Messiah — Christian View," 133). The interested reader might wish to consult the excellent source-book, *A Dictionary of the Jewish–Christian Dialogue* edited by Leon Klenicki and Geoffrey Wigoder [Stimulus Book. New York and Ramsey: Paulist, 1984], from where the two definitions, quoted immediately above, derive. In the Jewish prayerbook as in certain rituals, such as the weekly "Havdalah" (Hebrew for "separation") ceremony which acknowledges the separation from the holiness of the sabbath day to the ordinary time of the weekdays, the messiah and the future coming of the messiah are clearly mentioned. Within Judaism, historically there have been tensions between the idea of a personal messiah and the coming of the messianic age. "Jewish messianism, like so many other theological concepts in Judaism, is complex, contradictory, and confusing." Yet it is also clear that messianism is an idea that comes into its own *after* the period of the close of the Jewish Bible, sometime later than the middle of the third century BCE. Indeed, "there is no *personal* messiah in the [Jewish] Bible. Rather we detect in this notion *soteriology,* human messengers or mortal agents, who carry out God's will and pave the way for salvation. In the [Jewish] Bible, God *alone* is the king-redeemer; Moses, Joshua, Gideon, Saul, David, Hezekiah and others were merely his mortal messengers" (Gilbert S. Rosenthal, "Messianism Reconsidered," 552– 553). This is not the place to review the massive amount of material written on Judaism's views on the messiah. One place to delve further would be to refer to the article on "Messiah" in the *Jewish Encyclopedia* and the more recent *Encyclopedia Judaica* [*EJ*], as well as to references in the article by Gilbert Rosenthal [see Bibliography]. Two exceptional works, both mentioned by Rosenthal, might briefly be highlighted: Joseph Klausner's *The Messianic Idea in Israel* [New York: Macmillan, 1955] and Gershom Scholem's *The Messianic Idea in Judaism* [New York: Schocken, 1971].

This section begins with the question "Do the prophets, do any of the prophets of the Hebrew Bible, predict the coming of the messiah?" The clear answer to this question is "no." The idea of a personal messiah, or even of a messianic age, is one which develops after the period of the Hebrew prophets.

Chapter 2

THE FORMER PROPHETS

The books of the former prophets, Joshua, Judges, Samuel and Kings, as we have noted earlier, do not contain the earliest reference to either prophets or prophecy. Abraham, Moses, Miriam, and Aaron are each called prophets, and in a memorable episode in the book of Numbers, Moses remarks to Joshua his wish that more people were infused with the word of God, and would act the prophet (referring to Eldad and Medad's "ecstasy/prophecy" see Num 11:26–29). Yet these are the sole examples alongside the brief references in Deuteronomy 13 and 18 to future prophets and prophecy: the dual roles of Deborah as judge and prophet (in Judges 4:4–5), and an anonymous prophet who is mentioned in Judges 6:8. Aside from these examples there are no named prophets until one comes to the figure of Samuel. Then, in the late eleventh–early tenth centuries, a new phenomenon arises: people who are not only labeled prophets, but who can be *seen* prophesying. Of these examples, three names stand out: Samuel, Nathan, and Ahijah. Each of the three is labeled a *navi* (though Samuel is also a *ro'eh*) (1 Sam 3:20; 9:19), and each is associated with a monarch (1 Sam 15:1; 2 Sam 7:2; 1 Kgs 14:2). There *are* other prophets associated with monarchs (1 Sam 22:5, 28:15; 1 Kgs 22:11), but these three stand out above the rest.

1. Samuel

In the late eleventh–early tenth centuries, with the exception of David, perhaps no figure is as complex and as appealing as Samuel. From literally his youth onward, Samuel displays a sense of being God's special representative. Like his younger contemporary David, Samuel is not without faults and occasional bad judgment (his sons were nominated as judges and clearly were not up to this role — 8:1–3). Samuel begins his public career as an apprentice to the priest at Shiloh. "The word of the Lord was rare in those days; visions were not widespread" (1 Sam 3:1), the Bible explains. One evening, asleep, Samuel is called by God and told that the house of Eli is to be punished for its iniquity. From that time on Samuel was known as a trustworthy prophet and he was recognized as such from Dan to Beersheba (1 Sam 3:20).

The next major incident in Samuel's life comes just prior to his encounter with Saul. The people once again have grown restless. They sense that the loose confederation of tribes that required periodic charismatic leadership, the judges, is simply not an efficient form of national defense. "Give us a king to govern us," they demand of Samuel. The prophet-judge-priest-seer (Samuel fills all these functions and more) is appalled. He prays to God who comforts him by saying that the people are rejecting their deity, not their prophet, "...for they have not rejected you, but they have rejected me from being king over them.... Listen to their voice; only — you shall solemnly warn them, and show them the ways of the king who shall reign over them" (1 Sam 8:7–9). This Samuel does, though in chapter 12 he again tries to talk the people out of their decision. He is not any more successful on the second occasion.

The episode of Saul's and Samuel's first encounter (1 Sam 9) is followed by Saul's public anointment, first in chapter 10 (vs 24) and again in 11:14–12:2.

Saul turns out to be a disappointment. Though Samuel entreats on the new king's behalf (1 Sam 15:10–11), God indicates that a successor is needed. In short order, Samuel is sent off to find a proper replacement.

Suggested reading: 1 Sam 16:1–13

This incident in the life of Samuel is instructive of the role of the prophet. Clearly there is tension between Saul and Samuel. The prophet has been instructed to appoint a new king, but he says he fears for his life (1 Sam 16:2) and consequently he is told to disguise his true mission. When he arrives in Bethlehem he is greeted with alarm! "Do you come peaceably?" he is asked by the elders of the city. Were they aware of the Saul–Samuel conflict? Did they fear he was going to involve them in an uprising? The tradition of judge-as-charismatic leader was over a century old. The monarchy was perhaps a dozen years in existence. The multi-faceted roles of Samuel as judge, seer, priest, and prophet were a volatile combination. Samuel may have felt his power eclipsed by Saul, but the people knew that Samuel spoke the word of the Lord and they feared those consequences.

When describing a prophet's being infused with God's spirit or speaking God's word, it is understandable (albeit incorrect) to assume that *all* that is said and done has God's imprimatur. The very human side of a prophet is shown in this short narrative. Not only is Samuel fearful for his life, and he needs God to give him courage, but when it comes time for the selection he is ready to anoint the wrong person! The narrator of this episode is thus able to teach an additional important value: not outward appearance, but the heart is important to God (vs 7).

As noted above, Samuel is a judge, a seer, a priest. He is also a militant who is willing to take the sword into his own hand (1 Sam 15:33).

The strangest event recorded about Samuel takes place after his death and is found in 1 Samuel 28. This chapter informs the reader that at least as late as the period of Saul's monarchy, the Urim (and Thummim; see 1 Sam 28:6, Ex 28:30 and 1 Sam 14:41, some kind of oracles) were being consulted to understand God's will as were the methods of dreams and prophets (*nevi'im*, vss 6, 15). Note the word is in the plural, and that it cannot refer to Samuel as he has died. Saul is desperate to know the divine will, and when all else fails he seeks to speak to Samuel even though the latter is deceased. When Samuel "arises" from the earth he apparently has an unearthly form — "divine" (*elohim*) is the way the medium describes him (vs 13) — and his appearance is that of an old man wrapped in a robe (vs 14).

The incident allows Samuel one last prediction, which would again come true, as apparently was so of all his previous prophecies (see 1 Sam 3:19).

2. Nathan

As Samuel was associated primarily with Saul, so likewise Nathan is associated primarily with David. Though he is called "Nathan the prophet" about a dozen times (2 Sam 7:2; 12:25; 1 Kgs 1:10 et al.), his role is fairly limited to the terms of interacting with the monarch himself. To this extent, he is a narrower character than Samuel, but like his predecessor of the previous generation, he displays courage and a willingness to chastise his ruler for what is plainly a violation of the expected norms of behavior.

Before embarking on the three episodes recorded about Nathan's life, it is instructive to take note of what is missing. In 1 Chronicles 29:29 reference is made to "the records of the prophet Nathan" which tells of the acts, early and late, of King David. These "records" — one imagines scrolls or narratives — have long disappeared (see also 1 Kgs 11:41). Their very disappearance, however, highlights the fact that what we have in the Hebrew Scriptures is an edited version, an *incomplete* record of the ancient world. A cynic might suggest that the victors write the history they want remembered. This is not the case with biblical history. There is too much included of a negative nature, of self-condemnation, to say that what we have extant are only the heroic parts of the past. The fact remains, nonetheless, that we may have a great deal, but they are still only partial records.

Nathan appears in three instances: David's inquiry as to God's wishes if he should build the temple (2 Sam 7:1–17), the condemnation of David's adultery with Bathsheba (2 Sam 12:1–25), and finally the question of the Davidic succession (1 Kgs 1:1–49).

The first incident is instructive for it teaches again that there is a difference between the prophet-as-a-human being and the prophet-as-a-person-of-God. Earlier attention was drawn to Samuel making his own judgments (over the person to anoint as the new king) and how this differed from God's view. A similar instance is true with Nathan and David. When the monarch first asks the prophet if he should build a temple for the Lord, the prophet's "human" reply is in the affirmative. That same night, however, Nathan hears the word of the Lord and the prophet must now reverse himself and tell David that not he but his son shall build this structure (2 Sam 7:1–17).

The courageous stand that Nathan took with David in the second episode (berating him for his adultery) is well known.

It is the third incident in the lives of Nathan and David that is the most intriguing.

Suggested reading: 1 Kgs 1:1–49

In this episode Nathan is pictured in a role not dissimilar to one which Samuel played, and which will be played out again by Ahijah with Jeroboam and later Elisha with Jehu. The prophet here is seen intimately involved in the question of monarchical succession. It is a remarkable event as much for what it says as for what it does not say! In vss 11–14, and 22, it is patently clear that there is a firm alliance between Nathan and Bathsheba. This is somewhat amazing in the light of the first Nathan episode (2 Sam 12:1–25) where Nathan, *speaking as the Lord's prophet*, roundly condemns David and Bathsheba for their action. Now it is true that perhaps two dozen years or more have passed, and that conditions may well have changed. "Politics," it is said, "makes for strange bedfellows," and the former prime minister of Great Britain, Harold Wilson,

once remarked that "a week is a long time in politics." The Nathan–
Bathsheba alliance nonetheless is noteworthy!

What this third incident does *not* say is that Nathan is speaking in
a prophetic manner. At no point does he suggest that he is the Lord's
agent as he did specifically in 2 Samuel 7:17, "In accordance with all these
words and with all this vision [*hizayon,* not *nevua'h*], Nathan spoke to
David." Likewise Nathan does not claim, nor does the narration claim,
as in 2 Samuel 12:1, that the prophet is on a mission from God. What is
striking, however, is that Nathan is specifically referred to as "Nathan the
prophet" *nine* times in a space of less than fifty verses.

3. Ahijah

David seems to be the first king to have an *official* court prophet, but
the tradition seems to have been taken on by Solomon, for reference is
made (in 2 Chr 9:29) that Solomon's history is recorded in the chronicles
of Nathan the prophet, the prophecies of Ahijah, and the visions of Jedo
the seer (*hozeh*).

For all that, however, not only are these references or chronicles
long lost, but there is no mention of prophetic activity as such for most
of Solomon's monarchy. Only at the close of his reign does a figure arise,
and he does not bode well for the future of the Davidic dynasty.

Ahijah is associated with the shrine at Shiloh and "served as a rally-
ing point for the [northern] Israelite interests opposed to the [southern]
Judah-oriented united monarchy of David and Solomon" (M. A. Cohen,
"Ahijah the Prophet," *IDBS,* 13).

Suggested reading: 1 Kgs 11:26–40

Several points are worth noting. Ahijah, at the Lord's instigation, is
a king-breaker and a king-maker. He uses symbolic action, the tearing of
Jeroboam's garment, to convey his message. He outlines the wrongful
acts of Solomon, specifically worshiping other deities besides the true God
of Israel. In technical language this is known as *syncretism* — the combination of different forms of beliefs and practices. In short, Solomon
was guilty of either introducing pagan religious practices into his kingdom or permitting them, a crime not to go unnoticed or unpunished.
Notice that in his remarks to Jeroboam he consciously mentions that he
is speaking God's word and that furthermore Ahijah is identified as the
prophet (*navi*). His promise of success for Jeroboam, however, is conditional on the latter's following God's laws. The editor of Kings notes
parenthetically (1 Kgs 12:15) that Rehoboam is bound to fail in order to

insure the realization of Ahijah's promise to Jeroboam. Unfortunately, Jeroboam is also a syncretist and his dynasty is short-lived indeed.

One sees Ahijah in one other episode. As an old man, suffering from blindness, he is visited at Shiloh by Jeroboam's wife. She comes in disguise, which is ironic considering the prophet is sightless! The fact that Jeroboam had advised his wife to come in disguise does not mean necessarily that the king did not have any contact with the prophet. The Bible is silent about this, but her camouflage may have been to deceive others, to protect her against enemies imagined or real. In any case, God forewarns Ahijah that she is coming and tells him what to say to her even before she puts forward her question. It is not an optimistic message (1 Kgs 14:1–20).

4. Elijah

Some fifty to sixty years are to pass before another major prophetic figure comes to the fore. The Elijah narratives, however, make up for the missing years. In reality there are two Elijahs. There is the Elijah of the biblical text itself. This Elijah then takes on a new persona, a symbolic meaning in later literature, in the Hebrew Scriptures, in the Christian Scriptures (New Testament), and in Judaism and Christianity well after the biblical period. We shall return to this "second" Elijah further on in this chapter.

Elijah the prophet, also called Elijah the Tishbite [the man from the village of Tishbe], lived in the area of Gilead, east of the Jordan River. He was the first of three major prophets of the ninth century, whose period of prophecy coincidentally overlap in time: Elijah, his contemporary Micaiah, and Elijah's attendant-disciple, Elisha. There are *other* prophets in this period, yet these three men stand out among their colleagues.

The Elijah narratives are found in 1 Kings 17, 18, 19, and 21, and 2 Kings 1 and 2. "An element of mystery . . . surrounds the historical Elijah . . . it is difficult to isolate fact from legend . . . the episode of Naboth's vineyard (1 Kings 21) . . . can be defended as sober history, whereas the report of Elijah's miraculous feeding on his journey to the Sinai Peninsula (1 Kings 19:4–7) cannot" (Kuntz, 243–244; Kuntz's book incorrectly identifies Chapter 17, not 19).

The chapters on Elijah and the widow (and her son), Elijah and the Baal-Asherah priests, and Elijah confronting Ahab about Naboth's fields (1 Kgs 17, 18, 21 respectively) are very well known and often discussed. The encounter at Horeb therefore presents another opportunity to see the prophet in a different circumstance.

Suggested reading: 1 Kgs 19:1-18

The picture of Elijah that is presented here is a very different figure from the past. At Zarephath (chapter 17, the narrative about the prophet and the widow) Elijah is well-assured of his role. He states his wishes and they are followed. When the widow's son falls ill, Elijah knows exactly what to do and does it. Likewise, some three years later when he accosts Ahab and the pagan priests at Mount Carmel (chapter 18) the figure of Elijah is again self-confident, even on the edge of pride in his mission. He challenges the people and taunts the Baal prophets. He mocks their actions. He also subtly reminds the people of their distant tribal origins, taking *twelve* stones "according to the number of the tribes of the sons of Jacob" and he commands that four jars be filled with water and poured over the altar three times (4 × 3 = 12), again underscoring the amphictyony of the period prior to the monarchy (1 Kgs 18:31, 34).

In chapter 19, however, a very different Elijah is seen. The prophet may be the man of God, he may stand up to king and queen, but here his courage has failed him. He is frightened for good reason: he fears for his life. In time-honored fashion, as Moses and David had done before him, Elijah seeks protection in the wilderness.

At this point Elijah touches bottom emotionally and psychologically. He lacks purpose, he is ready to die, he feels he is a failure (vs 4). The first book of Kings makes no attempt to explain Elijah's depression. Was it merely a mood-swing? Dejection or depression following the manic experience on Mount Carmel? A more likely explanation is the sense of failure-of-mission. He had hoped to eradicate Baal-Asherah worship and discredit Queen Jezebel. To that extent he did not succeed. Her maintenance of power is clear not only in the threat she poses, but in her very words which tell Elijah that if he is caught he will be executed summarily. A further depressive state may have been induced from his reflection that, in his having the people dispatch the Baal prophets, on some level he was no more moral or celebrative of life than was Jezebel herself. After all, she "was killing off the prophets of the Lord" (1 Kgs 18:4). Another explanation is his realization that though the four hundred and fifty Baal prophets are gone, there remain the four hundred devoted to Asherah (who apparently, despite Elijah's challenge, did not come to Carmel; see 18:19, 22).

God appears impatient, unsympathetic with the prophet. "What are you doing here, Elijah?" the deity asks not once, but twice (1 Kgs 19:9, 13). Elijah explains that he is fearful for his life, and then exaggerates by saying "I alone am left [of the prophets]." Instead of replying in words, God demonstrates divine power and displeasure through nature via wind, earthquake and fire. Elijah finally understands and submits to the Lord's will. He is then commissioned to perform three related specific acts: anoint Hazael as king of Aram (Syria), anoint Jehu as king of Israel, and anoint as his successor Elisha ben Shaphat (vss 14–16).

The chapter ends with Elijah setting out on his way to accomplish these goals. "Curiously, he fulfills neither [the first nor the second] commission, although his successor Elisha does (2 Kings 8:7–15 and 9:1–13)" (Kuntz, 247).

This episode contains a number of clues which suggest that there are some important subliminal messages being sent. Elijah is pictured as a latter-day Moses. As Moses was *the* leader (the "prophet") of an earlier age, so is Elijah now *the* leader ("prophet") at this juncture in Israel's collective life. Put succinctly, 1 Kings 19 reads like a telescoped life of none other than Moses himself.

Consider these parallels:

a. *vs 1* Ahab tells Jezebel about how Elijah put the prophets of Baal to death. Moses (Ex 2:12) kills an Egyptian.

b. *vs 2* Jezebel seeks to kill Elijah. When Pharaoh learns of Moses' action "he sought to kill Moses" (Ex 2:15).

c. *vs 3* Elijah fled for his life. "Moses fled from Pharaoh" (ibid).

d. *vs 4* Elijah, *alone*, goes to the wilderness. Moses, *alone*, goes to the wilderness. Moses, *alone*, settles in the wilderness of Midian (ibid).

e. *vss 5–7* At a bush, in the desert, Elijah unexpectedly comes face to face with an angel of the Lord. He is told that there is a specific task to achieve. Moses likewise is met by an angel of the Lord, and the venue again is a bush (Ex 3:1ff, though the words for bush and broom bush are *not* the same).

f. *vs 8* Elijah walks "to Horeb the mount of God," a journey that takes him "forty days and forty nights." This immediately evokes the image of Moses on Mount Sinai (Ex 24:15–18), and Mount Sinai and Mount Horeb are understood to be the same mountain. "In the Elohist stratum and Deuteronomic literature another name for the sacred mountain appears: HOREB ... and the two must be reckoned as synonyms (cf. Exod. 3:1 ... Deut. 5:2)" (G. E. Wright, "Sinai, Mount of," *IDB*, 376). Furthermore, Moses' encounter with the angel is at Horeb (Ex 3:1–2).

g. *vss 9, 11* Elijah stays in a cave, and then is told to "stand on the mountain before the Lord." The cave is reminiscent of the cleft of the rock where Moses stood on Sinai (Ex 33:22).

h. *vs 11* The Lord passed by. God's presence "passed by" Moses (Ex 33:22).

i. *vss 11–13* Elijah hears the sounds of God and he wraps his mantle over his face; he knows he is not to see God's face. Moses also finds out he is not to see God's face (Ex 33:20–23).

j. *vss 15–16* Elijah is given certain commissions. Moses likewise is commissioned further (Ex 34:1ff). At Horeb Elijah learns the name of his successor, which Moses will not learn until later, but he will learn it in time.

k. As Elijah and Elisha are featured together, so earlier Joshua is the only person on Mt. Sinai with Moses (Ex 24:13).

The linking of this great, indeed the greatest of the ninth century prophets with the personage of Moses cannot be accidental. In the mind of his contemporaries and later editors as well, Elijah was a prophet figuratively larger-than-life. His acts were so important, for while there were others who had performed miracles, no one had so readily captured the popular imagination and left such an impression. Elijah's legacy would long outlive his days on earth.

A. *Elijah in the Christian Scriptures*

To say that Elijah's importance would continue through the centuries is an understatement. The Christian Scriptures' use of Elijah (and indeed Judaism's and Christianity's use of that figure) is rooted in a tradition that first appears in a line from the prophet Malachi. Ironically, the reference to Elijah, many scholars believe, is not from the original writing of Malachi, but the addition of a later editor (Sandmel, *The Hebrew Scriptures*, 213; W. Neil, "Malachi," *IDB*, 231; Newsome, 194–195).

Nonetheless, the reference to Elijah who is to be sent "before the great and terrible day of the Lord comes" (Mal 4:5 [3:23 H]) was understood by later generations to be the man who would announce the coming of the *messiah*! This Elijah figure was then interpreted by the gospel writers to refer to John the Baptist. Jesus does not exactly so identify John in Matthew 17:9–13, but the disciples reckon that this *is* his meaning. Luke likewise identifies John as Elijah long awaited (Lk 1:17). In the fourth gospel John the Baptist actually denies he is Elijah (Jn 1:21), but for many he still had this role. Others, including some of Jesus' contemporaries, saw Jesus as the Elijah figure (Mt 16:14; Lk 9:8).

At the transfiguration of Jesus, three of the disciples see Jesus actually speaking with *Moses* and *Elijah* (Mt 17:1–8; cf Mk 9:2–8, Lk 9:28–36). The combination of these three figures is neither simply fortuitous nor coincidental in Christian tradition. These two former foremost Jewish leaders give credence and stature to Jesus in the eyes of his disciples.

B. Elijah and Jewish Sources

Jewish tradition likewise saw Elijah as the one who would announce God's future rule over all the world. His name is infused with hope right through Jewish history, legend, and ritual. At the ritual which commemorates the weekly close of the sabbath, the *Havdalah* ceremony, Elijah is sung about as the personage who will announce the coming of the messiah. Likewise as part of the seder meal at Passover, Elijah is featured as the one who will herald the coming days of peace. At a ritual circumcision traditionally there is an "Elijah chair." Elijah is credited as being zealous to ensure that this sign of the covenant is performed generation after generation. Elijah is remembered in thousands of stories in the midrash and later literature. He is associated with Jewish eschatology and becomes an active partner with the messiah, not only his precursor. He overshadows other biblical and post-biblical figures in terms of folklore told or written about him (see Dov Noy, "Elijah [In Jewish Folklore]" in *Encyclopedia Judaica* [hereafter *EJ*]).

Among the thousands of Elijah stories and legends the following taken from rabbinic literature reflect several of Elijah's qualities. The first example comes from the Talmud. Elijah, having been translated to heaven, never has died. He is often present to help meritorious people. He is in close association with the messiah, and he knows the answers to seeming impossible questions.

> Rabbi Joshua ben Levi [a prominent Palestinian rabbi, c. 250 CE] met Elijah and then asked him, When will the Messiah come? Go and ask him, Elijah replied, he is at the gate of Rome. Then Rabbi Joshua went and asked him, When are you coming? *Today* (the Messiah) replied. Rabbi Joshua then went back to Elijah. He spoke falsely to me, the rabbi complained, for he said he would come today and he has not come! Then Elijah replied, he meant "*Today*, if you harken to my voice" (referring to Psalm 95:7) (abridged from Babylonian Talmud *Sanhedrin* 98a).

Next we find Elijah as a fountain of moral wisdom. This selection is from the rabbinic homiletic tradition, the midrash.

> Elijah taught, If people exalt God's glory, but diminish their own, God's glory is exalted, and theirs is also. If people diminish God's glory, God's glory remains, but their glory is lessened (*Midrash Numbers Rabbah* 4.20 near beginning, my translation).

5. Micaiah ben Imlah

A contemporary of Elijah is the prophet Micaiah ben Imlah. His moment on the stage of biblical history is centered in the final chapter of First Kings, chapter 22.

Suggested reading: 1 Kgs 22

King Ahab of Israel and King Jehoshaphat of Judah enter into an alliance against the Syrian king. They wish to recapture a piece of former Israelite territory east of the Jordan River, Ramoth-Gilead. Jehoshaphat requests a divine oracle before the troops set out. Ahab obliges by calling upon his four hundred prophets. "Go up," they say; "the Lord will give it into the hand of the king" (22:6).

King Jehoshaphat nonetheless remains skeptical; he wants a second opinion. Ahab says there is only one other man, "Micaiah ben Imlah, but I hate him, for he never prophesies anything favorable about me, but only disaster" (22:8).

Meantime one of the four hundred prophets, Zedekiah ben Chenaanah, performs a kind of mimetic ritual wherein he suggests that the two kings will be a rousing success (22:11).

Finally Micaiah is sent for and the man who brings him warns the prophet to prophesy only favorably. Micaiah demurs and says he will speak only what God tells him. When he stands before the kings he predicts *success*! "Go up and triumph; the Lord will give it [the territory] into the hand of the king" (22:15). When Ahab hears this unlikely prophecy he is immediately suspicious. It sounds too much like a mocking paraphrase of what his own four hundred prophets had said. He cautions Micaiah that he will only hear the truth from him. Micaiah then announces that the expedition will fail.

It is not easy to explain away Micaiah's first words. Having just told the messenger that he will only speak what God tells him, why does he then appear to do the opposite?

One reasonable response can be found in what takes place next. Micaiah tells Ahab and Jehoshaphat that he has seen God in conference with the host of heaven. Like a celestial committee meeting, they are planning how to entice Ahab to Ramoth-Gilead. Finally a certain spirit (*ha-ruach*) volunteers to be a conscious false witness. He will "be a lying spirit in the mouth of all his prophets" (vs 22). God approves the plan and sends the spirit on his way.

In any case, Ahab and Jehoshaphat reject the prophecy of Micaiah and the result is that the battle is lost and Ahab is mortally wounded.

The account discloses the commonly held prophetic view that Yahweh is responsible for all events in the world, whether they be pleasant or terrifying. Ahab's end on the battlefield is decreed by Yahweh and the "lying spirit." To be sure, Ahab had developed a strategy of his own (22:30). Yet ultimately Ahab was killed, Jehoshaphat survived, and Micaiah's prophecy was confirmed (Kuntz, 251).

6. Elisha

The figure of Elisha is eclipsed somewhat by that prophet's close association with his mentor, Elijah. They were, however, two very different men. Elijah is usually seen acting in solitary splendor while Elisha is often associated with the "company [disciples] of prophets" (2 Kgs 4:1, 38; 6:1, 9:1 *b'nai hanevi'im*). Elijah wears very sparse and rugged clothing (2 Kgs 1:8), and while less is known about Elisha's garments, he probably came from a wealthy family. When first called to prophesy he is seen plowing with twelve oxen, a notable number in itself. Then his family is able to sustain the financial loss of these oxen, for he slaughters the animals and shares pieces of them all around before he leaves with Elijah (1 Kgs 19:19ff).

Elisha comes into his own following the "ascendancy" of Elijah. This is such a remarkable moment it is worthwhile considering in greater detail.

Suggested reading: 2 Kgs 2:1-25

The time has come for Elijah's departure. This bodily ascension is a strange episode in its own right, but an analysis of that would more rightly be part of the Elijah legends.

Elijah's imminent translation to heaven apparently is either public knowledge, or at the very least it has been revealed to the disciples of the prophets residing at Bethel, and to another group of prophets residing at Jericho. Elisha is impatient and irritated when either group even raises the issue. Three times Elijah attempts to go on alone and three times Elisha protests. (In passing, Elisha's three-time affirmation of his relationship with Elijah is contrasted by Peter's three-time denial of Jesus in the Christian Scriptures — Mt 26:75; Lk 22:61, etc.)

Elijah and Elisha come to the Jordan, and Elisha asks for a "double share" (lit. a "two-thirds" share or portion). The reference to a "double share" is not coincidental. This is technical language, for the first-born son received this "double portion" (see Deut 21:15–17). Elisha is seeking or claiming this same kind of approval. Elijah's reaction is somewhat cautious. Even though he had been told to commission Elisha, he appears reluctant to suggest that the power of prophecy can be so easily transmitted. Consequently, Elijah proposes a test: only if Elisha can actually see Elijah being taken from him will he then be granted the gift of prophecy. In the event Elisha easily passes the test (vss 10–12).

Elisha then takes Elijah's mantle and immediately performs a similar miracle to that of his former master. Elisha's action here, once again, is not coincidental or unplanned. When Joshua succeeded Moses there was a public acknowledgment of the figurative passage of the mantle of leadership (Deut 34:9). Elisha takes the matter a step further. He literally takes up Elijah's mantle and the disciples of the prophet at Jericho acknowledge his leadership. "The spirit of Elijah rests on Elisha!" they exclaim in verse 15. Just as Moses had parted the sea in Exodus, so Joshua parts the Jordan in his day (Jos 3:9ff). Elisha will do the same. As shortly before Elijah had parted the Jordan, so Elisha's first act is to cause the parting of the Jordan (vs 14; see vs 8).

Immediately after the performance of this miracle, as noted above, the disciples of the prophets paid homage to Elisha. Yet apparently there were some skeptics. Some turn to Elisha and voice their concern that perhaps Elijah is still about. They wish to seek for the old master. Elisha refuses, but following their persistent demands he accedes to their request. They search for three days to no avail, and an exasperated Elisha says: "Did I not say to you, Do not go?" (vs 18). A small incident this, but indicative that while the prophet had the power to speak the word of God, and perform miracles, he was not unconditionally and unequivocally accorded respect from his contemporaries.

This lack of respect is underscored as Elisha retraces his steps from the Jordan, to Jericho, to Bethel. As he is going along some boys taunt him for his lack of hirsuteness. Elisha is in no mood to coddle such behavior. He curses them in the name of the Lord, and forthwith two she-bears come out of the woods and mangle the children. From Bethel Elisha goes to Mount Carmel, probably to vicariously associate himself with the Elijah–Baal prophets episode, and then he goes to Samaria, where he will function in the region of the northern kingdom.

In chapter 4 there is an anecdote that sounds similar to events in Elijah's life (1 Kgs 17:7–24), though they are further fleshed out here. The miracle of extending food that will be repeated in the narrative of Jesus' miracle of the loaves and fish (Mt 14:13ff; Mk 6:38ff; Lk 9:10ff; Jn 6:1ff) is also found in this chapter.

Chapter 4, like chapter 6, accounts for the modern readers the dire poverty and the true meaning of drought in the ancient Near East. The closest memory that many people in North America have of poverty and want is the period of the Great Depression and the Dust Bowl. That was a figurative paradise compared to the pain and deprivation highlighted by 2 Kings 4:1–2 and 6:24–30 as a perusal of those verses will reveal.

The episode with Naaman the commander of the army of Aram (Syria) described in chapter 5 is well-known. Once again, as Gehazi learns, Elisha is not a man who suffers wrongdoing lightly. A curious part of the narrative is that Naaman becomes "a believer" and takes back sacred earth with him to Aram (2 Kgs 5:17–19).

Chapter 6 features another illustrative incident about the life of Elisha. It reveals a great deal about his person and about prophecy as well.

Suggested reading: 2 Kgs 6:8–23

The king of Aram periodically would make raids on Israel and at several points planned to ambush Israel's king. Time and again "the man of God" warns the Israelite king and he avoids capture. The king of Aram suspects that there is a spy in his own camp. Not so, explain the king's officers; it is "Elisha, the prophet in Israel, who tells the king of Israel the words that you speak in your bedchamber" (vs 12). Go and seize him, the king counters. A large force of horsemen and chariots venture forth and surround the town where Elisha is staying. Elisha then asks God for a miracle, and the deity obliges. The Arameans are not only blinded, they are led into enemy territory into Samaria, where their blindness is lifted. The Israelite king then inquires of Elisha whether he should strike down the enemy. Elisha asks rhetorically: Did you capture them that you should have the right to attack them? Rather set food and drink in front of them. The enemy soldiers are lavishly feted and sent home to Aram. The episode ends with the explanation that peace was again established, for "the Arameans no longer came raiding into the land of Israel" (vs 23). The moral is even more important than the miracles. If you treat your captive enemy with kindness, even at times with generosity, it will redound positively to your credit. This notion is not without precedent. Exodus 23:4 suggests that if you come across your enemy's ox or donkey you must return it, and later in Proverbs it states clearly that you are to be kind to your starving foe. "If your enemies are hungry, give them bread to eat; and if they are thirsty, give them water to drink" (Prov 25:21; see also Prov 24:17). Elisha's action, moreover, is reflected in Jesus' sermon on the mount where he says: "Love your enemies and pray for those who persecute you" (Mt 5:44). Paul in Romans 12:14–21 echoes similar thoughts and quotes from Proverbs 25. (See the latter part of the article by J. A. Sanders, "Enemy," in *IDB*.)

The Elisha-related materials conclude on two events worth noting. In his dotage, Elisha suffers ill health and is soon to die. He must be of advanced age, for the late King Jehoash had ruled for thirty-seven years, and Elisha was prophesying before his reign. The young successor, King Joash, comes to pay his respects to the aging prophet. Seeing him so ill he quotes virtually the same words over Elisha as Elisha spoke when Elijah ascended to heaven (2 Kgs 13:14; see 2 Kgs 2:12): "My father, my father, the chariots of Israel and its horsemen!" The meaning of these words is probably a recognition of Elisha's (and earlier Elijah's) defense of the land and people against their enemies.

Finally, Elisha's power apparently lasted beyond his life. A strange incident is recorded where a man who died came in contact with Elisha's bones and then miraculously came to life and stood up (2 Kgs 13:21).

*   *   *

The ninth century saw the prophets Elijah, Micaiah, and Elisha and their contemporary rulers in Israel: Ahab, Ahaziah, Jehoram, Jehu, and Jehoahaz, and, in Judah, Jehoshaphat, Jehoram, Ahaziah, Athalia, Joash, and Amazia. Their primary ministry covered some fifty to sixty years, from c. 860–c. 810 BCE.

Another fifty years would pass, bringing new conditions and a new kind of prophet. When Amos would speak in the mid-eighth century BCE, less than four decades of existence were left for the northern state. Some one hundred years would separate the early years of Elijah and the prophecy of Amos. The classical prophets owed a great deal to their predecessors, but they were different people, with other concerns.

We shall take up their story in the next chapter.

Chapter 3

THE LATTER PROPHETS

The latter, literary, or classical prophets did not suddenly appear without precedent or precursors. We can "assume a core tradition of Yahwism maintained in an unbroken but fluid continuum from Moses to Malachi . . . [a] characteristically prophetic bent of mind long in advance of and in necessary preparation for the emergence of classical prophetism . . . [The] classical prophet . . . was debtor, and certainly conscious debtor to a core tradition already long established" (Napier, 905). The classical prophets cover a period of close to five hundred years (c. 750–250 BCE). The first two centuries form the high point of moral, literary and oratory messages. This includes, but is not limited to, the prophecies of Amos, Hosea, Micah, First Isaiah, Jeremiah, Ezekiel, and at least Second and possibly Third Isaiah as well. Taking the literary prophets (those whose names are associated with specific books) as a whole, we can see certain patterns which link them despite the fact that they lived in diverse times and under different conditions. This chapter will constitute an overview of the thought, messages and styles of these great religious leaders.

1. Some Similar Messages

Like their predecessors, the classical prophets were ready to denounce wrongdoing; they were ready to criticize syncretism (blending and mixing various religious traditions) and idol worship. Some would serve as advisors to monarchs, but others addressed the people Israel at large. The words that Samuel spoke to Saul concerning the need for obedience to God's ways in addition to a narrow definition of cultic ritual (1 Sam 15:22–23) would be paralleled in Amos' fifth chapter, "[The Lord says] I hate, I despise your festivals, and I take no delight in your solemn assemblies ... let justice roll down as waters, and righteousness like an ever-flowing stream" (Am 5:21, 24).

Like some of their predecessors, the classical prophets might serve as military or foreign policy advisors to the monarch. Certainly Isaiah does just this (Is 7:3ff; 37:21ff; et al.) and Jeremiah fulfills a similar role (Jer 37:3ff; 38:14ff; et al.).

2. Ecstasy

In the past ecstatic behavior was part of the prophetic tradition. In the classical period, however, Ezekiel is the primary exponent of such activity (Ez 2:2; 3:14–15, 23–27, et al.). Indeed Ezekiel's statement in chapter 3 of his book sounds a great deal like a description of Saul in 1 Samuel 19:24. Compare these words: "The spirit lifted me up and bore me away; I went in bitterness in the heat of my spirit, the hand of the Lord being strong upon me ... I sat there among them, stunned, for seven days" (Ez 3:14–15) with the earlier passage: "He [Saul] too stripped off his clothes, and he too fell into a frenzy. ... He lay naked all that day and all night. Therefore it is said, 'Is Saul also among the prophets?'"

3. Prophetic Courage

Certainly, like their antecedents in the earlier period, these latter prophets were willing to confront establishment figures and denounce them for their wrongful acts. Amos goes to the cultic center at Bethel to deliver his words (Am 7:13), Isaiah challenges King Ahaz (Is 7:13–16), and Jeremiah is imprisoned for his unpopular words (Jer 38:6). This took great courage.

> Priests were charged with failing to ... follow divine instruction and being eager to receive ... remuneration (Hos. 4:6–8; Mic. 3:11; Zeph. 3:4). Prophets were accused of violating the norms of their profession [Jer. 6:13; Zech. 13:2]. ... The "heads," "princes," or members of government, were criticized for ignoring basic morality, accepting bribes ... and exploitation (Amos 6:1–6; Hos. 5:10 ... Isa. 1:23). ...
>
> Other groups attacked are merchants, for cheating and insensitive rapacity (Amos 8:4–6; Hos. 12:7–8 [H 12:8–9]); Mic. 6:10–12) and city women for selfish or haughty luxury (Amos 4:1; Isa. 3:16–17). ... The list of specific sins castigated [includes

syncretism (Ezek 14:1ff)] ... idolatry, sacred prostitution (Hos. 4:14), sabbath violation, disrespect to parents (Mic. 7:6), murder, adultery, theft, falsehood, disloyalty to associates (Jer. 9:2–8 [H 9:1–7]) ... and incest (Amos 2:7) [and Ezek 22:9ff] (Buss, 696).

To be a prophet was to know social isolation, or worse physical abuse. The words from Isaiah 53:3 could fit many a prophet: "He was despised and rejected by others; a man of suffering ... he was despised ... held of no account."

4. The Prophet's Call or Initial Commission

A great deal more is known about the major prophets than the minor, simply because there is more biographical material about them. Some prophets simply prophesied, others explained how they came to this role.

Some prophets' "commission" or "call" followed the basic pattern set by Moses in Exodus (3:1ff; 4:10ff). Often these representatives of God are more than a little reluctant to take on their position (Jer 1:6, Jon 1:3), but nonetheless they know they have to do so. Other prophets, such as Amos, Ezekiel, and Hosea, simply get on with the task of prophecy without further ado (Am 7:15; Ez 3:1ff; Hos 1:2ff).

5. Prophetic Language

It seems redundant to point out that one major factor which distinguished the writing prophets from their predecessors was their "writing," yet it bears repeating. Not only were the words of the latter prophets collected and set down, either by themselves, their disciples, or later editors, but their very language was special. The classical prophets were orators, poets, people of powerful rhetoric. In addition, the prophecies of these leaders abound in imagery.

The relationship of God to the people Israel is expressed in a variety of ways: parent/child "(e.g. in addition to Hos 11; Is 1:2), owner/vineyard (Is 5; 27), shepherd/flock (especially Is 40:11), potter/clay (so Jer 18; see also Is 29:16; 64:8 – H 64:7), and of course predominantly, husband/wife (Is 50:1; 54:5; 62:4–5; Jer 2:1–7 ... Ez 16; 23; Hosea as the fundamental thesis)" (Napier, 913). Other relationships include: father (Jer 3:19), mother (Is 49:14–15), friend (Jer 3:4), warrior (Zeph 3:17), shepherd (Ez 34:31), metal worker (Ez 22:20), builder (Am 7:7), washer (Is 4:4), judge (Is 2:4), water-seller (Is 55:1–2), king (Jer 10:10), scribe (Jer 31:33), teacher (Is 2:3), provider of clothing (Is 61:10), and the one who metes out punishment (Am 3:14). (This list was expanded from one presented in E. W. Heaton, *The Old Testament Prophets*, 52.)

The prophets also used the imagery of the law courts, such as when Isaiah states that God "rises to argue his case.... The Lord enters into judgment" (Is 3:13–14), or in Micah, "for the Lord has a controversy with his people, and he will contend with Israel" (Mic 6:2).

The prophets would utilize rhetorical questions and then give appropriate answers. "Is such the fast that I choose, a day to humble oneself?... Is not this the fast that I choose: to loose the bonds of injustice ... to let the oppressed go free ... to share your bread with the hungry" (Is 58:5–7).

Questions are placed in God's mouth, as in Hosea's message of hope: "How can I give you up, Ephraim? How can I hand you over, O Israel? ... I will not execute my fierce anger; I will not again destroy Ephraim ... I will not come in wrath" (Hos 11:8–9).

Another use of prophetic language comes in the repetition of numbers and idioms. In the first two chapters of Amos we find a recurring pattern. "For three transgressions of Gaza, and for four, I will not revoke the punishment," "For three transgressions of Tyre, and for four, I will not revoke the punishment," "For three transgressions of Edom, and for four, I will not revoke the punishment" (Am 1:6, 9, 11 et al.).

"Both Isaiah and Jeremiah contrast the knowledge of the beasts and birds with Israel's lamentable lack of it" (Heaton, 55). Isaiah would complain that the "ox knows its owner, and the donkey its master's crib; but Israel does not know, my people do not understand" (Is 1:3). In a similar fashion, Jeremiah criticizes that even "the stork in the heavens knows its times; and the turtledove, swallow, and crane observe the time of their coming; but my people do not know the ordinance of the Lord" (Jer 8:7).

A metaphor drawn from the animal world is also utilized by Hosea when he contrasts God as a lion and the people like fluttering fowl. "They shall go after the Lord, who roars like a lion; when he roars, his children shall come trembling from the west. They shall come trembling like birds from Egypt, and like doves from the land of Assyria; and I will return them to their homes, says the Lord" (Hos 11:10–11).

6. Word and Symbol

Again and again in the classical prophets one reads this phrase: the "word of the Lord." (Is 1:10; 2:3; 28:13, 14; Jer 1:2, 4, 13; 2:1, 4; Ez 1:3; 3:16; 6:1, 3; 7:1; Hos 1:1; 4:1; Jl 1:1; Jonah 1:1; 3:1 et al.).

The "word of the Lord" is the phrase used most frequently in the OT to describe the medium of revelation. God speaks, and his prophet hears. Thus the books of Jeremiah, Hosea, Joel, Jonah, Zephaniah, Haggai, and Zechariah all have at, or very near, the beginning the formula: "The word of the Lord that came to . . ." or some slight variation of it, and the formula is frequently repeated in the course of the books. "Thus says the Lord" and "Hear the word of the Lord" also occur very often in the Prophets (J. N. Sanders, "The Word," *IDB*, 868–869).

This is not the only way that God communicates the divine will, for prophets also experience visions (Is 1:1; Nah 1:1; Ob 1, et al.). We also find that vision and word are intermixed: "The words of Amos . . . which he saw" [*hazah* — *connected to the older word for prophet "hozeh" — seer, gazer*] — Am 1:1). Likewise "The *word* of the Lord that came to Micah . . . which he saw [*hazah*]" (Mic 1:1). In the Jewish Publication Society's *TANAKH* the opening lines of these prophets read respectively, "The word of the Lord that came to Micah . . . *who prophesied*" and "The words of Amos . . . *who prophesied.*" Amos and Micah lived in the eighth century BCE. Between a hundred and a hundred fifty years later we find a similar mixture of word and vision in the speeches of Jeremiah. ". . . this is what [lit. "this is the word," *zeh hadavar*] the Lord has shown me" [*asher hir'ani Adonai. Hir'ani* is connected to the noun *ro'eh*, "seer"] in Jeremiah 38:21. In these examples, however, the "word" is usually present. The Bible knows of visions and visionaries, but hearing God's word is the primary mode of communication.

The emphasis on word rather than vision may be connected with the Hebrew rejection of idolatry and, indeed, mistrust of any visual aids to religious faith such as are found in most religions, including Christianity itself (J. N. Sanders, 869).

Visions were an alternate form of God making the divine wishes known, but that was a secondary, and far less frequent, form of communication. The "word" had a power that was lacking in a vision. While a "lying spirit" could come in the form of *words* (1 Kgs 22:22) we can detect a sense that visions, especially visions by themselves without the accompanying "word," had lesser regard. In the following passage from Isaiah one notes how he suggests that vision and sight are easily negated.

Stupefy yourselves and be in a stupor, blind yourselves and be blind! . . . For the Lord has poured out upon you a spirit of deep sleep; he has *closed your eyes*, you prophets [*nevi'im*], and covered your heads, you seers [*hozim*]. The vision of all this has become for you like the words of a sealed document. If it is given to those who can read, with the command, "Read this," they say "We cannot, for it is sealed" (Is 29:9–11).

That the word had power is demonstrated time and again in the Bible. God spoke and the world came into being. God said "Let there be light" (Gen 1:3), and there *was* light! In as varied texts as Genesis and Esther, examples can be given that once a mortal's word has been given, it cannot be retracted. Isaac blesses Jacob, unwittingly (?), but once the blessing is given he cannot retract it for Esau (Gen 27:33). Once Ahasuerus has given his royal edict and it is written into the laws of Persia and Medea, it cannot be abrogated (Est 1:19).

"The Lord God has spoken (*diber*); who can but prophesy (*vinav'ey*)?" explains Amos (3:8). God speaks and people are to listen. God *speaks* and the prophet must *speak out*. There is, however, a caveat that needs to be made. On one hand the Lord speaks and the word of God is understood to be unalterable (if the laws of the Medes and Persians do not change, presumably how much more so would this be true of God). Yet at the same time, apparently unlike the Medes and Persians, God can revoke the divine word, God's mind can change *if/when* people change their ways and repent. The possibility for change, for forgiveness, therefore, is part of God's greatness. With this understanding Isaiah's words take on a fuller and further meaning. God says: I do not speak without my words being accomplished, but one way of accomplishment is to get the people to repent and return to righteousness.

> For my thoughts are not your thoughts nor are your ways my ways, says the Lord.... For as the rain and the snow come down from heaven, and do not return there until they have watered the earth, making it bring forth and sprout ... so shall my word be that goes out from my mouth; it shall not return to me empty, but it shall accomplish that which I purpose, and succeed in the thing for which I sent it (Is 55:8, 10–11).

In the midrashic literature the rabbis suggest that at times God consciously revokes previous divine judgments. The word *can be* nullified. Developing prophecy found in Hosea 14:1 [14:2 H], "Return, O Israel, to the Lord your God," the rabbis teach that in the Torah (Deut 24:1–4) it explains that if people marry, get divorced, and then following this the wife remarries and is then subsequently divorced or widowed, the original couple cannot remarry. Even though Israel has forsaken God and worshiped others ("We have sinned against you, because we have abandoned our God and have worshiped the Baals" — Jgs 10:10), nonetheless God says, "Return in penitence: come to me, and I will receive you." The rabbis then note that Jeremiah took up this very issue by asking rhetorically: "If a man divorces his wife and she goes from him and becomes another man's wife, will he return to her? ... You have played the whore with many lovers; and would you return to me? says the Lord" (Jer 3:1). The rabbis explain that in answer to that specific question, God says "yes." "Come and I will receive you" — hence the line in Hosea, "Return, O Israel, to the Lord your God" (*Pesikta Rabbati, Piska* 44.6). As noted in the Introduction to this book, the concern of the prophets was "*faithlessness*," not the faithlessness of females-as-females. Jeremiah framed the question in terms of a man divorcing his wife, but the issue is of a couple being divorced.

Word and symbol for the classical prophets are often related. The symbol is an extension of the word, for it represents the word. While the greatest "audio-visual" prophet is Ezekiel, he certainly has precedents before his time.

One kind of symbol very intimately tied up with the "word" was word-as-symbol. Isaiah gave names to his children which conveyed unambiguously what he meant. His first-born is called "Shear-yashub," literally "a remnant shall return" (Is 7:3). Likewise, when conveying hope to King Ahaz he tells him that a child who will be born the next year shall be called "Immanuel," literally "God is with us" (Is 7:14). Hosea, a contemporary of Isaiah, was to call two of his children "Lo-ruhamah" — "not pitied," and "Lo-ammi" — "not my people" (Hos 1:6, 9).

In the Christian Scriptures the power of the word will be taken a quantum leap forward by the writer of the fourth gospel. There John begins with the majestic words "In the beginning was the Word, and ... the Word became flesh and lived among us" (Jn 1:1, 14). For John, the Word is Jesus as the Christ.

Other symbols that are found among the prophets are Jeremiah's almond tree, a steaming pot, two baskets of figs (Jer 1:11ff; 24:1-2) and Amos' summer fruit (Am 8:1-2), as well as the familiar images of the dry bones in Ezekiel 37, and the two sticks representing the northern and southern kingdoms in that same chapter (Ez 37:1-14, 15-28).

In addition, at times the prophets *by their very physical actions* conveyed their message. The prophets both figuratively *and literally* involved themselves with symbols. Contending for the starkest example would be Hosea who is told to (and then does) marry a prostitute. The symbolic action involved here is that the land and the people have strayed; they have committed "great whoredom [*zanoh tizneh*] by forsaking the Lord" (Hos 1:2). As Israel is "faithless," so does the prophet marry a "faithless" woman.

Isaiah garbs himself in sackcloth as a sign of mourning, and then walks about naked to symbolize despair and captivity (Is 20:2–6). Jeremiah wears a yoke to symbolize captivity and submission (Jer 27:2–7, 10–12) and Ezekiel in chapter 12 is filled with a variety of symbolic actions from collecting exiles' gear, covering his face, and eating bread and drinking water in a trembling manner (see also 4:1ff).

The image of Israel as collective sheep in need of a caring shepherd is also found in Ezekiel. Indeed Israel's corrupt leaders are depicted as careless shepherds, in contrast to God as a thoughtful sheep herder. There is also the promise of the Davidic successor as a shepherd in this same chapter (Ez 34:2ff, 11ff, 23ff). The sheep/shepherd image is found elsewhere in the Bible, most familiarly in Psalm 23 (cf. Jer 23:3–4).

The Christian Scriptures also reflect this sheep/shepherd theme (Mt 9:36; 26:31; Mk 6:34; Jn 10). It finds a full expression in the closing words of the epistle to the Hebrews: "Jesus, the great shepherd of the sheep" (Heb 13:20).

7. The Grand Design

As noted earlier the most notable of the classical prophets lived primarily over a two hundred year stretch from the mid-eighth to the mid-sixth centuries. Certainly this was the time of the prophetic careers of the figures of Amos, Hosea, Isaiah, Micah, Zephaniah, Nahum, Habakkuk, Jeremiah, Ezekiel and Second Isaiah. Given the fact that these were diverse figures viewing different situations it is difficult to offer an overview or a schema that would cover all of their prophecies. Certain trends or developments nonetheless can be ascertained. The question then remains merely how best to characterize biblical prophecy. There are many approaches we might take. Let us consider by way of examples how two standard and basic references approach the subject. Both are works that will be found in the reference section of many public, college or religious-oriented libraries. They are the *Interpreter's Dictionary of the Bible* (Abingdon) and *The Encyclopedia Judaica* (Keter/Macmillan). In each of these works under the article "Prophet" a general schema is offered. The following is a comparison of those rubrics:

IDB	EJ
Election and Covenant	Universalism and Election
Rebellion	Supremacy of Morality
Judgment	Attitude Toward Ritual
Compassion	Morality and Destiny
Redemption [Return]	Repentance
Consummation [Mission]	New Covenant
	Future of Israel

The two are not exactly the same, but they cover similar ground. A modified schema combining these rubrics will provide direction for our overview: Election; Morality; Change/Repentance; New Covenant; Future Mission.

A. Election

The people of Israel are elected or chosen by God. Why should this be? What is the reason or purpose of God's action?

For the prophets a *fundamental* concept was that GOD REVEALS THE DIVINE WILL THROUGH HISTORY. History itself has purpose, history *is* purpose. "The divine life confronts, is involved in, decisively qualifies, the life of history. To repudiate it ... to attempt to compromise with it ... is not mere folly, but unqualified disaster" (Napier, 910).

In contemporary times, for much of humanity, another worldview dominates. Generally people today would not say, as the prophets would and did, that "God directs the course of nations." Foreign policy decisions are not reached after the consulting of an oracle or the words from a prophet. Advisors to presidents or prime ministers in most countries do not preface their statements with the formula "Thus says the Lord" or "Hear the word of the Lord." This *is* a different age. Yet in the prophet's view that is exactly how history is to be understood. God works in and through history and historical personages. In Isaiah God "says of Cyrus, 'He is my shepherd, and he shall carry out all my purpose'" (Is 44:28; cf. Is 10:5–6; Jer 32:27ff). God appoints or has anointed both Jews and non-Jews to fulfill the divine will (cf. 2 Kgs 8:7–15; 9:1–10).

[The] characteristic prophetic phenomenon always presupposes (consciously or unconsciously, made explicit or taken for granted, immediately relevant or only of indirect ultimate pertinence) the decisive impingement of Yahweh upon history (Napier, 905).

Israel, therefore, is elected to fulfill a certain role. Israel is to learn God's message of morality and then, by precept and example, teach it to the world. Amos says it succinctly: "You only have I known of all the families of the earth; therefore I will punish you for all your iniquities" (Am 3:2). Israel is God's elect — in the words of Exodus, "a priestly kingdom and a holy nation" (Ex 19:6). Furthermore the people had responded "All that the Lord has spoken we will do" (Ex 24:7). "I am your God and you are my people" — this covenant, this contract, was spoken or expressed again and again in Israel's long history (cf. Jer 31:31–35; 32:38; Hos 2:23 [2:25 H] et al.).

B. Morality

At the core of God's teaching was a standard of morality that could be achieved by humankind. Micah stated the matter incomparably: Imitate God's ways!

> He has told you, O mortal, what is good; and what does the Lord require of you but to do justice, and to love kindness, and to walk humbly with your God? (Mic 6:8; cf. Jer 7:23).

As stated earlier in this book, the prophets were not "opposed" to ritual; indeed some were very favorably disposed toward it. Many of the major prophets have priestly links or interests. The classical prophets saw ritual as a way to bring humans closer to God. Yet ritual was a means, not an end in itself. "'God requires devotion, not devotions' (S. Spiegel, *Amos versus Amaziah* [1957], 43), right not rite. When cult becomes a substitute for moral behavior, it is to be condemned" (Paul, 1173).

Perhaps it was Jeremiah who came closest to causing a severe strain between priest and prophet. Time and again he stood near the temple in Jerusalem and urged the people to paths of morality. His message was: Do not "shed innocent blood in this place . . . do not go after other gods . . . [do not] steal, murder, commit adultery, swear falsely" (Jer 7:6, 9). At one point it is clear that he has so exasperated the priesthood that they literally call for his death for blasphemy, but the prophet responds that he is innocent, he is only speaking in the name of the Lord. This defense — that he is speaking in God's name — is sufficient on this occasion to protect him from harm (Jer 26:2–19).

Morality moves to center stage in the mind of the prophets. While in the past idolatry was *the* cardinal sin, now a whole spectrum of moral wrongs are condemned. "With the emergence of the classical prophets a new criterion became operative — moral rectitude. The destiny of the nation was bound up with it, and unrighteousness would spell the end of Israel" (Paul, 1173; cf. Am 8:4-14; Mic 6:8-16; see also Sandmel, *The Hebrew Scriptures*, 60ff).

A higher moral standard for the nation of Israel was expected simply because, as has been delineated earlier, Israel is God's chosen. In describing the classical prophets notice was taken earlier of the language of relationship and how this underscored the bond between Israel and God. Various metaphors were suggested for God's relationship to Israel: Parent/child; Owner/vineyard; Shepherd/flock and the like.

C. Change Is (Usually) Possible/Repentance

Israel: Israel as the beloved; Israel as the one-held-more-responsible; Israel is to be judged on her actions. A day of reckoning will come, and God will use the surrounding nations, predominantly Assyria, but later Babylon, as rods of chastisement. Such is literally what the prophet prophesies:

Suggested reading: Is 10:5-6, 12-15, 21-22

In this passage it is clear that Assyria is *only* a tool in God's hands and, when its role is over, that "a remnant shall return" to the land.

> [The Lord spoke to me:] "Ah, Assyria, the rod of my anger — the club in their hands is my fury! Against a godless nation I send him. . . ." When the Lord has finished all his work on Mount Zion and on Jerusalem, he will punish the arrogant boasting of the king of Assyria . . . [yet even after your punishment, Israel,] a remnant will return. (See also Jer 32:27-41 — Jerusalem will be punished, but this punishment is limited in time.)

Judgment is certain, yet time and again the prophets urge the people to repent and return to the path of morality. Though the "sin of Judah is written with an iron pen" (Jer 17:1) yet can Israel also seek to repent of her ways. God tells Jeremiah to preach to Israel. "It may be that they will listen, all of them, and will turn from their evil way, that I may change my mind about the disaster that I intend to bring on them because of their evil doings" (Jer 26:3).

In the minds of the rabbis who set the scriptural lectionary lessons which are read on the various sabbaths and holy days in the Jewish year, it was the prophet Hosea who stood out above all to set the tone for repentance. On the sabbath between Rosh Hashana (the Jewish New Year) and Yom Kippur (the Day of Atonement), during that period of the

Jewish year specifically dedicated to repentance, it is Hosea (14:1–9 [14:2–10 H]) along with Micah (7:18–20) and Joel (2:15–17) who is read in the synagogue.

Suggested reading: Hos 14:1–9 [14:2–10 H]

Prophet after prophet hoped for a repentant nation. They preached, at times with little hope of success, but with an unfailing belief that even though many would deservedly suffer, God would eventually take back their people. This ultimate forgiveness shall be discussed below. In the meantime, however, Israel's punishment was deserved. It was not a matter of a capricious God.

Isaiah explains that God will judge against the sinners. God will wreak vengeance on the wicked (Is 1:24–31). The people shall be sent into exile, explains Jeremiah (Jer 25:8–11, 30–38), because of their wrongdoing.

Yet it is not Israel alone who shall know the wrath of the Lord. The surrounding nations, for their wickedness, shall well learn that they too must pay for their evil ways, that they are to be punished for their crimes. There are denunciations of cities such as Damascus, Gaza, Ashdod, Ashkelon, Ekron, and Tyre, and nations as well: Edom, Ammon, Moab (Am 1:3–2:3; see also Is 15:1; 17:1; [Egypt] 19:1; [Philistia] Jer 47:1; 48:1; and Nineveh in Jonah; and Nineveh is the subject in the whole book of Nahum).

In a unique prophecy in early Isaiah a new image was suggested. The people are so decadent that the freedom to repent at times must be taken away from them. Such a suspension of free will is difficult to accept, much less understand, but it is the unmistakable message of the prophet. Since the people will not hear, they must suffer until only a few remain. "Since Israel had so often spurned the words of God and since they had not returned to Him, the privilege of repentance was to be denied them (until only one-tenth of the population remained). The only "cure" for obdurate hardness was to intensify it" (Paul, 1174).

Suggested reading: Is 6:10–13

D. A New Covenant

The election of Israel with a set of moral demands had set her apart from other nations. Yet as is the way with humankind, we are apt to stray. In the words of the later Wisdom literature, "Surely there is no one on earth so righteous as to do good without ever sinning" (Eccl 7:20). Or one might reflect on the even more pessimistic statement in Genesis "that the wickedness of humankind was great in the earth, and that every inclination of the thoughts of their hearts was only evil continually" (6:5). Israel, and the nations as well, would be accused and judged. Eventually Israel *would* repent and God would take Israel back, even as a spouse receives back an erring mate. Poignantly phrased by Hosea:

> How can I give you up, Ephraim? How can I hand you over, O Israel.... My heart recoils within me.... I will not execute my fierce anger; I will not again destroy Ephraim; for I am God and no mortal.... I will not come in wrath (Hos 11:8–9).

A time was coming when God would establish "a new and/or renewed covenant with Israel" (Napier, 917), a covenant grafted to the very hearts of the people. It is very easy to understand how Christianity could read the words of a Jeremiah (31:31–34), an Ezekiel (34:23ff; 36:26ff) or a Second Isaiah (55:3–5) and understand this to refer to the work of Christ on behalf of a new people of God, the church. It was perfectly understandable — viewed through the prism of Christianity — for the writers of the Christian Scriptures to feel that these prophetic words were realized in Jesus and the nascent Church.

Luke (22:20; cf. 1 Cor 11:25) has Jesus speak of the "new covenant" which is mentioned in Jeremiah 31:31, a covenant to be written on the hearts of the people. The writer of the epistle to the Hebrews (8:8–12; 10:16–17) likewise makes reference to these words from Jeremiah. Coincidentally, Jeremiah 31:31–34 is so central to the theology of the Christian Scripture that it has the distinction of being the longest sustained quote from the Jewish Bible.

Suggested reading: Jer 31:31–34

While it is easy to understand how and why Christianity appropriated these lines, as well as similar ones, there is nothing in the original text which indicates other than the thought that God will re-establish the divine covenant with the Jewish people. As explained earlier, the Hebrew prophets were speaking to contemporary audiences. Both prophet and people expected these prophecies to come about within a short time of their being uttered. For a Jewish understanding of Jeremiah 31:31–34 see Text Study in the Jeremiah chapter below.

E. The Future Mission

To be God's people in a new fashion, to renew and/or re-establish the relationship with God was seen by many of the prophets as but the first step of a larger role for Israel. A better day was coming, a time when the knowledge of God would fill the earth, "as the waters cover the sea" (Is 11:9). Jerusalem will become the center of world learning, and God's message of righteousness will flow to the ends of the earth (Mic 4:2; see also Is 2:2–3; 51:4ff).

In the words of Second Isaiah, God is specifically sending Israel to be a "light to the nations" (42:6; 49:6), for her role is to be wider than just the restoration of Israel in her homeland (49:5–6).

Second Isaiah also would offer the image of a "servant of the Lord" who would bring this message (Is 42:1–4; 49:1–6; 50:4–9; 52:13–53:12). This servant first would be reviled, but then the message would be accepted. Again it is easy to understand how, some six hundred years and more after Second Isaiah's words, the nascent Church could appropriate this prediction to refer to Jesus. The fact remains that the prophets saw this as an internal *Jewish* phenomenon, even though the message was for the world at large.

The classical prophets saw a wider role for Israel than their predecessors. No doubt their historical experience deeply influenced their judgment. The fact that there also were viable Jewish communities in Egypt and Babylonia/Persia helped to establish a worldview. They never, however, eclipsed their belief that the beacon, the light itself, God's teaching of light, emanated from Zion in Jerusalem. Though Isaiah (and Micah) are relatively early among the classical prophets, their words reflect their contemporaries and their heirs (see Napier, 918).

Suggested reading: Is 2:2–4 and Mic 4:1–3.

The classical prophets owed a great deal to their predecessors, leaders such as Samuel, Nathan, Elijah and Elisha. Broadly there is a living link between a Moses, a Micaiah and a Malachi. The classical/literary/latter prophets also often shared moral concerns; they were involved in social and religious issues. They were orators and poets, speakers of the word of God. Let us now turn to that pivotal figure who flourished in the last half of the eighth century, the prophet known as First Isaiah.

Chapter 4

FIRST ISAIAH

The book of Isaiah, some sixty-six chapters, is generally recognized to be a composite work of at least two and possibly three voices. These divisions are based on several criteria, including historical context, stylistics, and grammatical analysis. The three generally agreed divisions are chapters 1–39, called "First Isaiah," chapters 40–55, "Second Isaiah," and chapters 56–66, "Third Isaiah." Other scholars divide Isaiah into only two parts, First Isaiah (1–39) and Second Isaiah (40–66).

First Isaiah lived in Jerusalem in the last half of the eighth century. His period of prophecy covers at least four decades, 742–701 BCE.

1. Geo-Political Background

The geo-political background to Isaiah is the rise of Assyria, and that empire's expansion westward aiming to challenge and hopefully conquer Egypt. "Since the route of conquest lay through Palestine, the two kingdoms of Israel and Judah were menaced" (Sandmel, *The Hebrew Scriptures*, 83). In an effort to stave off Assyria, the northern kingdom of Israel (which is often called Ephraim) forms an alliance with her neighboring country, Aram (Syria). Knowing that the addition of another partner to this alliance would help, Judah is invited to join. She refuses, and so Aram (Syria) and Israel (Ephraim) lay siege to Jerusalem. This is known as the Syro–Ephraimitic war of 734 BCE. King Ahaz of Judah refused the invitation to join the Syro–Ephraimitic alliance, but then, apparently ignoring Isaiah's advice of absolute neutrality, Ahaz opts to become a vassal of Assyria (2 Kgs 15:37–16:9; Is 7:1–9). Tiglath Pileser III (745–727) attacks and subjugates Aram and Israel. About a dozen years later King

Hoshea of Israel (732–724) — who should not be confused with the prophet Hosea — rebels against Assyria. It is a fatal mistake. In 721, under the leadership of Sargon II (722–705) Israel, the northern kingdom, is utterly destroyed and the people taken into exile. This marks the *end* of the ten tribes as a separate entity.

The two-decade-long rule of King Ahaz of Judah (735–715) is followed by an even longer reign by King Hezekiah (715–687). Vassalage to Assyria meant economically difficult days for Judah. The rich continue to tax the poor to pay the heavy tribute. Meantime pagan worship has entered the land again, though Hezekiah does bring about some religious reforms. In 705 Sargon II is killed. Using his death as a pretext a number of countries revolt against Assyria. Against Isaiah's advice (chapters 30 and 31) Hezekiah joins the revolt against Sennacherib and sides with Egypt. It was a politically unwise decision, for the Assyrians then march against Judah.

> The Assyrian armies brought destruction upon forty-six of Judah's fortified cities, killing many of their inhabitants and deporting others. Jerusalem itself was besieged.... The siege ended with Hezekiah's total submission, increased tribute ... and the loss of most of his territory (2 Kings 18:13–16) (A. S. Herbert, Cambridge Bible Commentary, *Isaiah 1–39*, 7).

The last one hears from Isaiah is toward the end of the eighth century, about 701, when Hezekiah submits. Coincidentally it is at this time that the famous underground tunnel is cut through nearly 1800 feet of rock to the spring of Gihon (2 Kgs 20:20; see also 2 Kgs 18–20; Is 36–39).

2. The Central Ideas of Isaiah

God is a deity who works in and through history. Consequently Isaiah teaches trust in God and not in "foreign alliances" (chapters 7, 37). God directs Israel's history and that of the other nations as well (chapters 10, 13–23, 37). God is an exalted God, and at the same time the deity demands faith and righteous living of the people (chapters 1–3, 5). God will call the people to repentance and demand that they change (1:18, 25–28). As Abraham Joshua Heschel remarked, "Isaiah's primary concern is not Judah's foreign policy, but rather the inner state of the nation" (1.77).

The people will be punished for their wrongdoing, but in the end a remnant shall be saved and Jerusalem shall stand (10:20–23, 27, 32;

37:31-32). Further, teaches Isaiah, the future will eventually be peaceful, and the Davidic dynasty will rule in justice and equity (11:1-13; 12:1-6).

3. Reading Isaiah

Like so much of the Bible, Isaiah cannot be read chapter after chapter as if this book were a novel with a beginning, middle and end. Isaiah is composed of a collection of prophecies which were set down, some at his time, some later. It "is necessary to distinguish the words (and the biography and autobiography) of the prophet ... from the words of his disciples ..." (Winward, 73).

That some of Isaiah's prophecies were delivered orally is clear from their context (see 7:1ff; 38:1ff), and that some were literally written down — at God's command — is equally clear, for the text reports as much (8:1ff; 30:8).

Isaiah is not an easy book; it is a country of its own, and therefore, as one studies, it is very helpful to do so with a commentary, or, to carry the metaphor further, it is prudent to read and study with a guide, a road map.

4. First Isaiah in the Christian Scriptures

The most famous passage from Isaiah that appears in the Christian Scriptures is taken from Isaiah 7. These are the famous "Immanuel" verses. We shall return to a more detailed analysis of this passage in the "Text Study" section. What is at issue? The setting takes place in Jerusalem. The city is under siege. King Ahaz is fearful and does not know how to respond. Isaiah wishes to provide comfort to the king, but Ahaz is distant and tries to ignore the advice of the prophet. Incensed, Isaiah explains that like it or not, a sign will be given to the court. Isaiah then points to a young woman nearby who is pregnant. She is about to give birth, says Isaiah. Call his name "Immanuel" — literally "God is with us." Isaiah goes on to suggest that before the child is weaned the siege will be lifted. Since Ahaz did not have faith in God, Jerusalem will be punished nevertheless.

The word for "young woman" in the Hebrew of vs 14 is *almah*. The term *almah* means "young woman," a post-pubescent female as distinguished from a *betulah* which is the word for "virgin." The note to Isaiah 7:14 in the NRSV *New Oxford Annotated Bible* explains:

Young woman, Hebrew "'almah," feminine of "'elem," young man (1 Sam 17.56; 20.22); the word appears in Gen 24.43; Ex 2.8; Ps 68.25, and elsewhere, where it is translated "young woman," "girl," "maiden."

It was through a *mistranslation* that the word "virgin" appears. When "'almah" was translated into Greek, the word "*parthenos*" or "virgin" was used. In the gospels, Matthew (in 1:23) relies on this late tradition. Professor Otto Kaiser, the internationally known and respected Christian scholar, and author of the commentary on *Isaiah 1–12* published in the Westminster Press "Old Testament Library" series, states the case clearly:

> Against the ancient christological interpretation, it can be shown that the whole context demands an event which is shortly to come about, and that the Hebrew word *'alma,* like its Ugaritic equivalent *glmt,* does not simply correspond to the word "virgin" but signifies a young woman without regard to whether she is married or single. The messianic interpretation of the verse is refuted by v. 17, as well as by the whole context of the passage (Kaiser, 101–102).

As we pointed out in the Preface, readers need to bear in mind that the prophets were speaking to a *contemporary audience* that readily understood their allusions and references. The prophets fully expected that God's role in shaping history would be realized in the near future, perhaps a decade of years if not even earlier. Punishment, and latterly repentance and salvation, were *near* events, to come about in a short period of time, prophecies to be known not hundreds of years, much less thousands of years in the future. Jews understand Isaiah to be addressing an event in his own day. Clearly some Christians understand his words as predictive of Jesus.

Professor Kaiser also dismisses the claim that this boy who is to be born the following year refers to Hezekiah, for Hezekiah already "was sixteen or seventeen years old" at this time (102). Does Isaiah really suggest that Immanuel refers to the "good news" of Jesus? The answer is no. *In its context* the reference to Immanuel is in the nature of a threat, not a happy prediction. There will be temporary relief from the problems at hand (hence "God-is-with-us" — Immanuel) but the wrath of Assyria will follow. Likewise, as Christopher R. North, professor emeritus of University College of North Wales, explains, there is no indication that

Jesus was "called Immanuel, except subsequently, and occasionally, in the language of devotion" ("Immanuel," *IDB*, 687).

5. Isaiah and Jewish Sources

Isaiah's commission in chapter 6 forms part of the "Text Study" below. It contains the familiar words "Holy, holy, holy is the Lord of hosts." This phrase has been incorporated into the liturgies of both the Synagogue and the Church. In the Bible these words are recited by seraphim (angels) on high. According to Jewish tradition they are angels whose specific role is to do God's will (*Midrash Exodus Rabbah* 25.2). Another midrash explains that as these seraphim proclaim God's greatness three times, so do Jews praise God in their daily service with the words "God of Abraham, God of Isaac, God of Jacob" to correspond to the angels' Trisagion (*Midrash Exodus Rabbah* 15.6).

In the biblical text it mentions that the seraphim are six-winged. With two they fly, and the other pairs cover their faces and legs. The reference to covering their eyes presumably is to protect them from seeing the heavenly appearance. Covering their "legs" or "feet" has been explained as referring to their calf-like feet (*Midrash Leviticus Rabbah* 27.3 based on Ezekiel 1:7), for exposing such hooves would remind God of the blasphemy of the golden calf (Ex 32:1ff).

In that same passage, a seraph takes a burning coal and touches it to Isaiah's lips to purify him (Is 6:6–7). The rabbis linked this passage to the words in Deuteronomy (30:11–12): "Surely, this commandment . . . is not too hard for you, nor is it too far away. It is not in heaven that you should say, 'Who will go up to heaven for us, and get it for us so that we may hear it and observe it?' There is a double message here. The angels wanted God's laws and blessings, but it is too abstruse for them, they are for humankind" (*Midrash Deuteronomy Rabbah* 8.2). Further, now that humans have God's instruction, they are responsible for following it and able to receive the blessings which go with it.

6. Text Study

Suggested reading: Is 6:1–8 — Isaiah's commission

This passage is best known by vs 3 ("Holy, holy, holy is the Lord of hosts") because it has been incorporated into the liturgy of Judaism and many Christian churches. The whole scene suggests the prophet Isaiah's familiarity with the temple in Jerusalem, its precincts and rites. It "is of great importance to notice that the prophet does not actually describe Yahweh himself, but only the hem of his garment and the seraphim. Thus he has not actually seen God himself, but 'has only been aware of His presence in what he has seen'" (Kaiser, 74, quoting E. Brunner, *Revelation and Reason*, 97).

Vs 1 This reference to a specific time sets Isaiah's "call" in the year 742 BCE.

Vss 2–3 The seraphim seem to be some extra-celestial beings whose function is primarily to attend upon the deity. Earlier we explained a midrashic explanation of why their legs or feet were covered. The word "legs" may actually refer to genitalia. In a note to this verse, the Roman Catholic volume *The Jerusalem Bible* suggests that "feet" here are a "euphemism for sexual organs."

Vss 4–7 The smoke refers probably to the incense which was part of the temple cult (Lev 16:12ff). An echo of it is found in special masses found in the Roman Catholic and Orthodox as well as the Episcopal churches where burning incense is part of the ritual.

Isaiah's recognition that he is but human, and therefore flawed, echoes Abraham's statement that he is but "dust and ashes" (Gen 18:27). That the seraph touches Isaiah's *lips* is appropriate symbolic action, for it is with his lips that he will give expression to God's words. Only after he has been purified and sanctified does he become God's messenger.

Vs 8 Isaiah's lack of hesitation is in contrast to the lack of enthusiasm of taking on the prophetic role displayed by a Moses, Jeremiah or Jonah. The Hebrew literally translated says "Who will go for *us*?" This can be understood as either the magisterial plural, or recognition that Isaiah like his forebear Micaiah (1 Kgs 22:19) has stood before the heavenly council.

Isaiah's alacrity in accepting this commission is not unnoticed by the rabbis (*Midrash Leviticus Rabbah* 10.2). Whereas other prophets offered single words of comfort and cheer, they explain that Isaiah will double those efforts ("Comfort, O comfort my people; Awake, awake, put on strength; I, I am he who comforts you; Rouse yourself, rouse yourself! Stand up O Jerusalem" — Is 40:1; 51:9, 12, 17).

Suggested reading: Is 5:1–8, 18–21 — Social justice

Another facet of Isaiah is the prophet who is concerned with social justice. In the opening lines of chapter 5 (vss 1–6) Isaiah lays out the groundwork for his message. He begins with the pastoral image of a wedding feast, where the poet sings of a friend who has built a beautiful vineyard. It has been planted with choice vines and a winepress has been hewn out. Yet instead of grapes, it yields wild grapes. God then asks rhetorically: What else could I have done? "When I expected it to yield grapes, why did it yield wild grapes?" (vs 4). Next God explains that the wall will be trampled; it will become a desolation and a ruin. "For the vineyard of the Lord of hosts is the house of Israel. . . . [God] expected justice, but saw bloodshed; righteousness, but heard a cry!" (vs 7). In this instance the Jewish Publication Society translation of the Bible, *TANAKH*, certainly comes closer to capturing the word-play in the Hebrew. There verse 7 reads:

> [God] hoped for justice, but behold injustice, for equity, but behold, iniquity.

Note the conscious play-on-words: justice/injustice and equity/iniquity. This excellent translation of the Hebrew reflects the sense of the biblical text. As Samuel Sandmel noted, the Bible "has no disdain for puns" and these last "lines contain two, which come as a gripping climax of denunciation at the end of this love song:

> *He hoped for* mishpat [justice] *but there was* mispah [injustice],
> *For* tzedaqa [equity], *but there was* tze-'aqa [iniquity]" (Sandmel, *The Hebrew Scriptures*, 92).

Then in vss 8 and 18–21 Isaiah lays out in stark detail the immorality, the rapaciousness, the traders in malevolence and evil who stand before him. Not only are they venomous and corrupt, but they are irredeemable hypocrites. They piously call for God to execute divine justice (as if they were innocent of any wrongdoing), and on top of it they falsify the very meaning of words, calling evil good, and good evil, bitter as sweet, and sweet as bitter (vs 20).

As Abraham Joshua Heschel explained, while the purpose of the vineyard had been to plant and produce righteousness and justice, "the fruit it yielded was violence and outrage, affecting God, arousing His anger. . . . Isaiah pleads for the meek and the poor, condemning the ruthless and scoffers. . . . It is the moral corruption of the leaders that has shattered God's relationship to His people" (1.85–86).

Coincidentally, in the Christian Scriptures, Jesus' denunciation in Matthew 23:13ff "of some, not all, Pharisees" (NRSV, *The New Oxford Annotated Bible*, note to Mt 23:13) reflects a similar sevenfold cataloging of woes, again featuring hypocrisy as a major misdemeanor (see Kaiser, 63ff).

Rabbi Akiva who lived a generation after Matthew, during the Roman oppression of Judea in the first third of the second century CE, explained that at first sin is like a spider's web, but eventually becomes as thick as a ship's rope. His "prooftext" is from Isaiah 5:18, "Ah, you who . . . drag sin along as with cart ropes" (*Midrash Genesis Rabbah* 22.6).

Suggested reading: Is 7:10-17 — The "Immanuel" passage

Isaiah was speaking to a contemporary audience. They immediately understood his allusions. Living close to three thousand years later, it is not surprising that these references are unclear to us. Without an explanation of who is involved, this remains a very confusing passage.

The background to these verses is the Syro–Ephraimitic war of 734 BCE. Vss 1–9 are fairly easy to understand once the major characters are delineated. Judah is under siege from Israel and Syria. Isaiah says simply: Ignore them; they are no real threat to you. They are bluffing; they are, to use the prophet's image in vs 4, smoking stumps of wood. Their smoke creates the illusion of fire, but it is only an illusion.

Pekah	= son of Remaliah = king of Israel
Israel	= Ephraim
Samaria	= the capital city of Israel (Ephraim)
Rezin	= king of Aram
Aram	= Syria
Damascus	= the capital city of Aram (Syria)
Son of Tabeel	= an otherwise unknown figure who would be placed as a "puppet" ruler to succeed King Ahaz of Judah.

Isaiah meets the king along with the royal entourage at a location near the fuller's field. A fuller is someone who is involved in the preparation of wool into cloth. The fulling process took the wool and thickened it after cleaning it of its natural oils. The location of the fuller's field may be ironic because the same word used here as a noun, is used in

Jeremiah in its verbal form to speak of Jerusalem washing [fulling] "your heart clean of wickedness" (Jer 4:14; see also Ps 51:2 [51:4 H]). Likewise in Malachi, the messenger is likened to a fuller's lye or soap. In the Christian Scriptures, during the transfiguration, Jesus' garments are described as whiter than any fuller could bleach them (Mk 9:3).

The issue at hand in vss 10–17 is whether or not King Ahaz is going to be faithful to God, or whether he is going to ally himself either with his besiegers or the Assyrians. Isaiah counsels/prophesies neutrality, but Ahaz disregards this advice and allies himself with the Assyrians under Tiglath Pileser III (2 Kgs 16:5–9; 15:29).

Vss 10-12 On the face of it King Ahaz is being respectful of both God and prophet. "I will not ask ... I will not put the Lord to the test." His use of the word "test" is the same verb as is found in Deuteronomy 6:16 ("Do not put the Lord your God to the test as you tested him at Massah" — see Ex 17:1-7). Yet behind his refusal is not faith but faithlessness, not respect but disrespect. Four hundred years earlier, the judge Gideon had asked for a sign and he was given it without any censure (Jgs 6:17ff). "It is evident that Ahaz knew that the sign would be given, that it would point to a way of life already declared in verse 9, and therefore would condemn the policy, reliance upon Assyria, on which he was already determined" (Herbert, 64).

Vss 13-17 Since Ahaz refuses to accept the sign, what was to be a sign of hope now becomes a note of coming disaster. In vs 13 Isaiah addresses the royal entourage as much as King Ahaz when he says that it is bad enough to treat humans as helpless, but far worse to treat God as helpless. Then comes the scathing "Immanuel" passage, offering not succor but despair.

Suggested readings: Is 9:2-7 [9:1-6 H] and 11:1-10 — Two possible messianic passages

To what extent is it even correct to refer to "possible messianic passages" in Isaiah? The very brief answer is that while the biblical prophets had no intention of their words being construed as "messiah-oriented," nonetheless certain passages were considered by *later* religious leaders to be messianic, to refer to a human "savior." This is not the place to rehearse the many reasons, but we can repeat Gilbert S. Rosenthal's astute analysis (mentioned earlier in Chapter 1, Section 9, that "there is no *personal* messiah in the [Jewish] Bible. Rather we detect in this notion *soteriology,* human messengers or mortal agents, who carry out God's will and pave the way for salvation. In the [Jewish] Bible, God *alone* is the king-redeemer."

What, then, were some of the verses that were taken by later religious leaders, both Jewish and Christian, to refer to a [or to "the"] messiah? The key verse in this first section under consideration is from Isaiah 9:6 [9:5 H].

> For a child has been born for us, a son given to us ... named Wonderful Counselor, Mighty God, Everlasting Father, Prince of Peace [*sar shalom*].

While Christianity saw this as referring to Jesus, and being directly linked to Isaiah 7:14, Jewish commentators in the Talmud and midrash were just as sure that it referred to Hezekiah (*Midrash Genesis Rabbah* 97 [NV]; Babylonian Talmud *Sanhedrin* 94a; *Midrash Ruth Rabbah* 7.2). Another possibility in Jewish tradition was that the "child ... son ... Prince of Peace" was also seen as the future messiah (*Midrash Deuteronomy Rabbah* 1.20) or to the peace of the Davidic line (*Midrash Numbers Rabbah* 11.7 on Isa 9:7 [9:6 H]).

In the case of Isaiah 11:1–9, there are clear connections between these verses of psalm-like quality and the verses dealt with above in Isaiah 9. A number of scholars have noted the similarities between these two passages (Newsome, 77; Herbert, 89; Kaiser, 158–159; Winward, 85–87). These prophecies of a Davidic line which shall be filled with "the spirit of wisdom and understanding, the spirit of counsel and might, the spirit of knowledge and the fear of the Lord" (Is 11:2) are meant to contrast with the shallow faith and lack of courage of King Ahaz. "Whether the poem was composed by Isaiah, quoted or adapted by him from a temple psalm, or included here by the disciple who edited this collection of prophecies, it is impossible to say" (Herbert, 89–90).

What is remarkable about this particular piece is how scholars have read into it a sure messianic flavor which is not necessarily part of the text itself. A. S. Herbert (89) states unambiguously that "The word 'anointed' (messiah) does not actually appear in these verses," but then he goes on to say "but it is implied in the description of the investiture of the Davidic king" (see Newsome, 78; Winward, 87). Jewish sources also have regarded this as a messianic foretelling (see I. W. Slotki, *Isaiah*, 56). Certainly it is correct to point out that often in the midrashic literature the verse "the spirit of the Lord shall rest on him" (11:2) is taken to refer to the messiah (*Midrash Genesis Rabbah* 2.4; *Midrash Numbers Rabbah* 13.11; *Midrash Ruth Rabbah* 7.2), but that verse also was explained as referring more generically to prophets (*Midrash Numbers Rabbah* 14.10).

There are also obvious parallels between vss 2–3 and the Wisdom literature such as Proverbs 8 where there are references to wisdom (*hochma*), understanding (*tevunah/bina*), counsel [righteousness] (*tzedek*) and fear [reverence] (*yirah*) for the Lord.

The images of peace in the world of humankind and animals, and peace between humans and beasts, is indeed endearing and with the closing words that "the earth will be full of the knowledge of the Lord as the waters cover the sea" (vs 9). It is a wonderfully poetic reference and counterpart to the days following Noah and the flood where humankind was given dominion over all the animals, fish and fowl (Gen 9:1–2). In Isaiah's words, there will be a future time of true peace between *all* God's creatures, for peace is to cover the earth, not water, to heal, not to harm, and evil and vile actions shall be no more.

Chapter 5

JEREMIAH

He has been called a prophet of doom, a man of lamentation, some-one who was deeply burdened by the condition of his people. His con-fessions and inward reflections have been compared to Paul, Augustine and Martin Luther (J. Muilenberg, "Jeremiah the Prophet," *IDB*, 824). Abraham Joshua Heschel speaks of Jeremiah as a prophet whose soul was in pain, stern with gloom (1.105). He was all this and more. His name lives on in the English word "jeremiad" which is defined as a lamenta-tion or lugubrious complaint. Jeremiah was one of the greatest of the Hebrew prophets, a man of vision, stature and leadership, of powerful rhetoric and beautiful poetry. He prophesied over a period of four decades, from c. 627/626–585 BCE, speaking his words in Jerusalem.

As was true of First Isaiah, and before him the former prophets Samuel, Nathan, and Elijah, Jeremiah dared to stand up to power. He would suffer for his heroism, but he would not shirk from his duty. As his predecessors, Jeremiah knew that "the prophet was not a *primus inter pares*, first among his peers. By his very claim, his was the voice of supreme authority. He not only rivaled the decisions of the king and the counsel of the priest, he defied and even condemned their words and deeds" (Heschel, 2.260).

1. Geo-Political Background

A. *Changes in World Empires; Reactions in Judah (c. 630–580 BCE)*

The geo-political background to Jeremiah is the steady decline of Assyrian hegemony, and the corresponding ascendancy of the Babylon-ian empire. In terms of Jewish history the two most important events were the "discovery" of the scroll of the Torah (Deuteronomy) in 622/621 BCE during the reign of King Josiah and the fall of Jerusalem in 586 BCE with the corresponding destruction of the first temple. Those events are so central to the life, times, and prophecy of Jeremiah that they need to be developed further.

The Assyrian empire had come into its own in the latter part of the eighth century. The fall of the northern kingdom of Israel in 722/721 BCE during the life of First Isaiah also signaled what was to be roughly a hundred year state of vassalage to the rulers of Assyria. Tiglath Pileser III and his successors, Shalmanneser V and Sargon II, had taken control of the Near East, and among many others the Hebrew kingdoms were no match for them. By the period of 627 BCE, however, Assyrian power was in severe decline. The death of their ruler Ashurbanipal (669–627) marked the imminent collapse of this era. The Babylonians (Chaldeans) under Nabopolassar (626–605) filled this vacuum as we see the rise of the neo-Babylonian empire.

In Judah, under the leadership of King Josiah (640–609), certain changes were taking place. There was an attempt to declare independence from Assyria. In addition, important work began toward religious reform. About 615 Assyria, in an attempt to stem the Babylonian tide, allied itself with Egypt. Egypt sought to regain its former control over the land mass just east of the Mediterranean, including Judah-Phoenicia-Syria. In 612 BCE the Assyrians were crushed by the Babylonians, and Nineveh, the Assyrian capital, was destroyed. In 609 the Egyptians, under Pharaoh Neco, sought to assist their ally, the Assyrians.

> At Megiddo ... [King] Josiah tried to stop him. Whether Josiah acted as an ally of Babylon, or independently, is unknown; but he could hardly have wished an Egypto-Assyrian victory, the result of which would have been to place his country at the mercy of Egypt's ambitions. Be that as it may, it was a futile and suicidal action. Josiah was killed and brought dead in his chariot to Jerusalem amid great lamentation (II Kings, xxiii, 29 f; II Chron. xxxv, 20–25). His son, Jehoahaz was made king in his place (John Bright, *Jeremiah*, xlvi).

King Jehoahaz (609) ruled but a few months and was followed by his brother King Jehoiakim (609–598 — not to be confused with his son, Jehoiachin, who came to the throne in 598 BCE).

In short order King Jehoiakim became a vassal of Babylonia about 604. In 601 he rebelled, but tactically it was a fatal error. The Babylonian army devastated the outlying areas of Judah. Jehoiakim died late in

598, and was followed by Jehoiachin who was forced to capitulate early the next year. The ruler Nebuchadnezzar "behaved with relative leniency. Contenting himself with deporting the King [Jehoiachin], the queen mother, the court officials, military leaders, and skilled artisans to Babylon, and seizing considerable bounty, he allowed the little state to continue in existence, placing the king's uncle Zedekiah, another one of Josiah's sons, on the throne as his vassal (II Kings xxiv 10–17). Judah had been granted a brief respite" (Bright, xlix).

Zedekiah's rule was disastrous for Judah. Not strong enough to suppress their activities, he allowed a rebellious group to agitate for independence. Finally Babylonia decided to put an end to the matter. In 589 they invaded, and by 587/586 the southern kingdom had ceased to be, and the temple built by Solomon was razed to the ground.

B. Josiah's Religious Reform (c. 622 BCE)

To appreciate the messages of Jeremiah we need to return to the last quarter of the seventh century BCE. King Josiah's religious reforms often are mistakenly associated with the "discovery" of the book of Deuteronomy (as detailed in 2 Kings 22–23) in the eighteenth year of his reign, 622/621 BCE. Without doubt Josiah welcomed this "find" but the religious reformation began some five years earlier. The Bible differs on the dates of the reform.

> According to Kings (II Kings xxii 3; xxiii 23) the entire reform took place in Josiah's eighteenth regnal year (622) and was based on "the book of the law," a copy of which had been found in the temple in the course of repairs to that structure. But … the very fact that the temple was being repaired when the lawbook was found indicates that reform was already in progress, for the repairing and purification of the temple was itself a reform measure (Bright, xxxix).

This latter contention is supported by the writer of Chronicles who explains that the reform had been going on for several years before the lawbook was found (2 Chr 34:3–8).

In any case a definite move against syncretism was undertaken, with Josiah rooting out Canaanite and probably Assyrian idol worship as well (see 2 Kgs 23:4–14, 24; 23:15–20; 2 Chr 34:6f). In addition Josiah sought to centralize political *and* religious power in Jerusalem. He invited religious leaders from the outlying areas to come to Jerusalem to take their place among the Jerusalem priesthood, to function at the temple (2 Kgs 23:8).

The reforms, the changes in ritual regulations, were linked to a growing sense of nationalistic fervor. As Assyria went into political decline, Judah flexed its political and religious muscle. Whether the religious reform led to the nationalistic ambitions or the nationalistic ambitions led to religious reform is really a moot question. No doubt, they affected and were effected by each other. They were ideas and actions in symbiosis.

The meaning and background to the "discovery" of the "Book of the Teaching" (*Sefer haTorah* — 2 Kgs 22:8) and its being the kernel of our present book of Deuteronomy are too complex to deal with here. The obvious question of why neither Jeremiah nor his contemporary Zephaniah was consulted remains a mystery. The enigma extends to the one prophet who was consulted, namely the female prophet Hulda, about whom we know nothing aside from this incident.

Finally, the key question might be asked: How successful were the Josianic reforms? It is difficult to know how to answer, for there is insufficient material dealing with it in the Bible. The writer of Kings (2 Kgs 23:25) felt that Josiah and his reforms were excellent. That it had some good effect is sure. That others, including the displaced priesthood, resented it is also likely. Unfortunately the reforms, no matter how effective they were, did not sufficiently (and the key word is "sufficiently") change the national character because, as we learn from Jeremiah's words (Jer 6:16–21), what repentance did take place was simply not as thorough as was necessary. Likewise, as shall be shown, the wealthy as well as the powerful continued to pay only lip service to the covenantal relationship with God (see Jer 7:1ff). They were far from moral in their actions.

Following Josiah's death in 609, the country slipped back (see 7:16–20, 30, 31) and the results, in the mind of the biblical writers (as well as in the mind of the rabbis during Talmudic times), would be the reason for the destruction of the temple and the fall of Judah.

C. The Temple's Destruction

It is almost impossible to gauge deeply enough the feeling of depression, dejection and downright devastation that would describe accurately the feelings of the Jerusalemites and Judeans following the temple's destruction. God's house which had stood for nearly four hundred years was no more. The building which symbolized God's presence, God's care for the people and the nation, was gone. Razed, burnt, smoldering ruins, the holy of holies had been violated and obliterated! It would be equivalent to the destruction of the major historical buildings of a country's capital, destroyed: for example, the buildings of Washington, DC: the White House, the Congress, the Supreme Court; in Ottawa, the Parliament, Supreme Court or the Public Archives; in London, the Houses of Parliament, Buckingham Palace and the National Gallery; in Paris, the Chamber of Deputies, the Sorbonne and the Louvre — all destroyed and the leadership there taken into exile by the enemy. As American, Canadian, British or French morale would be at the lowest ebb ever, so was the morale and will of this ancient people. Jeremiah's voice had prophesied this day, but the people had not believed. Now, following this devastation, Jeremiah reversed his stand. He began to speak of a day of redemption and of hope. That, too, would be difficult to appreciate, but as shall be shown below, it gave the people succor in the weeks, months and years of their grief.

2. The Book of Jeremiah

The book of Jeremiah is a collection of collections, a group of books by and about the prophet Jeremiah. It contains poetry, preaching, narrative, history, and biography as well as prophecy. There have been numerous ways suggested how to divide the text we have received. While at its simplest we could consider the categories as poetry, biography and prose, a more detailed division offers a clearer picture.

Chapters 1–25 *Poetry and preaching* — much written in these chapters is in the first person. It includes prophecies against Jerusalem and Judah.

Chapters 26–45 *Prose and biography* — this section includes the subdivisions of chapters 30–31 and 32–33 which together have been labeled "The Book of Consolation" (Bright, 284) or the "Little Book of Comfort" (Muilenberg, 834). It contains a great deal of material by Baruch ben Neriah, Jeremiah's disciple or secretary.

Chapters 46–51 *Prophecies against foreign nations* (Egypt, Philistia, Moab, Ammon et al.).

Chapter 52 *Historical appendix* — this is taken almost verbatim from 2 Kings 24:18–25:30 and describes the fall of Jerusalem and the early years of Babylonian exile.

Jeremiah came from a priestly family in Anatoth, a village a few miles north of Jerusalem (1:1). His years of prophecy probably began in 627/626 BCE (though some scholars argue for a later date; see Jer 1:2ff; Bright, lxxxviiff; Muilenberg, 825; Heschel, 1.103; Sandmel, *The Hebrew*

Scriptures, 127). In any case the preponderance of his prophecies would seem to come after the year 609, which means they were spoken during the last year of King Josiah, or more likely during the reigns of Josiah's successors Jehoiakim, and then Jehoiachin and Zedekiah.

Jeremiah's ministry begins with his summons by God in the first chapter. Assuming that this is at 627/626, the next few chapters deal with an unknown foe from the north (2–6).

Early on in Jeremiah's prophecy came the Josianic reform. As noted earlier, Jeremiah certainly supported it, but felt that it did not go far enough, nor was it taken sufficiently seriously by the people.

"Soon after the accession of [King] Jehoiakim [in 609], Jeremiah preached what is now called his Temple Sermon. The event is recorded in Chapter 26, but the sermon delivered on that occasion is outlined in Chapter 7:1–15" (Winward, 131; see also Bright, 58; Muilenberg, 826). The message was simple and succinct: reform your ways, behave justly, renounce immorality and idolatry, or God will bring utter destruction!

This sermon shall be analyzed below, but suffice it to say that it was *not* well received by the priests and nobles and Jeremiah nearly forfeited his life for giving it.

In the next few years (609–605) Jeremiah continued to preach and prophesy against the rule of Jehoiakim. At one point (Jer 22:13–17) he actually contrasts the wickedness of the king against the virtues of the former King Josiah. Then in 605 BCE Jeremiah is told by God to dictate a book (scroll) to Baruch, detailing his prophecies from the day of Josiah until the present. God says: "It may be that when the house of Judah hears of all the disasters that I intend to do to them, all of them may turn from their evil ways, so that I may forgive their iniquity and their sin" (Jer 36:3).

This chapter also will be considered in more detail below. In the event, King Jehoiakim and his inner coterie are totally disinterested in Jeremiah's prophecy. For this insolence and contempt God promises that Jehoiakim will die "and his dead body shall be cast out to the heat by day and the frost by night. And I will punish him and his offspring and his servants for their iniquity ... [for] they would not listen" (Jer 36:30–31). The importance of this chapter is that it follows upon the Babylonians' crushing defeat of the Egyptians at Carchemish in 605 and signals the coming invasion of Judah.

Jehoiakim first accepts vassalage to Babylon and then rebels (see 2 Kgs 24:1). Caught up with other, more pressing matters the Babylonians did not immediately respond, but then by 598 BCE Jerusalem was besieged. Jehoiakim died (he may have been assassinated) and was followed briefly by his son Jehoiachin. Just prior to the king's death Jeremiah uses mimetic action to indicate God's will.

Described in the opening verses of chapter 13 Jeremiah takes a loin-cloth of linen and is told to symbolically bury it by the river Euphrates. Clearly God means this as a symbol and Jeremiah is not to go to the real river, many hundred miles distant, but a river nearby with a similar name. After a period of time he is told to go and retrieve it. In the mean-while it has disintegrated. In similar manner says God, as that loincloth now has no worth, it "is good for nothing," so are the people of Judah worthless. The symbolism of the Euphrates points to the coming exile where the Judeans will be deported (Bright, 95). Other symbolic action takes place later in chapter 13 and also in chapter 19.

In 597 Jerusalem capitulates and the new king and the queen mother are taken into exile. Jeremiah offers them no hope, but tells them they will die in a foreign land (Jer 22:24–27). Only a decade is left for the fate-ful kingdom. Zedekiah sits on the throne, but he is a weak and indecisive sovereign. Friendly toward Jeremiah, he seeks his counsel but in fact does not or cannot follow it. Moving inexorably to its dramatic conclu-sion, the actors play out their various parts. In 594 a group of rulers from around Judah come to Jerusalem to plan a revolt against Nebuchadnez-zar of Babylonia (Jer 27:2–4). Again utilizing symbolic action, this time straps and bars as a yoke upon his neck, Jeremiah explains that whoever does *not* submit to the yoke of Nebuchadnezzar will be visited by the Lord with sword, famine and pestilence (Jer 27:8). Unfortunately another prophet, Hananiah, prophesies the exact opposite of Jeremiah. Who is to be believed, who is speaking the true word of God? (In some ways this echoes the confrontation between the prophets Zedekiah ben Chenaanah and Micaiah ben Imlah in 1 Kings 22, described above in the chapter on the former prophets.) This is where Jeremiah spells out the notion that great prophets in the past prophesied disaster, and that the only way to know if a prophet who speaks good fortune is true or not is to see if the prophecy actually is realized (Jer 28:1–9).

When some years later the Babylonians lay siege to Jerusalem, Jeremiah is accused of wishing to defect to the enemy. He denies this strenuously but is imprisoned in any case (chapters 37–38). Jerusalem finally falls, and against his will Jeremiah is taken to Egypt where he dies (chapters 43–44).

3. Jeremiah's Theology

"Israel's distress was more than a human tragedy," explained Abra-ham Joshua Heschel in *The Prophets*. With "Israel's distress came the affliction of God, His displacement, His homelessness in the land, in the world.... Israel's desertion was not merely an injury to man; it was an insult to God" (1.112).

Jeremiah's contributions were many. He not only spoke of the need for morality, but on another level he spoke of how the people needed to know God in a different manner. Trust God. Know God. Have a deeper faith. A term that appears again and again in Jeremiah is the word "heart." We read: "The heart is devious above all else; it is perverse — who can understand it? I the Lord test the mind and search the heart, to give to all according to their ways..." (Jer 17:9–10). Yet if people change their ways, if they turn their thoughts to God, they shall be like a tree planted by the water, rooted in the soil, not afraid of the drought (17:8).

Furthermore, says Jeremiah, trust in the Lord, for that is the way to achieve salvation. "Thus says the Lord: Do not let the wise boast in their wisdom, do not let the mighty boast in their might, do not let the wealthy boast in their wealth; but let those who boast boast in this, that they understand and know me" (Jer 9:23–24 [9:22–23 H]).

Finally, as shall be discussed below, God says that in a future time there will be a new covenant between Israel and God. "... I will make a new covenant with the house of Israel ... I will put my law within them and I will write it on their hearts..." (Jer 31:31–33).

Jeremiah predicted defeat, but beyond defeat, like his younger contemporary Ezekiel, Jeremiah predicted a future of hope. It would be a different community, not based on a political unit or a set geographical area.

> Such a community did in fact emerge, in the Exile and after. And the very fact that Jeremiah — and Ezekiel — stressed, perhaps to a unique degree, the inward and personal nature of man's relationship to God surely prepared for its formation (Bright, cxv).

Jeremiah taught the people that God wanted their trust and obedience, even more than their cult. Indeed God did not need the house in Jerusalem. This message gave comfort and hope, not only in his day and immediately thereafter, but again following the destruction of the second temple in the year 70 CE.

4. Jeremiah in the Christian Scriptures

Jeremiah 31:31–34 is an important passage for Christianity. On the face of it, taken out of context, one can understand how and why it was appropriated by the writers of the Christian Scriptures. The "new covenant" of which Jeremiah spoke was understood as *the* "new covenant" or "New Testament" with the "new Israel," that is, the followers of Jesus. The writer of Luke has Jesus offer just this image of a "new covenant" (Lk 22:20) and the image is repeated in the First Corinthians description of the Last Supper (1 Cor 11:25). Further, in Second Corinthians Paul speaks of " ... God, who has made us competent to be ministers of a new covenant, not of letter but of spirit; for the letter kills, but the Spirit gives life" (2 Cor 3:5–6). That this is a faith statement and consciously and viciously disassociates Christianity from Judaism is noteworthy (see also 2 Cor 3:7ff).

Likewise, in the epistle to the Hebrews, a letter to former Jews, who are now Christians, the words of Jeremiah 31:31–34 find full expression (Heb 8:8–12; 10:16–17).

Jeremiah's denunciation of Jerusalem's citizens at the temple is certainly a likely basis for the incident recorded in Mark 11:11–21 (see Mt 21:12ff; Lk 19:45ff; Jn 2:13ff): Jesus' remark that the temple has become "a den of robbers" (vs 17) is the same phrase as Jeremiah's "den of robbers" in 7:11. Likewise Jesus' curse of the fig tree, which then dries up from the roots (Mk 11:12–14, 20–22), is not only a symbolic statement about the changing times as understood by the writer of the Christian Scriptures, but also reflects Jeremiah's statements in chapter 17:5–8 where Jeremiah speaks of the person of faith being compared to a tree which is planted by water, and how it shall never fear its roots drying, but the person who trusts in mortals shall be barren.

Finally Jeremiah's rough handling by priests and prophets, and being protected by the princes and the people (Jer 26), is echoed in Mark 11, for the scribes and chief priests are opposed to Jesus and the people are in awe of Jesus. Likewise Pilate seems, like the princes in Jeremiah's day, to be sympathetic to the accused man (Mk 15:8–15; see Lk 23:13ff). The connection between Jesus and Jeremiah is further strengthened by the fact that at one point a number of people assume Jesus *is* Jeremiah redivivus (Mt 16:14). For a development of the connections between Jesus and Jeremiah see D. J. Zucker, "Jesus and Jeremiah in the Matthean Tradition," in *The Journal of Ecumenical Studies* (see Bibliography).

5. Jeremiah and Jewish Sources

In the section above we drew attention to connections between the rough handling of Jeremiah in chapter 26 and a passage in Mark 11. The prophet's temple sermon also provided material for the rabbis of the Talmudic era. The reference to the otherwise unknown prophet/ martyr Uriah ben Shemaiah (26:20ff) and his prediction of the destruction of Jerusalem is heralded as true prophecy and is linked to the prophecy of a positive future by Zechariah. The rabbis say that just as Uriah was correct (in Jer 26:18) so will Zechariah's prophecy also come about in time: "Old men and old women shall again sit in the streets of Jerusalem ... the city shall be full of boys and girls playing" (Zech 8:4–5) (*Midrash Lamentations Rabbah* to Lamentations 5:18; see also Babylonian Talmud *Makkot* 24b end [though there seems to be some confusion between Uriah and Micah the Morashite]).

The Book of Consolation, Jeremiah 31, shall be analyzed in the "Text Study" section below. In it the prophet refers to Rachel weeping for her children (vss 15–17). The rabbis offered two differing homilies on the significance of this figure of Rachel. In one they explain somewhat fancifully that Rachel was buried purposefully by Jacob where she was, for he knew (nearly a thousand years earlier! — see Gen 35:19) that the exiles would pass by her grave and her voice would arise and plead their case (*Midrash Genesis Rabbah* 82.10; see also *Midrash Genesis Rabbah* 97 [MSV]).

This midrash is thematically connected to an even more powerful (and contemporary in its gender-consciousness) midrash. The explanation is given that when the temple was destroyed Abraham himself was so upset that he came before God and lamented these events. How could you do this? Abraham asked. The ministering angels, likewise, were so moved that they too composed lamentations. God, it is related, tersely replied that the people "transgressed the whole of the Torah." God then calls the Torah to come and testify against Israel. The Torah comes forward, but Abraham challenges the Torah, and points out that each letter of the alphabet points to a word where Israel has been righteous. Abraham recalls to God that the deity was willing to call for the sacrifice of Isaac, and surely this should account for merit for Abraham's children, the people of Israel. Next Isaac and Jacob come before the heavenly throne and argue on behalf of Israel. Then Moses presents a long case, and apparently to no avail. Moses calls upon Jeremiah, and he is no more successful. Finally Rachel breaks into speech and presents her case. She says that as she was not jealous of Leah, so likewise God, "a ruler who lives eternally and is merciful, should not be jealous of idolatry in which there is no reality" [a reference presumably to the idol-worship of the Jerusalemites — see Jer 7:17ff, 8:19; 11:10; et al.].

Never undervalue the word of a woman! God hears her plea and immediately capitulates. The midrash ends on this wonderful note:

Forthwith the mercy of the Holy One, blessed be God, was stirred, and [God] said, "For your sake, Rachel, I will restore Israel to their place." And so it is written, "Thus said the Lord: A cry is heard in Ramah, wailing, bitter weeping, Rachel weeping for her children. She refuses to be comforted for her children, who are gone" (Jer 31:15). This is followed by "Thus says the Lord: Restrain your voice from weeping, your eyes from shedding tears; for there is a reward for your labor, declares the Lord; they shall return from the enemy's land" (Jer 31:16) (*Midrash Lamentations Rabbah* Proems 24 end section).

Earlier in that chapter, in Jeremiah 31:3, it states that God's love for Israel is to be "an everlasting love." The rabbis suggested that there were important lessons to be learned from some of these verses. "It does not say, 'with abounding love,' but 'with eternal love.' For you might think the love with which God loves Israel was for three years or two years or a hundred years. But it was a love for everlasting and to all eternity" (*Tanna Debe Eliyyahu,* Chapter [6] 7, p. 31, 114).

Coincidentally this very line "with an everlasting love" (*Ahavat olam*) is incorporated into the Jewish evening service liturgy, the second paragraph following the "Call to worship" (*Barchu*).

The rabbis also taught that there was a special meaning to vs 9 where God speaks of being a parent to Israel. Israel knew it had sinned and was ashamed to return. An example was given from the everyday world (if you will, a parable). The child of a monarch took to evil ways. The ruler sent a tutor urging the child to repent and return. The child wished to, but was ashamed. The monarch then sent the message: How can a child be ashamed to return to one's parent? In like manner God (the ruler of rulers) sent Jeremiah (the tutor) with a message of repentance. Israel was ashamed (see Jer 3:25) and so God said: Are you not returning to your parent? And hence the words in Jeremiah 31:9: "I have become a father to Israel" (*Midrash Deuteronomy Rabbah* 2.24; *Pesikta de Rab Kahana* 24.16).

6. Text Study

Suggested reading: Jer 7:1-20, 30-31 — The temple sermon

Chapter 7, verses 1–15, mark the famous "temple sermon" which caused such consternation in the opening period of the reign of King Jehoiakim. It is filled with important material, and suggests that the Josianic reforms, at least by this point, were more in form than content.

Vss 1-2 Three times in the first two verses one finds the characteristic term "devar" — the *word* of the Lord.

Vss 3-4 In vs 3 is the familiar phrase "Thus says the Lord." This then continues with an abrupt message: Mend your ways and your actions, reform the whole pattern of your conduct! Do not assume that a mere building will save you! It is an illusion to cry "The temple of the Lord, the temple of the Lord, the temple of the Lord." This trifold repetition is a powerful rhetorical device.

Vss 5-7 The need for true justice, protection for the stranger, orphan and widow, and the rejection of other gods show how the covenant with God explained in Exodus 22–23 was not being followed.

Vs 9 "Note that the crimes listed are violations of the eighth, sixth, seventh, ninth, first and second commandments, i.e., constitute an almost total breach of the covenant stipulations" (Bright, 56).

Vss 16-18 In vs 16 there is an echo of the rejection of the people found in Isaiah 6:8–10. The reference to the queen of heaven and the dough cakes are probably for an Assyrian-Babylonian goddess, Ishtar.

Vss 30-31 It appears from these verses that the abominable pagan rites which were featured in King Manasseh's day (2 Kgs 23:10), including child sacrifice, were reinstituted, under the impression that God actually desired this (see Mic 6:7). "Had they misunderstood the command to dedicate all first-born to Yahweh (Exod xiii.2)?" asks John Bright (57).

Suggested reading: Jer 26:1-24 — The temple sermon continued

Vss 2-6 contain an abridged version of the "temple sermon" of chapter 7.

Vss 7-9 explain how Jeremiah is seized by *priests* and prophets (court prophets? — the term used is *nevi'im*). They demand his execution for sedition.

Vss 10-19 The officials (princes) and the people contradict the priests and prophets and say: No, this is not a crime. Indeed there is precedent in the days of King Hezekiah and they refer to the words of Micah (see Mic 3:12).

One must say that the conduct of these princes certainly reflects
credit upon them, and warns us against accepting Jeremiah's
pessimistic evaluation of this people (e.g., v 1–5; ix 1–8) without
qualification. There *were* good men in Judah! (Bright, 172).

The fact that some nineteen chapters separate the "original" temple
sermon and its shortened version here with its "in situ" description is a
clear indication of how this book of Jeremiah is really an edited version
of several different sources. The "patchwork quilt" nature of the book of
Jeremiah is also seen in the fact that chapters 26 and 27 are said to come
in the reign of Jehoiakim, as are chapters 35 and 36. In the meantime
chapters 29, 32 and 34 clearly come from the period of King Zedekiah
(N.B. Bright argues that chapter 27 is erroneously applied to Jehoiakim
and should be connected to Zedekiah — Bright, 199, 201).

Suggested reading: Jer 36:1–32 — The burnt scroll

This chapter in the life of Jeremiah shows again the lengths to which
this prophet dared to go in order to speak the Lord's word. Since he is in
hiding there is no doubt that he knows that his life is in danger, yet speak
he must, even if it is by his proxy, Baruch ben Neriah. Bright states that
this "chapter is one of the most noteworthy in the entire book" of Jeremiah (Bright, 181).

The message of the scroll is read three times. Baruch reads it twice:
once to the people at the temple, a second time, by their own request, to
a group of court officials. The people's reaction is not recorded, but the
officials were perturbed and fearful. Whether their fear and upset is
because the prophecy details their wrongdoing and future calamity, or
whether they are concerned about such seditious talk, is unclear. The
latter seems to be the case, for they tell Baruch to go into hiding with
Jeremiah, and then one of them takes the scroll and reads it one final
time to the king and his closest advisors. King Jehoiakim and his coterie
show neither fear nor dismay, but rather open contempt. Though the
court officials beg him not to, Jehoiakim listens to the prophecy and then
burns it in a brazier (Jer 36:20–25).

These events took place in 605, following the victorious battle of the
Babylonians over the Egyptians at Carchemish, and just prior to a Babylonian invasion of this area.

Vs 4 Once again we see here how the text we have today came to
us. Jeremiah literally dictates it to the scribe. Inasmuch as it covers over
twenty years of prophecy (from the time of Josiah until now), it must
cover a fair number of columns.

Vs 16ff The officials are excited, but fearful. They also want re-assurance that this is really God's word and not something made up by Baruch himself. Note the reference to *scroll* and *ink*.

Vss 21-25 The picture of the scroll being read, and the king's lit-erally cutting the scroll after three or four columns are read and tossing it into the brazier before him, has an eyewitness flavor that makes the whole narrative entirely believable. The king and his advisors blatantly disregard the other court officials who are horrified at the king's action.

Vss 27-32 As explained earlier, for his contempt for God's word Jehoiakim is condemned to death by God and his courtiers will know only disaster.

Suggested reading: Jer 31:1-3, 15-22, 31-37 — The Book of Consolation

These verses contain some of the strongest words of hope that we find in the book of Jeremiah. Though the present looks dismal, do not despair, do not give in to your dejection. God cares. A bright future still awaits the people of Israel. The covenant is eternal and a time of renewal will yet come.

Vss 15-17 According to biblical tradition (1 Sam 10:2ff) Rachel's tomb was near Ramah. Jeremiah here evokes the spirit of Rachel who is the mother of the Joseph (Ephraim) tribes. She is still in mourning for her "children" who had been dispersed by the Assyrians over a hundred years earlier in 721. God promises that they shall return again. The lines in vss 16b–17 will be echoed in Second Isaiah's words (Is 62:10ff).

Vs 18 "You disciplined me, and I took the discipline." This active/passive image is also seen in 17:14: "Heal me, O Lord, and I shall be healed; save me, and I shall be saved." This verse also refers to Ephraim. In the prophet's mind, as also with Ezekiel 37:15ff, there was the hope/expec-tation that the tribes would be reunited. This leads one to believe that it is at least possible, if not probable, that the ten northern tribes did not "disappear" but were living in scattered cities in the Near East. It is not beyond imagination that members of the northern tribes then joined the exiles in Babylonia and integrated themselves and intermarried with their cousins, thereby becoming again one united people, if not a united kingdom.

Vs 22 A woman encompasses a man (NRSV); when a woman courts a man (*TANAKH*); a female shall compass a man (Bright, 276); a woman protects a man (RSV); a woman turned into a man (*New English Bible*). The Hebrew is obscure. In the note to his translation, Bright explains that there have been numerous emendations to this text, but that none commands confidence. "*A female shall compass a man:* This is a literal translation, but the meaning is wholly obscure. . . . Quite possibly we have here a proverbial saying indicating something that is surprising and difficult to believe, the force of which escapes us" (Bright, 282).

Vss 29–30 This phrase about parents, children and guilt is paralleled in Deuteronomy 24:16 and Ezekiel 18:2ff.

Suggested reading: Jer 31:31–34 — The new covenant

The Book of Consolation is a jewel in the diadem of biblical literature, and vss 31–34 contain a unique and special message. The noted Jeremiah scholar John Bright termed these verses possibly "the high point of his [Jeremiah's] theology. It is certainly one of the profoundest and most moving passages in the entire Bible" (287).

These verses have been understood very distinctively within Judaism and within Christianity. We dealt with a Christian understanding above. Judaism, naturally, understands these words (Jer 31:31–34) in a different way. They were an in-house message to the Jewish people: a time will come when there will be an updated covenant, but it is still with the same partners: God and Israel. The plain meaning of these verses indicates as much, for the concluding words of vs 34 are: "I will forgive their iniquity, and remember their sin no more." Indeed in vss 35–36 the text says plainly that as there is a set order to the world of nature, so only if those laws were abrogated would "Israel cease to be a nation" for God. In vs 37 a similar thought is expressed.

Generally it was assumed by the rabbis that the "new covenant" referred to the world to come. Being but human, one learns here, but forgets. Not so in the world to come. There God will teach humankind directly and it will be inscribed on their hearts (*Midrash Ecclesiastes Rabbah* 2.1; *Midrash Song of Songs Rabbah* 1.2.4). According to another source many ceremonial laws will cease, but praise of God will remain in force forever (*Midrash Leviticus Rabbah* 9.7 though this is based on Jer 33:11).

Chapter 6

EZEKIEL

1. Introduction

The biblical book of Ezekiel, some forty-eight chapters in length, contains many of the most memorable images found in sacred literature. His vision of the "valley of dry bones" (in chapter 37) has provided the text for many an orator. Ezekiel's commission as a sentinel (in chapters 3 and 33) who is required to warn the people of their wrongdoing, lest that figure also share in their guilt, has inspired many religious leaders.

The words of Ezekiel are correctly assessed as passionate and fertile. "He is the master of the dramatic, representational action. . . . He was famous for his (often lurid) imagery (21:5). His actions and his images are more numerous and more complex than those of any of his predecessors" (Moshe Greenberg, "Ezekiel," *Encyclopedia Judaica* [*EJ*], 1092).

Ezekiel ben Buzi, whose period of prophecy spans the years prior to the destruction of the temple in Jerusalem to some years thereafter (c. 592–572 BCE), might be characterized as the "audio-visual specialist" of the Bible. "As a visionary too he has no peer; indeed he innovated a genre: the transportation-and-tour vision, so common in later apocalypse. It is no wonder that people flocked to his 'entertainments'" [33:30ff] (Greenberg, 1092).

For all these positive comments about Ezekiel and the book, it also contains some of the most difficult chapters to translate which are found in all the Bible. This applies to both the prose sections and the poetry (Greenberg, 1089; Sandmel, *The Enjoyment of Scripture*, 267f).

2. A Brief History

A. *The Setting of Ezekiel*

The historical background for Ezekiel is fairly parallel to that of his (probably older) contemporary, Jeremiah. Judah had already been defeated by King Nebuchadnezzar ([Nebuchadrezzer] Ez 26, 29, 30). The best of the Judean/Jerusalem leadership, the "craftsmen, the warriors, the state officials, the cream of the population, together with the treasures of the Temple and city" (Winward, 135), had been sent into exile into Babylonia in the year 598/597. Among these refugees was probably Ezekiel himself, though as shall be noted presently, Ezekiel's whereabouts are a matter of dispute. King Jehoiakim had been killed and was followed briefly by his son Jehoiachin and then latterly by Jehoiakim's brother King Zedekiah. In 594/593 BCE King Zedekiah joined an anti-Babylonian coalition. This was about at the same time that Jeremiah fought with those whom he labeled as "false prophets," those who predicted the imminent fall of Babylon and return of the exiles (Jer 27–28).

About 589 Judah actually revolted against Babylonia, and in 588 Nebuchadnezzar laid siege to Jerusalem. As was noted earlier in the chapter on Jeremiah, Jerusalem finally fell victim to the siege and famine and was destroyed in 586.

Ezekiel, if he was not totally in Babylonia for his prophecies prior to this, certainly now found himself among the exiles. For years he had been predicting the destruction of Jerusalem and Judah. He lived to know of the fall of the city and the razing of the temple. In the remaining, perhaps fifteen years of his prophecies, as shall be shown, he would alter his message from doom and devastation to comfort, hope and consolation.

B. *Ezekiel as a Person*

In the opening line of the book there is a reference to "the thirtieth year," but of what is not known. If it refers to the thirtieth year of his life it would mean that he was born about the same time as the "discovery" of the Deuteronomy scroll during the reign of King Josiah. In any case Ezekiel certainly grew to maturity during the Josianic reform, and his familiarity with the temple and its rituals (see chapters 40–48), along with a reference to his being of a priestly family (1:3), places him in an important position at this time. One knows little else of the biography of the man himself. He was married, though no children are mentioned. His wife died during the siege of Jerusalem, and though she was called the "delight of (his)... eyes" he is told not to mourn for her, for a greater mourning is to come, that for the city, the temple and the people (chapter 24).

The locale of Ezekiel's prophecies is the matter of great debate. Clearly it begins in Babylonia in the community of exiles (1:4–3:15). Did he actually travel to Jerusalem, or merely direct his prophecy there? The question is intriguing, but academic. Various analyses are found in articles in the *Interpreter's Dictionary of the Bible* (*IDB*) and *Encyclopedia Judaica* (*EJ*) and elsewhere as well. James Newsome's contention that "Ezekiel remained physically present in Babylon ... [but that] he felt himself to be psychologically and spiritually in Jerusalem at times" makes a great deal of sense (127).

3. Messages of Doom and Consolation

Though one can always subdivide still further, there is some consensus on the following scheme. *Chapters 1–24* form the early prophecy of Ezekiel and lead up to the destruction of Jerusalem (c. 593/592–587/586 BCE). *Chapters 25–48* are "after the fall" and deal with Israel's restoration. The latter chapters are then further divided: *25–32*, denunciation of foreign nations (Ammon; Moab; Edom; Philistia; Tyre; Sidon and Egypt); *33–39*, the future restoration of Israel; and finally *40–48*, the restored temple in Jerusalem with a messianic priestly code (see Greenberg, 1079–1080; Sandmel, *The Hebrew Scriptures*, 153; Newsome, 133; C. G. Howie, "Ezekiel," *IDB*, 208–209).

Though, as shall be noted later, Ezekiel was influenced by other prophets, his prophecies are very unique in addition to their being so visually remarkable. Most of Ezekiel's prophetic predecessors (Isaiah and Jeremiah, Hosea and Micah, and certainly the pre-literary giants) were actively involved in society. Prophets often were both visible and vocal. Ezekiel was just the opposite. To begin, Ezekiel was placed under "house arrest" by God (Greenberg, 1082).

In 3:24–25 Ezekiel is told by the Lord to "shut yourself inside your house. . . . Cords shall be placed on you, and you shall be bound with them, so you cannot go out among the people." Furthermore, Ezekiel is told he is to be dumb and *only* speak when God specifically orders him to do so (3:26–27).

The prophet's withdrawal is borne out by every notice of his contact with others (8:1; 14:1; 20:1; 33:30ff). He is visited at home; he is never on the street or in the market, no reflex of daily life outside makes its way into his utterances. "For the most part

Ezekiel lives in a separate world. Other people drift in and out of the book, but there is little direct contact" (Freedman). The only conversation recorded with other human beings is by the command of God (24:18ff). . . . "Ezekiel's account is more a spiritual diary of personal experience of God and his inner reaction to it than a record of objective occurrences" (*ibid.*) (Greenberg, 1082–1083. Both quotations from D.N. Freedman, cited as *Interpretation* 8 [1954], 446–71).

After the actual destruction of Jerusalem Ezekiel is instructed to change his role from mute to a more traditional speaking prophet. He is specifically told by God that only after he learns of Jerusalem's fall "your mouth shall be opened . . . and you shall speak and no longer be silent" (24:27).

To explain that Ezekiel was restricted both to where he could go and what he could say is *not* to say that he failed to communicate his message. He did so through symbolic acts, and at times he did speak aloud, but always at God's specific behest (12:21–24). Indeed as shall be shown in the "sentinel" allegory, were Ezekiel not to have given warning to the people he would share their guilt.

Much of Ezekiel's prophecies in the first half of the book are denunciations of Judah and Jerusalem. In his serving as the sentinel, warning them of the consequences of their wickedness, Ezekiel is told that he is "not accountable for the reaction of his audience — an important release for a prophet anticipating an indifferent or hostile reception" (Greenberg, 1081).

4. Ezekiel's Theology

Ezekiel's theology has been described as addressing four major points: God will judge human wrongdoing; God's presence will remain with the people, even in exile; individuals, like the nation itself, have an obligation to respond to God; and a messianic ruler will arise (see Newsome, 134–136).

A. God Will Judge Human Wrongdoing

That God will judge human wrongdoing is not a new idea with Ezekiel. Ezekiel *is* concerned with the proper worship of God, as chapters 6–7 and 40–48 indicate, but he has wider concerns: prostitution (16:15–19), child sacrifice (16:20), and adultery 16:32ff; 23:11–21) are also on his mind.

God stands in judgment of human sin, and Ezekiel records in great detail the wickedness of the people. In chapter 8 he addresses the abominations that are going on in the temple itself. Creeping things, beasts and fetishes are depicted on an entire wall (8:9–10); women are worshiping Tammuz, a Babylonian deity (8:14); sun worship has succeeded the worship of God (8:16ff). This syncretism all came about (or was reintroduced) during the reign of Jehoiakim (609–598 BCE). In the city of Jerusalem degenerate prophets offer false messages (13:4ff). Jerusalem is called a city of bloodshed (22:2); fathers and mothers have been humiliated, orphans and widows wronged, sabbaths profaned; sexual immorality is rampant (22:6–11). Ezekiel is concerned with cultic as well as moral issues.

God has sought someone to effectively protest, to "repair the wall and stand in the breach," but no one has been found; hence God promises that destruction will come. "I have consumed them with the fire of my wrath; I have returned their conduct upon their heads..." (22:30–31).

B. God's Presence Will Remain with the People, Even in Exile

As is evidenced again and again in Ezekiel, much if not all of his prophetic life is actually spent in Babylonia. God speaks to him there, and he in turn addresses (on command) the exiles in Chaldea (11:24–25; 33:21–22).

The exiles, of both 597 and 586, were weary and dispirited (see Psalm 137: "By the rivers of Babylon — there we sat down and there we wept..."), but Ezekiel buoys them up and says that God is not limited, God is a God of history, there is a future time of hope. The images of the good shepherd (chapter 34), the resurrected valley of dry bones (chapter 37), and the life-giving stream issuing from the restored temple (47:1–12) are all conveyed to give hope to the exiles.

Underlying the fact of hope for the future is that *God is the God of history*. This theme is also seen in Jeremiah and shall be expressed in Second Isaiah as well. Ezekiel addresses the nations all about and predicts what will happen to them (chapters 25–32). The fact that these prophecies did not come about exactly as Ezekiel suggested is less important than the notion that God is portrayed as the ruler of all of the world (see 39:27–28 as well).

Furthermore, an important concept in Ezekiel is that God acts *for God's own name's sake*. God will return many of the exiles, but it is not alone because of their repentance, but because God has *consciously* chosen to do so. This fact is specifically delineated in 36:22–23, "It is not for your sake, O house of Israel, that I am about to act, but for the sake of my holy name ... the nations shall know that I am the Lord ... when through you I display my holiness before their eyes."

C. Individuals, Like the Nation Itself, Have an Obligation to Respond to God

Two of the great messages of Ezekiel are the concepts of "individuation" and "God's desire for human repentance." Ezekiel is not the only biblical figure to speak about individual guilt. As noted in the chapter on Jeremiah, he too rejected the notion of children or parents being responsible for each other's actions (Jer 31:29–30), and likewise a similar point is brought out in Deuteronomy (24:16).

> [Yet, nowhere] in Scripture is there as clear an exposition of individualism as that which appears in Ezekiel 18 and 33.... Ezekiel answers the implied question of how Yahve can continue His relationship with the Israel which forfeited His benign providence and underwent the terrible destruction at the hands of the Babylonians. The old covenant was collective; the new covenant is individual.... The emphatic assertion of individualism and the possibility of repentance are [how God and Israel continue their bond] (Sandmel, *The Hebrew Scriptures*, 162).

Yet the notion of individualism should not be overstated. God is going to create a new nation from the exiles, but it is in part because God in effect "declares that He cannot permit Israel to dissolve into nothingness" (Sandmel, *The Hebrew Scriptures*, 163). God will choose among the people and create a new Israel. Using the metaphor of a shepherd, God says: "I will save my flock ... I will judge between sheep and sheep" (34:22ff; see also 37:22ff). Yet what is a primary concern for God is, as noted above, that God acts because it is part of the divine plan, not alone because of Israel's merit. Indeed God explains that the people will be given a new heart (11:17–20; 36:26, see also Jer 31:31ff). Furthermore, as is evidenced by the multitude of bones in the valley (37:1–14), this is a *group* restoration, not one of individual acts. In Ezekiel there remains an important and creative tension between the individual and the group.

D. A Messianic Ruler Will Come

While a ruler in the Davidic line is suggested in Ezekiel 37:24ff (see 34:23–24) and a restoration of both parts of the monarchy of Israel-Judah is mentioned, what was of much greater concern for Ezekiel than a political return was the restoration of the temple and specific details about the temple, the cult and its personnel. This is the major theme of the final nine chapters of Ezekiel.

The prophecy of the Davidic ruler in chapters 34 and 37, the restoration of the temple and theocracy in chapters 40–48, and the specific mention of the twelve tribes at the end of chapter 48 (vss 23–35) all underscore the notion that Ezekiel, unlike Second Isaiah, or even First Isaiah, was *not* a broad universalist. Ezekiel's concern was primarily for Israel. God controlled history and was validated through history, sometimes using the "nations" as tools. In the end, however, Ezekiel's "messianic" future prophecies are centered alone on his own people. He does not specifically deny a future for the other nations, he just is not concerned with them beyond their recognition that God is triumphant in all the world, and that God is bringing Israel back to the land — not because of Israel's repentance, but in order to glorify God's own name and fame.

> [When] I have brought them back from the peoples and gathered them from their enemies' lands, and through them have displayed my holiness in the sight of many nations, then they shall know that I am the Lord their God because I sent them into exile among the nations, and then gathered them into their own land. I will leave none of them behind (Ez 39:27–28).

5. Images, Symbolism and Allegories in Ezekiel

It is difficult to write succinctly of the varied and wonderful images, symbolism and allegories found in Ezekiel. From the "wheels within wheels" and the multi-faced, multi-winged, multi-formed beasts of chapter 1, to the occasion of his lying on his side for well over a year (4:4–8), to his scanty eating of food (4:9–17) and to cutting and dividing his hair (5:1–4), there is much to describe.

He comes into his own with his allegories: in chapter 15 Judah is depicted as a useless vine good only for fuel as opposed to the good vine in Jeremiah 2:21, Hosea 10:1 and Psalm 80:9, 15 [14 H]. In chapter 16 Jerusalem is a "nymphomaniacal adulteress" (Greenberg, 1084), and in chapter 17 among other allegorical figures are two great eagles. Chapter 23, like chapter 16, is written in lurid detail, narrating the sexual improprieties of Judah's citizenry. Whether one takes this literally or figuratively, it is eyebrow-raising reading, as provocative and titillating as anywhere in the Bible.

Another characteristic of Ezekiel is the use of the term *"ben adam"*

which in the Christian Scriptures is often a synonym or appellation for
Jesus as the "Christ" or messiah, but in the context of this book it is only
a phrase meaning "mortal!" or "O man!" (See note to Ezekiel 2:1 in *The
New Oxford Annotated Bible.*)

6. Influences on Ezekiel

Ezekiel draws upon several sources for his prophecy. Some are linked
to Leviticus and the holiness code (Lev 17–26), and like Moses, Ezekiel
"not only envisions the future but lays down a blueprint and a law for it"
(Greenberg, 1092). The image of being taken by the hand of the Lord and
transported by divine wind echoes similar images with Elijah and Elisha
(Ez 3:14, 22; 37:1, etc.; 1 Kgs 18:12, 46; 2 Kgs 2:16; 3:15).

Ezekiel may well be indebted to Hosea for the imagery of a whor-
ing Israel, but unquestionably the most direct influence is that of his
contemporary Jeremiah. The two have in common a vocabulary and a
stock of concepts and figures including eating God's words (Ez 2:8–10
and Jer 15:16); the harlot sisters (Ez 16, 23 and Jer 3:6ff), the bad shepherds (Ez 34 and Jer 23:1ff), the sentinel (Ez 3:16ff and Jer 6:17), and
many more examples beyond what may be explained by mere contem-
poraneity. That Ezekiel heard (or heard of) Jeremiah before 597 is to be
assumed (see Ez 9:4); that he continued to receive word of his prophecies
afterward is likely, since such a word did reach the exiles (Jer 29:24ff)
(Greenberg, 1093).

7. Ezekiel in the Christian Scriptures

While the "Gospel of John and the Revelation are most directly akin
to" Ezekiel, it is likewise clear that "Jesus was well acquainted with the
book of Ezekiel, from which he drew expressions to frame the new picture of Christian faith" (Howie, 212). The image of the divine presence
in Ezekiel provided much material for the writer of Revelation. The
multi-faced, multi-winged animals are found in Revelation 4:6–8, and
the different stones of Ezekiel 1:26–28 are reflected in Revelation 4:1–3.
As in Ezekiel, so in Revelation 21:9ff Jerusalem is spoken of specifically, and there are details about its dimensions (see Ez 40:2ff and 48:31–35).

The breath of God's spirit in Ezekiel 37 and God's sprinkling clean
water (36:25) find echoes in the gospel of John 3:1–8. The image of the
good shepherd (34:11ff) is picked up by Matthew (18:12–14), Luke (15:3–7)
and John (10:2–18).

Likewise there are connections between the vine image in Ezekiel 15 and John 15.

In Ezekiel Gog and Magog make their appearance in chapters 38–39. In the Hebrew Scriptures Gog is a person and Magog a country. In Revelation 20:7–10 Gog and Magog became two nations. In both instances the figures face defeat by God.

Though Ezekiel was a great influence on the Christian Scriptures it needs to be stressed that he was speaking to a contemporary, not a later audience. Nonetheless, as with several texts in the Isaiahs, some words of Ezekiel have been interpreted as pointing the way to the ultimate Davidic ruler (see Newsome, 136)

8. Ezekiel and Jewish Sources

The book of Ezekiel has had a mixed reaction within Judaism. To begin, it nearly did not make it into the Jewish canon (the "officially recognized" scriptures), for the description of the temple and its activities was at such variance with past tradition as described in the Torah that some rabbis voted against its acceptance.

According to the Talmud, only through the diligent efforts of Hananiah ben Hezekiah (c. 50 CE) were the contradictory passages reconciled. Medieval exegetes explained that Ezekiel's references were for a future messianic time. Furthermore Ezekiel's descriptions were patently ignored when the second temple was built and functioning (Babylonian Talmud *Shabbat* 13b; Greenberg, 1094).

The rabbis note that both Ezekiel and First Isaiah describe the heavenly throne (Ez 1:4ff; Is 6:1ff) and that Ezekiel's description is far more elaborate. They dismiss these discrepancies by explaining that, compared to Isaiah, Ezekiel was a country hick who was that much more in awe than the sophisticated city dweller (Babylonian Talmud *Hagiga* 13b). Furthermore there is a midrashic explanation that God shows Ezekiel the divine chariot and the glory of God to prove that even though Israel has been banished, God's own glory is not diminished. Even though the temple and temple ritual of praise no longer exist, the celestial beings continue to worship and praise God as before (*Midrash Leviticus Rabbah* 2.8).

The "chariot" of Ezekiel becomes a code word for certain mystical studies (the *Ma'aseh Merkavah*) which were certainly restricted by the rabbis.

The midrash also claims certain honors for Ezekiel. When, at the time of Daniel, Hananiah, Mishael and Azariah (Shadrach, Meshach and

Abednego) ask Daniel if they should bow before Nebuchadnezzar's fiery statue, Daniel refers them to Ezekiel for an answer (*Midrash Song of Songs Rabbah* 7.8.1).

The rabbis further explain that Ezekiel's great miracle of prophesying and bringing about the revival of the dead (Ez 37) took place on a sabbath which was also the Day of Atonement. The image built by Nebuchadnezzar was toppled by a divine wind (the divine spirit) which then entered the dry bones and gave them life (*Midrash Song of Songs Rabbah* 7.9.1).

There is a variation on this story which also seeks to answer the question of literally whose bones were those in the valley. According to that explanation, when Nebuchadnezzar saw that the fire did not destroy the three young men, the Babylonian king turned to all those Jews who *had* bowed down and berated them sorely: Not only were you so corrupt as to destroy your own homeland, now you bring evil to my country. You do not believe in the might of your God, but are content to worship an idol. Consequently Nebuchadnezzar ordered the 600,000 exiles slain. Twenty years pass and then Ezekiel is brought to the place where they are buried and he witnesses the "miracle" of their resurrection in Ezekiel 37 (*Pirke de Rabbi Eliezer*, chapter 33; the story here is even more convoluted with Ezekiel being chastised for his lack of full faith, and the newly resurrected also having certain doubts about their return to Israel).

Ezekiel is also credited by the rabbis as having contradicted Moses' statement in the recital of the ten commandments that God visits the sins of the parents onto the children (Ex 20:5) by the famous prophetic line "the person who sins shall die" (Ez 18:20) (Babylonian Talmud *Makkot* 24a).

9. Text Study

Suggested reading: Ez 18:1–32; 33:1–20 (see also 3:16–21)

Chapter 18 sets out most clearly Ezekiel's well-known theology and teaching, the notion of individual responsibility. As noted before, Ezekiel did not "invent" this concept, but he was the prophet who took it to its greatest development (see Jer 31:29; Deut 24:16).

Vss 1–3 The "sour grapes" proverb and its rejection.

Vs 4 Note how different translations suggest variant words: life (NRSV, *TANAKH*); soul (*New English Bible*, RSV), i.e. the living being, the actual person.

Vss 5-9 Laws of correct living. The fifteen laws described here have a close affinity to Pentateuchal law. They govern relationships between God and humankind including idolatry as well as laws that focus on human interaction, sexual morality, cleanliness (menstruation), business dealings, and matters of judgment. These laws reflect a sure knowledge of the ten commandments *and* the holiness code (Lev 17-26) and the book of the covenant (Ex 20:23-23:33).

Vss 10-19 Ezekiel deals here with three generations. If a righteous person has a violent, wicked child, the violent, wicked child alone shall die. In turn, in the case where this violent, wicked child has a righteous child (i.e. the grandchild of the righteous person), the violent, wicked parent shall die, the righteous child shall live.

There are some variations on the sins, and they are not in the exact order as in vss 5-9. It follows that "there was apparently no necessity to test a man's behavior minutely against a standard list of laws" (Keith W. Carley, *The Book of Ezekiel, Cambridge Bible Commentary on the NEB*, 119).

Vs 20 "The person who sins shall die. . . ." This verse summarizes the aforementioned relational non-responsibilities.

Vss 21-24 Ezekiel takes morality and responsibility a quantum leap forward. Righteousness spurned brings punishments, just as wickedness rejected brings reward. The rabbis linked vs 22 to Malachi 3:7 and offered this explanation:

> See how wonderful a thing is repentance! God says "If you return to Me, I will return to you" (Mal 3:7). For however many sins a person has committed, if one returns to God, all is forgiven, God accounts it as if the person had not sinned (Ezek 18:22). But if one does not return, God gives warning once, twice, and a third time. Then if there is no repentance, God exacts punishment (*Midrash Tanhuma, Genesis, Wayyera*, Buber Edition 4.16, Gen 19:24ff, Part I [slightly modified]).

Vss 25-29 Israel questions God's justice and God basically repeats the notions just enunciated.

Vs 30 God explains that there will be *individual* judgment, and repentance again is stressed.

Vss 31-32 A new heart and new spirit are called for (see Jeremiah's similar comment in 31:31-34 and God's statement in Ezekiel 11:17-20 and 36:26 that God *is* placing a new heart in the people. Note that in vs 32 God says explicitly: "I have no pleasure in the death of anyone. . . . Turn, then, and live").

Suggested reading: Ez 33:1-20

Vss 7-9 This, as in 3:16-21, refers to the sentinel who at least needs to give warning. Once the warning is given, the guard's duty has been discharged.

Vss 10-11 These verses may sound similar to 18:29-30, but there is a *radical* difference. Here (in 33:10) Israel admits its wrong and voices its longing to change. "Our transgressions and our sins weigh on us . . . how then can we live?" Then God repeats the call for repentance that the people may live.

Chapter 7

SECOND AND THIRD ISAIAH

The consensus of scholarly opinion for over two centuries has spoken of several divisions within the sixty-six chapters of the book of Isaiah. The accepted units are that Chapters *1-39* constitute *First Isaiah,* or Isaiah ben Amotz, the Isaiah of eighth century Jerusalem. His period of prophecy was c. 741-701 BCE. Chapters *40-55* are from *Second Isaiah* (or Deutero-Isaiah) whose prophetic period is c. 550-540 BCE in Babylonia. Finally there is *Third Isaiah* (or Trito-Isaiah) who functions in Jerusalem after c. 537 BCE and whose words are found in chapters 56-66. Some argue that the anonymous Second and Third Isaiah are the same person whose prophecies, therefore, range from 550-c. 516 (?) BCE, and these prophecies would then be found in chapters 40-66.

1. Historical Background

A. *From Nebuchadnezzar to Cyrus*

The major background for the prophecies of Second Isaiah are the five decades c. 588-538 BCE. These years mean prior to the final fall of Jerusalem (586) through the destruction of the Babylonian empire in 538 BCE.

Babylon had been at the height of its power under Nebuchadnezzar and his successors (605-539) but it was to succumb to the upcoming power of Cyrus the Persian, who was to move decisively beginning about 550 BCE. In 546 Cyrus had attacked and conquered Lydia in Asia Minor, the kingdom of the legendary ruler Croesus with his hoards of gold. The "oracles of Deutero-Isaiah are very probably to be dated at or shortly after the date of Cyrus' conquest of Lydia, when the magnitude of Persian power and Persian ambitions had become apparent" (John L. McKenzie, *Second Isaiah*, Anchor Bible, xxviii).

Next on Cyrus' list was Babylon, which he took with surprising ease in 539. A year later in 538 BCE "he issued a decree permitting the resettlement of a Jewish community in Palestine and the restoration of the cult (Ezra i 1–11, vi 3–5). This decree could hardly have been issued except as a response to a petition from the community in exile" (McKenzie, xxix).

Cyrus and his Persian successors were essentially benevolent rulers who, in specific contrast to their empiric predecessors the Assyrians and Babylonians, allowed conquered nations to function in the old manner as long as they were loyal to their "masters."

B. The Jewish Community in Babylon

To understand the meaning of the prophecies of Second Isaiah we need to appreciate the life and condition of the exiled Jewish community in Babylon. "It is quite impossible to dissociate the prophetic word from the time at which it was uttered" (Claus Westermann, *Isaiah 40-66: A Commentary*, 9). The cream of Judah's society had been forced to leave home and hearth and forcibly resettle in a foreign land more than a thousand miles distant. Though some prophets had claimed that this would be merely a temporary displacement (Jer 27:16–19) it became abundantly clear that this was not to be the case. The literal destruction of Jerusalem, including the razing to the ground of the four hundred year old temple, the capture of the holy vessels, and the end of the monarchy were all painful reality. As mentioned in the chapter on Ezekiel, the painful plaint of Psalm 137 ("By the rivers of Babylon — there we sat down and there we wept…") reflects the woe of the refugees. These people were devastated psychologically and emotionally. Having said this, however, the community-in-exile made the best of their situation. From verses in Jeremiah one learns that the people settled, built homes and gardens, and farmed the land (Jer 29:5ff). Furthermore, from Ezekiel's descriptions it becomes apparent that there were several Jewish communities (Ez 3:15; 8:1; 33:30f). They were able to maintain a "consciousness of continuity … no other ethnic or religious group of the Assyrian and Babylonian period" was able to do following a similar series of disasters (McKenzie, xxv). This is the period where the former Hebrew community reconstitutes itself as a Jewish community, based on Jewish culture, history and ethnicity. Judaism moves from a religious/ethnic group solely centered in the land of Israel to a religion/people which would be international in scope. This is the time of the development of the synagogue. No doubt there were some local Jewish cultic gatherings and certainly it was in Babylon that the Torah reached its final shape. The words of Second Isaiah probably were spoken at some of these gatherings.

Second Isaiah is exclusively an *exilic* (as opposed to pre-exilic or post-exilic) prophet. As shall be noted shortly, the prophet's role was to give a message of hope to the community of refugees.

C. The Life of Second Isaiah

While certain biographical details are known about some of the prophets such as Jeremiah, Ezekiel, Amos and Hosea, virtually *nothing* is known about Second Isaiah. We do not know Second Isaiah's name, if the prophet was male or female, young or old. How then can one speak of a separate authorship for chapters 40–55 (or 40–66)? The key is found in the message itself. Second Isaiah is addressing a despondent community. The prophet calls for a restoration of Judah and Jerusalem. The community is invited to leave Babylon, to rebuild Jerusalem, and God is said to be bringing the people to Zion (Is 48:20; 51:11–12; 49:14–52:12; 40:9–11). If those who are hearing Second Isaiah's message are not in Babylon, this prophecy makes little sense. Further, Cyrus is specifically mentioned, and as noted before, Cyrus lived in the sixth century BCE, some two hundred years *after* First Isaiah (Is 44:28; 45:1; see McKenzie, xvi).

Third Isaiah again presents a different message. This prophet was probably centered in Jerusalem in the early years following the restoration, c. 538–516 (?) or perhaps still later. Though some people have returned, the promise of a glorious salvation as suggested earlier by Second Isaiah has not been realized. There is a sense of possible changes to come, but the destruction of Israel's foes has clearly not materialized. The prophecies of Third Isaiah are more restricted than those of Second Isaiah. The area of concern is centered on Israel itself. Third Isaiah does not perceive of Israel being a "light to the nations" and there is, therefore, a narrower focus, a considerably lesser "universalistic" image in these final chapters of the book (see Westermann, 297).

2. The Messages of Second Isaiah

There are several messages in Second Isaiah. We need to bear in mind the prophet's audience or "congregation" now forced to live in Babylon. These were refugees, people astounded at being exiled from their land. They surely wondered: Why has this happened to us? What is the purpose of our being here?

Second Isaiah explains that the exile in Babylon, and the soon-to-be-realized triumph of Cyrus is *part of God's plan.* God has not forsaken Israel. Quite the contrary. A new era is about to begin. Israel has a different role to play than in the past. Israel is to proclaim God's absolute rule over the earth, over all people and all nations. Furthermore the exiles will soon return to their land, and Judah and Jerusalem will be rebuilt.

James Newsome (148ff) speaks of the "salvation" of Israel, yet he uses this term carefully, correctly suggesting that salvation is a synonym for "redemption." Though "salvation" is a word that can be and is used properly within a Jewish framework, for many people, and more specifically for many Jews, there is a mistaken "Christian" sound to that word (see "Salvation" in L. Klenicki and G. Wigoder [eds.], *A Dictionary of the Jewish-Christian Dialogue,* 179ff).

While Isaiah does present several points to those who hear this prophecy, the over-arching message is that *God is a universal deity and Israel's role is to be God's messenger to the world.* One way that Israel is to accomplish this goal is to be a "servant of the Lord." Indeed an important subsection of Second Isaiah encompasses the servant songs (42: 1–4; 49:1–6; 50:4–9; 52:13–53:12) which shall be dealt with subsequently.

Another part of the message is that God is granting Israel a release from her past wrongdoing even if Israel is not fully deserving of these blessings. This is a gratuitous act on God's part:

> It is not granted because of the merits of Israel. Yahweh has chosen Israel, he loves Israel, and he saves Israel on his own account and for his own glory [43:25; 48:9, 11] (McKenzie, lxiii).

This renewal of God's favor is then tied to the restoration of Judah to Jerusalem.

Among other points, Isaiah also strongly puts the case for God being the one and only creator of the world.

3. Structures, Characteristics and Themes in Second Isaiah

A. *Structures*

Second Isaiah's utterances are all presented as poetry. They are a series of pronouncements which do not necessarily fall neatly into the chapter divisions which only came about at a later date. Scholars will debate how many separate oracles were spoken, and how to divide them.

Generalizing about chapters 40–55 we can divide them into two major groupings.

Chapters 40–48 address a group often designated as Jacob or Israel. This assuredly refers to the exiled community in Babylon. The broad message is that hope is coming, redemption and restoration will soon be realized.

Chapters 49–55 have been called the Zion poem where, though still spoken in Babylon, the direction of Isaiah's attention is toward Jerusalem and Zion, a city ruined and abandoned awaiting a glorious restoration (McKenzie, xxxii).

That these are but general rubrics should be understood, for the four servant songs are split between these sections, one in the first group and three in the second. Indeed the servant songs, like other prophecies, do not form chapters in their own right, but only parts of chapters. We shall deal with the servant songs below.

B. Characteristics

Second Isaiah differs from both prophetic predecessors and successors in the unremitting word of hope, the promise for the future. The prophet "proclaimed that the great change from judgment to salvation was already accomplished fact" (Westermann, 11). "Comfort, O comfort my people.... Speak tenderly to Jerusalem, and cry to her that she has served her term, that her penalty is paid..." (40:1–2).

Another characteristic, following from the sense of future hope, is the very "upbeat" nature of these words. God is openly becoming known among the nations. This is to be a public celebration. God says: "I will go before you ... level the mountains ... break into pieces the doors of bronze ..." (45:2). God exclaims clearly: "To me every knee shall bow, every tongue shall swear" (45:23). "Awake, awake, put on your strength O Zion! Put on your beautiful garments..." (52:1).

A third characteristic to Isaiah's message which makes it distinctive is the immediacy and personal sense to it: the individual and the people are as one, and together they are the object of God's love and concern. "The audience addressed by the prophet is the entire nation taken as a unit; nevertheless, the word of God given him to proclaim is meant to affect every individual member at the most personal and existential level" (Westermann, 13).

Some authors write of a "trial" motif in Second Isaiah. There is a sense of coming before the divine judge to give account, but this sense of a "trial" may be overstating the case. Likewise in the article on "Isaiah" in the *Interpreter's Dictionary of the Bible* the author there speaks of an "assize-inquest" and being "summoned to the bar of judgment" (C. R. North, "Isaiah," *IDB,* 739). A closer sense of these "debates" between God and the foreign nations or between God and Israel is captured in the softer tone of Father McKenzie when he writes that if "any would dispute the prophet's claim, he challenges them to a legal contest with him; he can prove his case" (McKenzie, 27).

C. Themes

The Exodus; the Psalms

The exodus from Egypt was a very appealing image to Second Isaiah. Time and again the prophet either speaks directly of the exodus experience or alludes to it (43:16–21; 51:10–11; 52:11–12).

Isaiah, sitting in Babylon, a desert wilderness away from Judah, naturally saw the parallels to the desert wilderness of the Sinai which also had to be traversed. Second Isaiah's "Zion," which shall become the hope of the world, on some level is a latter-day Sinai. As at the "first" Sinai God's sovereignty and contract with Israel-the-people was proclaimed, so at Zion (the "second" Sinai) will God's worldwide sovereignty and contract with the world be proclaimed. In Isaiah 52:7ff a messenger or herald is welcomed announcing good fortune: God has returned to Zion. This then leads into the fourth servant passage which in its opening lines speaks of righteousness coming to the nations (52:13–15). Then even foreign nations shall come forward (55:5) and the old promise of First Isaiah shall be realized: "For out of Zion shall go forth instruction, and the word of the Lord from Jerusalem" (Is 2:3).

A major influence on Second Isaiah was the Psalms. Isaiah draws frequently on the psalter. There are parallels between Isaiah 40:31 and Psalm 103:5 (youth/eagles); Isaiah 41:18 and Psalm 107:35 (lakes/desert); Isaiah 45:2 and Psalm 107:16 (breaking bronze gates); and many other examples could be given.

4. The Servant Passages

Some of the strangest and certainly most provocative lines of the Bible are found in Second Isaiah's servant songs. These verses are set in four chapters of Isaiah.

[These] poems reflect a unique thought — that the death of the "servant" enables the total community to live. He bears their guilt; hence, they become guiltless. Such human "vicarious atonement" appears only here in Jewish literature and tradition; it is, of course, central to Christianity (Sandmel, *The Hebrew Scriptures*, 190).

These four sets of verses are referred to variously as the servant songs or the suffering servant songs. The word "song" is not meant as it relates to melody, but rather as a synonym for the word poem, for all of Second Isaiah is written in poetry. The Hebrew word for "poem" is the same as the word for "song."

The first three servant songs are (1) 42:1–4 with their response 42:5–9; (2) 49:1–6 with their response 49:7–13; (3) 50:4–9 with their response 50:10–11. The fourth song is 52:13–53:12.

These passages are difficult to understand. One can easily have an immediate sympathy with the Ethiopian eunuch who in the Christian Scriptures reads some of the lines from the fourth song and then asks the apostle Philip, "About whom, may I ask you, does the prophet say this, about himself or about someone else?" (Acts 8:34; see also vss 26ff). Who is the servant? A number of possible answers can be given. Philip suggests the answer is Jesus, but that is a faith statement within the context of the Christian Scriptures.

Who are the (other) possible identities of the servant? Put very briefly they include a figure or figures of:
1. the past, present, or future;
2. an individual or a collective;
3. real or mythical.

Among the many answers given have been Moses, Jeremiah, King Hezekiah, Isaiah himself, collective Israel, the pious of Israel, an unknown prophet, a future messiah, and as noted above, in traditional Christian thought, Jesus of Nazareth. To claim, as does one Christian scholar, that since no one can "prove" once and for all the identity of the servant, the answer needs to be supplied by Christianity, lacks objectivity ("The tools of Old Testament scholarship have never succeeded in providing a satisfactory answer to this question [the identity of the servant] which has caused the answer supplied by the faith of the Christian church to assume all the more significance" (Newsome, 145).

Scholarly analyses of these passages are found in many standard references which deal exclusively with Second Isaiah. A good summary of the servant passages is found in James King West's *Introduction to the Old Testament* (399–404). One of the best discussions is found in the Anchor Bible Series, the volume on *Second Isaiah* (xxxviii–lv), as well as McKenzie's notes and comments on the various songs themselves. Some of the salient points that McKenzie mentions include the following thoughts. The title itself, a servant of God, is an honorific. It means one who is specifically commissioned by God. Though the title "servant" is certainly used elsewhere in the Bible, in Second Isaiah the title is applied to the people of Israel. Yet, in "spite of the superficial attractiveness of the Servant-Israel theory, the theory raises more problems than its solves" (McKenzie, xliii).

There are various "voices" in these passages. In the first song (chapter 42) God is the speaker. In the second and third songs (chapters 49 and 50) the servant is the speaker. In the final song (chapters 52–53) the speaker is not identified, but it is clearly not God. This final passage is the most "controversial," for it unambiguously presents the servant as vicariously atoning for the sins of others.

> The Servant, a figure of affliction, has died. His death has brought an atoning value for "the many," with whom the speaker is identified. The Servant was regarded as guilty, but he will see his own vindication and the fruit of his atoning death (McKenzie, xxxix).

A great deal has been written about these poems, and the interested reader can spend months, indeed years, perusing the relevant literature.

5. Third Isaiah

Third Isaiah lived in Jerusalem following the return of those limited numbers of people who took up the privilege of going back to the land. The section of Third Isaiah is probably made up of "a collection of pieces from different authors" (McKenzie, lxvii). The core seems to be chapters 60–62. These chapters reflect the fact that the temple has not yet been rebuilt but probably will be soon (61:3ff). There will be worship and sacrifice (60:6ff). God is further removed than in Second Isaiah (Is 65:15); and while God's house will be a "house of prayer for all peoples" (56:7), there is a greater sense of pessimism (58:1–14), and occasional vengeance (63:1–6). Nonetheless, there are also passages of great hope, of coming redemption, such as 60:1ff, which reflect a kinship with the more optimistic views of Second Isaiah.

6. The Later Isaiahs in the Christian Scriptures

If one counts up the quotations from the Hebrew prophets that are featured in the Christian Scriptures, the collective Isaiahs stand second to none. Among the standard three Isaiahs the ranking puts Second Isaiah in first place, followed by the chapters of his successor.

In the synoptic gospels (Mt 3:3; Mk 1:3; Lk 3:4–6) as with John (1:23) the ministry of Jesus begins with a quotation from Second Isaiah (40:3–5). During Jesus' ministry as recorded in Matthew (12:17ff) there is an extensive quotation from the first servant song (42:1–4).

According to some Christian interpretations, the "sequence of thought in the four Songs is reproduced in the ministry, death and resurrection of Jesus" (Winward, 186). Christianity certainly has traditionally understood the servant passages to refer to Jesus. One of the most famous instances underlying this is, as noted before, the episode of Philip the apostle and the Ethiopian eunuch as recorded in Acts 8:26–35. Likewise in the Matthean account, Jesus seems to refer to the servant when he suggests that suffering is a necessary part of his life (Mt 16:21–23). There are other images as well. In John (7:37f) Jesus paraphrases Isaiah 55:1: "If any man is thirsty, let him come to me" (see also Is 44:3), and in James (2:23) one finds a paraphrase of the statement concerning "Abraham, my friend" (Is 41:8).

Third Isaiah contains some very beautiful and poetic imagery, words which lent themselves to quotation in the Christian Scriptures. "For I am about to create new heavens and a new earth" (65:17) is quoted in Revelation (21:1), and "for my house shall be called a house of prayer for all peoples" (56:7) is quoted by Matthew (21:13), Mark (11:17) and Luke (19:46).

Parts of Third Isaiah also suggest apocalyptic times (Westermann, 364; Newsome, 173), and this theme is taken up in Revelation 21:23: "And the city has no need of sun or moon to shine on it, for the glory of God is its light, and its lamp is the Lamb" (see Is 60:19). Likewise the apocalyptic-like images in Isaiah 63:1ff are taken up in Revelation 19:13ff and 14:19–20. Further, Romans 10:20–21 features a quote from Isaiah 65:1–2.

7. Second and Third Isaiah and Jewish Sources

In Jewish tradition on each week in a given year a set lectionary reading from the prophets follows the Torah portion. Among those chosen, one-fourth are taken from the Isaiahs, and the overwhelming number (ten out of fifteen) come from Second Isaiah. When reading in the book of Deuteronomy, several portions are linked with chapters from Isaiah. Though these feature predominantly chapters 49–55 they consciously omit reference to the fourth servant song found in chapter 53. This is because of the "christological interpretation given to the chapter by Christians... the omission is deliberate and striking" (Herbert Loewe, *The Rabbinic Anthology*, 544). This reading of a weekly section from the prophets is mentioned in the Mishna as a familiar practice (*Mishna Megillah* 4:10), and the Christian Scriptures support this when Jesus reads from Isaiah (61:1–2) during a synagogue service (Lk 4:16–21).

Words from Second Isaiah and Third Isaiah have influenced synagogue liturgy in a major prayer of the morning service. In the "*Yotzer*" which praises God as creator of light and darkness the first sentence is adapted from Isaiah 45:7 (see Babylonian Talmud *Berachot* 11b). Likewise in the sabbath hymn "*Lecha dodi*," a number of phrases are taken from both Second Isaiah and Third Isaiah (52:2; 51:17; 60:1; 54:4; 49:19; 62:5; 54:3).

On the Day of Atonement, Yom Kippur, in the morning service, the prophetical reading is taken from Third Isaiah, a passage which suggests certain parameters for righteous behavior, and that God is ever ready to hear the prayers of the repentant (57:14–58:14).

We shall consider, in the "Text Study" section below, Isaiah 51:1–11. In this passage, Second Isaiah refers to Abraham. In the midrash the rabbis offered a further reason why Abraham is specifically mentioned here. Hearkening back to Genesis 15:17 they noted that God had shown Abraham a smoking oven and a flaming torch when they concluded their covenant. The rabbis explain that God told Abraham that the smoking oven was Gehenna (hell) and the flaming torch was Torah. As long as your descendants study Torah and offer sacrifices they will be saved from Gehenna, but when they fail in their duty they will be punished. Then God gave Abraham a further choice: Should their future punishment be Gehenna or captivity? Abraham opted for captivity. Hence even as the exiles are returning they should remember that as unpleasant as was their captivity, it was preferable to Gehenna (*Midrash Exodus Rabbah* 51.7).

The rabbis were also intrigued with this notion of God comforting Zion, and the waste places turned into Eden-like freshness (Is 51:3). From their own life experience they knew that this had not in fact come about. Did this mean that Isaiah had prophesied incorrectly? To avoid that explanation they simply moved the time sequence. God will comfort Zion and turn the desert into a garden, but it will be part of the schema of the world to come (*Midrash Genesis Rabbah* [New Version] 97 end; 100.13 end).

In the "Text Study" section we shall also consider Isaiah 61:1–11. The rabbis saw a special message in these verses. In *Pesikta Rabbati, Piska* 34.1, Isaiah 61:9 is quoted and the rabbis suggest that these are words of comfort to those who are mourners for Zion. Do not understand the word to be "their descendants" (*za'rm*) but rather "their arm" (*z'roam*) — and who is their arm? The Holy One, blessed be God, shall stand by them, as it says in Isaiah 33:2: "Be our arm every morning, our salvation deliverance in time of trouble."

In that same midrash collection the rabbis address Isaiah 61:10, "I will greatly rejoice in the Lord ... for [God] has clothed me with the garments of salvation, he has covered me with the robe of righteousness." The "rejoicing" refers alternately to the days of the messiah, being delivered from punishment in Gehenna, when the inclination to do evil will have been rooted out of Israel, or when the angel of death will no longer have power over Israel (*Pesikta Rabbati, Piska* 37.2).

8. Text Study

Selection from Second Isaiah

Suggested reading: Is 51:1-11

Some would divide up these lines and suggest that there has to be a rereading (see Westermann, 232ff); others feel there is a sufficient unity here to consider it as a whole (McKenzie, 124).

Chapter 51 follows directly upon the third servant song (50:4-9) and its response (50:10-11).

Vss 1-2 These lines suggest to the exiles that even if they have some lingering doubts, they should think of their ancestors Abraham and Sarah. They too were promised a brilliant future. Initially they were doubtful, but God's promise was kept.

The reference to Abraham/Sarah has several levels of meaning. They also came from Mesopotamia, they too had to begin anew, and they had to traverse the desert wilderness before they could come to the promised land. In addition Isaiah utilizes very powerful imagery here, evocative (and sexually provocative): Abraham is the "rock" and Sarah is the "quarry" (vs 1) of the preceding verse. The genital allusions, however, are subtle, unlike those pictured in Ezekiel 23.

Vs 3 The image of God comforting Zion and the presence of joy and thanksgiving are quintessential Second Isaiah. The verb "comfort" (*Nun-Het-Mem*) is the same as that which begins his words in chapter 40:1: "Comfort, O comfort my people." Notice here that in this one sentence that same verb appears *twice*, just as it did in 40:1.

The allusion to Eden-like lushness is a striking contrast to the waste places, ruins and desert. It echoes a similar vision in Ezekiel (36:35 and 47:1ff).

Vss 4–6 In these verses the prophet turns from Israel and addresses the *peoples*. This is another major concept in Second Isaiah (in addition to comfort/hope), for God is to be understood in increasingly universalistic terms.

The phrase in vs 4, "a light to the peoples" (*l'or amim*), differs but slightly from the "light to the nations" that is so familiar in the servant passages which preceded it in Isaiah 42:6 and 49:6 (*l'or goyim*).

This is really a paraphrase of the first servant song. It is a striking example of the way in which the songs lived on and were handed down. The post-exile community, or a section within it, took up the possibility of salvation for non-Israelites which Isaiah 42:1–4 had opened up, and in the servant's name proclaimed to the heathen that God's salvation was available for them, and that light which they had been awaiting was now there (Westermann, 235). (N.B. In view of Harvey Falk's thesis in *Jesus the Pharisee* [New York, Mahwah: Paulist, 1985] this corresponds well with the notion that Jesus had at least some Pharisaic support to teach God's words to the heathens.)

There is also another, somewhat more ambiguous reference to vs 6. Rabbi Judan said in Rabbi Aha's name: What did the children of Noah think, that the covenant with them would endure to all eternity? (*Midrash Genesis Rabbah* 34.11). He then goes on to explain that God's covenant with the heathens (children of Noah) would *not* last forever, and he cites Isaiah 51:6 and Zechariah 11:11. This might suggest that in his view the heathens who follow the basic seven Noahic laws really do not have a place in the world to come. Alternately this may mean that in order to achieve the world to come, the heathens who previously followed the Noahic code will now need to be even more righteous. The rabbis cite seven precepts, which they suggest were given to Noah and to his children. These seven rules are basic laws for a moral life. The usual classification is as follows:

> 1) Not to worship idols; 2) Not to commit murder; 3) Not to commit adultery or incest; 4) Not to eat a limb torn from a living animal; 5) Not to blaspheme; 6) Not to steal; and 7) To have an adequate system of law and justice (Louis Jacobs, *A Jewish Theology*, 285; see also *Midrash Rabbah Genesis* 34.8).

In another collection of midrashim, the rabbis interpreted the statement in vs 6 that "the earth wear out like a garment" to be a reference to the world to come where God shall simply fold up the earth like a garment and then unfold it out anew (*Pirke de Rabbi Eliezer*, chapter 51 beginning).

The images of the heavens/earth being destroyed, but God's words enduring, are echoed in Matthew 24:35, 2 Peter 3:7–12 and Revelation 20:11.

Vss 9-11 Now Isaiah addresses God. These verses end up on a triumphal note (vs 11) similar to vs 3, but in the immediately preceding two verses some very powerful allusions appear.

The arm of the Lord (*zeroa Adonai*) brings the immediate echo of the exodus. The same word (*zeroa*) is used in Exodus 6:6: "I will redeem you with an outstretched arm ..." and in the song of the sea: "by the might of your arm, they became still as a stone ..." (Ex 15:16).

The exodus theme continues directly in vs 10, "Was it not you who dried up the sea ... a way for the redeemed to cross over?" — a clear reference to Exodus 14:16, 22.

Then in addition there are references to God who is also the creator who made short shrift of the legendary monsters of the deep. Featured here are four separate entities from Near Eastern mythology: Rahab, Tannin, Yam and Tehom Rabbah (Westermann, 241; see T. H. Gaster, *Myth, Legend, and Custom in the Old Testament*, 576). These references are particularly appropriate, for the exiles are living in Babylon, where they would be familiar with the Babylonian epic *Enuma Elish* which features a defeat of similar monsters.

The rabbis took note that in vs 9 there is a repetition of the word "awake," just as later in the chapter (vs 17) there would come the words "rouse, rouse yourself" and similar repetitions in 40:1, 51:12 (and 61:10). Since these repetitions are fairly rare (see Gen 22:11; 46:2; Ex 3:4; 1 Sam 3:10) the rabbis concluded that Isaiah was specially favored by God (*Midrash Leviticus Rabbah* 10.2).

Selection from Third Isaiah

Suggested reading: Is 61:1-11

Vss 1-3 These verses are part of Third Isaiah's message of hope and salvation that are found in chapters 60–62. These three lines, however, have an echo of the servant songs which were discussed earlier. Here again the prophet is speaking to the depressed and dejected.

Vss 4, 7-11 Here again is a message of hope. The ancient cities shall be rebuilt, and since you suffered so much, you will inherit double portions. You shall be like brides and bridegrooms.

Chapter 8

AMOS, HOSEA AND MICAH

AMOS

1. The Importance of Amos

The prophet Amos is a pivotal figure in biblical thought. Historically, that is chronologically, he is the first of the *classical, literary,* the *written* prophets. As shall be shown, Amos sets down many of the patterns that shall be followed by the prophets whose books are found in the Hebrew Scriptures. As would be said of another "prophet" more than two thousand five hundred years later, he was the "beginner of the great work" (the remark is attributed to George Whitefield about Theodore J. Frelinghuysen, the "source" of The Great [religious] Awakening in colonial America [quoted by L. J. Trinterud, in Winthrop S. Hudson, *Religion in America,* 62]). We cannot overestimate the importance of Amos.

> [The] practice of collecting and preserving the oracles of a prophet in a separate book came to begin with Amos. It was to have far-reaching results, first in the raising of the prophetic office to a consistently high level, which it was to hold for two centuries, then in the consolidation and crystallization of Israel's faith in a series of prophetic books (J. D. Smart, "Amos," *Interpreter's Dictionary of the Bible* [*IDB*], 117).

What motivated the writing down of Amos' addresses or prophecies is not recorded. It has been suggested that "the swiftness with which his words were validated by disastrous historical events" induced people to preserve his words and something of the occasion surrounding them (Smart, "Amos," 117).

That this may not be the full answer, for Elijah and Elisha's words were also validated with swiftness, does not detract from its being one important factor. Unlike the book of Jeremiah, in Amos there is no record of a disciple recording the prophet's exact words. It may be that Amos spoke extemporaneously and some time may have passed before his words were collected and set down (Sandmel, *The Hebrew Scriptures*, 60). It is likely, as with those who would follow him, that the prophet said a great deal more than was ever recorded, or perhaps it was set down, but lost.

Amos sets the pattern for his literary successors. His work falls into four categories: a prophecy against the nations, a prophecy against Israel, stories about the prophet, and finally a prophecy of comfort for Israel, a kind of epilogue. "The remaining prophetic books of the Bible are built on the same four categories, but they are not necessarily arranged in the same order and not every one has left prophecies in all four categories" (Menahem Haran, "Amos," *Encyclopedia Judaica [EJ]* 881).

Amos was also unique in his teaching and his prophecies. He was the first classical prophet to suggest that a consequence of Israel's sins will mean exile (Haran, 887). The book of Amos is special, for it contains a statement by the prophet about his commission. While this would not be true of all of his successors, it certainly provided not only important information about this mid-eighth century figure, but furthermore gave incentive to Hosea, Isaiah, Jeremiah, Ezekiel and Jonah to do likewise.

Amos was the beginner of the great work but he also "was the inheritor of a great tradition" (Smart, "Amos," 121) that reached backward in time for about two centuries. He is the first *literary* prophet, not the first biblical prophet.

2. Historical Background and Biography

A. *Historical Background*

In comparison to the tumultuous days of First Isaiah, Jeremiah and Ezekiel, Amos lives in an outwardly peaceful and prosperous land. In the period of Amos' prophecies, c. 750 BCE, Uzziah the king of Judah (783–742) is well into his forty-one year reign, and the same is true of Jeroboam II of Israel (786–746) who also provides great stability in his forty year reign. While Jeroboam II's rule does not get much notice in the historical books of the Bible (2 Kgs 14:23–29) he was a very successful ruler. He was the great-grandson of Jehu who had overthrown the Omride dynasty. Jeroboam II and his father Jehoash had both recovered land which had been lost to the Syrians in former times. The major power of Assyria was still concerned with internal problems closer to home, so this too permitted opportunity for some expansion.

Relations between Israel and Judah were cordial, and this allowed for advances in business and trade. A leisure class was very much in evidence. From Amos one learns of well-built winter and summer residences, luxuriously decorated (3:15; 5:11). Bethel and Gilgal are very active as cult shrines (4:4-5; 5:21-25) but the flourishing cult is only a screen for deeper ills in society. Judges take bribes (5:12), the powerless and the needy are without advocates, injustice is sovereign in the land (2:6-7; 5:12), and sexual immorality is rife (2:7). The women are as profane and profligate as their spouses (4:1; see 2:7).

B. Biography

Into this society came Amos, the herder and agriculturalist (7:14-15). A great deal has been written about Amos' life and the town of his origin. It is all speculation. There are those who claim he was a complete rustic, with no professional training for religious office (Smart, "Amos," 117; see S. R. Driver, *The Books of Joel and Amos*, 105 — the comments of W. Robertson Smith). Others claim that Amos was an "owner of an agricultural enterprise" with some "formal education" (Newsome, 19). Nearly all scholars would place his home in the southern city of Tekoa, in the general vicinity of Jerusalem and Bethlehem (Smart, "Amos," 117; Newsome, 19; Driver, 95). The fact that he traveled to and prophesied in the northern kingdom is explained away by saying that he was concerned about the people of God and was indifferent to regional borders. Though a minority view, much can be said for the argument that Amos is a northern prophet. If a Tekoa in the north is not known from the biblical period, there is such a village mentioned in the Talmud. If America can boast numerous Springfields, Portlands, et al., why not more than one Tekoa (see Haran, 879)? It is intriguing that the priest Amaziah at Bethel urges Amos to *go* to the land of Judah and prophesy there; he does *not* say "return" to Judah (7:12 — *lech b'rach l'cha el eretz yehudah* — lit. "go, flee away").

In any case Amos takes great umbrage, for Amaziah suggests that he, Amos, is a "professional prophet." Not so! he says. God has sent me on this specific mission! He then attacks Amaziah directly and predicts the coming humiliation of Amaziah's wife and the priest's dying in exile (7:12-17).

As to Amos' formal education, we simply have no evidence one way or the other. "Rudeness of occupation does not necessitate rudeness of thought and speech" (Smart, "Amos," 117; see also H. Graetz, *History of the Jews*, 1.231). Many a country person has a wonderful command of language, for incisive words and insight are not the sole preserve of the city-dweller. To be unlettered is not to be ill spoken.

3. Divisions of the Text and Amos' Messages

A. *Dividing the Text*

When dividing the prophecies of Amos, the fourfold pattern referred to above serves us quite well.
   a. A prophecy against the nations (1:2–2:3);
   b. A prophecy against Israel (and Judah 2:4–6:14);
   c. Stories about the prophet (7:1–9:6);
   d. A prophecy of comfort, a kind of epilogue (9:7–15).

B. *Amos' Messages: Rulership; Relations; Responsibility*

Central to Amos' thinking are three interconnected points: God's rulership over the universe, God's special relationship with Israel, and God's holding Israel responsible for having broken the covenant.

Certainly there is in Amos a strong sense of what will be developed in later prophets, the notion that God reigns and is creator of all the world. Universalism (the idea that God's concerns are widespread, that God cares about other nations in addition to Israel, as opposed to "particularism" which presents God as solely concerned with Israel) is clearly visible with Amos (see 9:7; Sandmel, *The Hebrew Scriptures*, 67). God is concerned not only with Israel but with foreign nations as well.

There is, nonetheless, an ongoing and unique relationship between Israel and God. Amos points out for the first time that "the people's fate is determined solely by its social and moral perfection" (Haran, 888–889). God demands more of Israel, for "only you have I known of all the families of the earth ..." (3:2).

Clearly God is disappointed with Israel. Israel has spurned the covenant, it has rejected God. Consequently Israel shall be called to account because of its sins (3:2). This statement is then followed by the powerful call to prophecy, the cause and effect speech (3:3–8).

Amos' promises of doom are based on social and moral corruption (see "Historical Background" above). "The heart of Amos' faith was the conviction that only a nation in which the dealings of men with one another are just can be in any true sense a people in covenant with God" (Smart, "Amos," 121). God demands justice, not merely outward signs of the cult. "Seek good and not evil, that you may live ... establish justice in the gate..." (5:14–15). "Let justice roll down like waters, righteousness like an ever-flowing stream" (5:24).

Have no doubt, says Amos, destruction is coming, "I will make the sun go down at noon ... I will turn your feasts into mourning and all your songs into lamentation..." (8:9–10).

For all that, the book ends on a note of hope. Chapter 9:11f speaks of the restoration of the Davidic rule and vss 13ff suggest a glorious future ("the time is surely coming ... the mountains shall drip sweet wine ... I will restore the fortunes of my people Israel, and they shall rebuild the ruined cities..."). Did Amos really offer consolation, or were these verses merely added on later? In all probability Amos predicted destruction and exile, but felt a saving remnant would survive and return, both to the land and to God (3:12; 5:3, 15).

4. Amos in the Christian Scriptures

Amos (5:25–27) is paraphrased in Acts 7:42 to suggest that the Jews were idolaters from long ago, and at the Jerusalem conference James quotes from Amos 9:11–12 in Acts 15:16–18. These, however, are exceptions, for generally the Christian Scriptures only rarely refer to Amos' words.

J. D. Smart, however, in the article on "Amos" in *IDB* is ready to compare Amos to John and Jesus.

Amos' primary call to Israel, like that of John the Baptist and Jesus, is: "Repent and return to God."... Like Jesus he could say "Do this, and you will live" (120).

5. Amos and Jewish Sources

In a pun on the word "Amos" the rabbis suggest that this prophet was a stutterer (from the word *'amus*, literally "burden, heavy," i.e. he had a heavy tongue — *Midrash Leviticus Rabbah* 10.2). Furthermore, the rabbis, in an effort to add to the lineage of Amos, credit his father with being a prophet. Their explanation goes against the simple and plain meaning of the text, but it enhances the prestige of Amos. In the relevant line in the Bible Amos says to the priest Amaziah: "I am no prophet, nor a prophet's son ..." (7:14). That is its *literal* meaning, but in this case the Jewish Publication Society translation *TANAKH* more clearly captures the sense of what Amos is saying. He is not speaking about his literal parentage. The Hebrew phrase *ben-navi* can be translated literally as "a prophet's son" or "the son of a prophet" but in its context it means "a prophet's disciple." Thus *TANAKH* renders this passage: "I am not a prophet, and I am not a prophet's disciple." Amos' reply is a retort to the priest Amaziah who had just said: "Seer, off with you to the land of Judah. Earn your living there, and do your prophesying there" (Am 7: 12) The plain meaning is that Amos is saying that he is not a professional prophet, he is only here on a commission from God. The rabbis, however, take Amos' words *very literally* and supply some extra words: "I am not [*that is to say, I have not always been*] a prophet, and I am not a prophet's son [*that is to say, my father was not always a prophet (— when I was born, my father was not a prophet)*]" (*Midrash Leviticus Rabbah* 6.6).

Elsewhere Amos is lauded for reducing the essential commandments of God to one line (Am 5:4), "Seek me and live!" (Babylonian Talmud *Makkot* 24a).

Amos' prestige is further attested to in another midrash where it explains that when the messiah comes there will be a committee of advisors made up of fifteen notables. Among Adam, Abraham, Jacob, Moses and David will be the figure of Samuel and *Amos*! (*Midrash Song of Songs Rabbah* 8.9.3; Babylonian Talmud *Sukkah* 52b. This midrash has echoes in the Christian Scriptures. See Mt 19:28 and 1 Cor 6:2.)

6. Text Study

Suggested reading: Am 3:1-8

Vs 1 Reference to the exodus — there is a subtle irony here. God reminds the people of the exodus which led to Sinai, but in fact they have, by their action, rejected the covenant. Furthermore, as they were enslaved in Egyptian "exile," so will they be exiled again.

Vs 2 Amos' point that "You only have I known of all the families of the earth . . ." was quoted by the rabbis to explain God's partiality for Israel. The rabbis, however, were not unmindful of the second part of the sentence: "therefore I will punish you for all your iniquities" (Babylonian Talmud *Avodah Zarah* 4a; *Tanna Debe Eliyyahu* — Chapter [15] 16, p. 76, 210–211). In both these midrashic sources just mentioned it is clear that they recognized that the people had done wrong. Elsewhere they quoted other verses from Amos to explain why Israel was being punished. They understood Amos' words and explained that Israel deserved to be disciplined, but there were mitigating circumstances, namely because they associated with evil people. The proof-texts for this latter assertion come from Amos 6:1–4 (*Midrash Leviticus Rabbah* 5.3).

Vss 3 ff Throughout the next lines "cause and effect" are repeated. The examples are primarily of a pastoral nature (lion/forest; young lion/den; bird/snare; prey/trap; lion's roar/fear) which underscore the author's rural background. Amos is "impelled and coerced" by God; it is "impossible for him not to speak" (Lindblom, 194).

Vs 7 God reveals the divine purpose to the prophets. This line was quoted by the rabbis as a proof that while the prophets may not have seen the totality of the future, they were able to see some of it. In the words of Rabbi Berekiah, "As [one peeps] through a crack in the door" (*Midrash Ecclesiastes Rabbah* 1.8.6 — based on Amos 3:7. See also *The Midrash to Proverbs*, chapter 14 beginning).

Vs 8 The image of God as a lion also appealed to the rabbinic mind, for this certainly is a powerful concept. In the *Avot de Rabbi Natan*, chapter 2, this verse is quoted and the comment is that "God is not merely like one lion, but like all the lions in the world!"

HOSEA

1. Introduction

Even as we begin to analyze the prophecies of Hosea, a special note is in order. Throughout this book I have endeavored to be sensitive to gender issues. In an earlier chapter I wrote about the fact that when a prophet offered the image of Israel as a "faithless wife" the key issue was "faithlessness" and not faithless women. A central metaphor in Hosea is Israel-as-God's-faithless-spouse. In Hosea, the prophet himself is portrayed as the cuckold, just as God is abandoned by the people Israel. In the real world in which we live, just as in the real world addressed by the prophets, at times men violate their marriage vows, just as on occasion do women. The received text of Hosea casts Israel as an errant wife. These images and metaphors would be offensive if understood as an attack on womankind. Hosea's intent, I believe, was otherwise. His concern was generic faithlessness, just as his hope was for a time of reconciliation ("Return, O Israel, to the Lord your God, for you have stumbled because of your iniquity. . . . I will heal their disloyalty; I will love them freely, for my anger has turned from them" (Hos 14:1, 4 [14:2, 5 H]. Hosea is a book rich in metaphors and allusions. I would hope that the reader will appreciate Hosea's messages and the skill of his language.

In actual fact, one of the most baffling mysteries of the Hebrew Scriptures is the question surrounding the true identity of Hosea's wife Gomer. Was she or was she not a prostitute, a cult prostitute, and/or an adulteress? Indeed, was she a real person or does she really represent a prophetic metaphor? The divisions generally break into two schools: the "historicizers" who hold that she was real and the "symbolists" who suggest Hosea began the "practice, followed increasingly by later prophets, of dealing in symbols" (Sandmel, *The Hebrew Scriptures*, 78). We will never know for sure, just as we will not be able to settle the question whether the woman of chapter 1 — specifically named there as Hosea's wife Gomer — is the same woman who is mentioned in chapter 3 as the prostitute. Chapters 1 and 2 are biographical accounts, chapter 3 is autobiographical. Is chapter 3 authentic Hosea, and if so does it repeat material from chapter 1 or not? In any case, both "historicizers and symbolists agree on the symbolic significance" of this woman, which is to depict Israel's *unfaithfulness* to God (Sandmel, *The Hebrew Scriptures*, 78–79).

2. Historical Background

Hosea was a prophet located at and concerned with the northern kingdom. He focuses primarily on Israel (called most often "Ephraim" in his book). Significantly the city of Jerusalem is not mentioned once in Hosea. Nevertheless "Judah falls within the immediate area of his interest . . . as a member of the ancient twelve tribes (10:11) standing together with Ephraim before Yahweh (5:12, 13, 14; 6:4)" (Hans Walter Wolff, *Hosea, A Commentary on the Book of Hosea*, xxii). He lived and prophesied about 745–725 BCE, coming after Amos and before the final destruction of the northern kingdom by the Assyrians under Sargon II in 722/721 BCE. Hosea's prophecies in the north come in the same period as that of Isaiah's and Micah's in the southern kingdom of Judah.

Hosea and Amos complement each other well. Amos lashed out at specific abuses in society — the wide chasm between the rich and the poor, the perversion of the justice system, sexual immorality, gluttony, and a corrupt priesthood, to name just some of his concerns, Yet Amos is virtually silent when it comes to matters of ritual worship. Here Hosea takes up the slack, for Israel's widespread worship of the pagan god Baal is both fact and symbol of its infidelity to God.

The political background to Hosea's pronouncements is the deteriorating condition of Israel. Jeroboam II (d. 746) had ruled for four decades. This had been a time of relative peace and fair prosperity. Over the next period there would be a succession of kings and assassinations. One of these kings was Pekah who ascended to the throne through bloodshed and was to rule for five years (737–732). It is this selfsame Pekah ben Remaliah who is mentioned in Isaiah (7:1ff; see 2 Kgs 15:25ff) in connection with the Syro–Ephraimitic war (734 BCE) and the siege of Jerusalem at the time of King Ahaz. Ahaz, king of Judah, would defy Isaiah and call on King Tiglath Pileser III of Assyria. It would be only a matter of time before the fall of the northern kingdom.

3. Hosea's Message

Hosea's message can be summarized fairly briefly. Israel has turned from a fidelity to God to the false worship of Baal. Chapter 4 paints a vivid picture:

> They sacrifice on the tops of mountains, and make offerings on
> the hills, under oak, poplar, and terebinth, because their shade
> is good. Therefore your daughters play the whore, and your
> daughters-in-law commit adultery (4:13).

This faithlessness has come about because Israel has turned from God, the very source of morality. Infidelity has brought about foreign entanglements and with it foreign religious cults. There is no recourse but punishment. Specifically this means exile from the land. In Hosea's own words, "They shall not remain in the land of the Lord; but Ephraim shall return to Egypt, and in Assyria they shall eat unclean food" (9:3). This will come about not because of God's lack of compassion but because Israel deserves and needs this chastisement. Israel has sown the wind, and is now reaping the whirlwind (8:7). As a parent laments a wayward child, and as a spouse laments a faithless partner, so does God grieve over this turn of events (11:1ff; 2:2ff [2:4ff H]). Israel will know destruction, but after a time repentance will come (14:1ff [14:2ff H]) and eventually reconciliation. The restoration, however, will take on a new aspect. God will set the covenant in such a way that Israel will remain faithful forever.

This eternal reunification is epitomized in two sentences that, as shall be noted subsequently, have been well incorporated into Jewish tradition. The sentences come from the second chapter:

> And I will take you for my wife forever; I will take you for my wife in righteousness and in justice, in steadfast love, and in mercy. I will take you for my wife in faithfulness; and you shall know the Lord (2:19–20 [2:21–22 H]).

This is another passage where there are similarities, yet significant differences between the NRSV and *TANAKH* translations. Therefore consider here the version found in the *TANAKH:*

> I will espouse you forever: I will espouse you with righteousness and justice, and with goodness and mercy, and I will espouse you with faithfulness. Then you shall be devoted to the Lord (2:21–22 H).

A cluster of concepts are found here which explain the relationship between Israel-the-people and God: take you for my wife/espouse (*erus*); righteousness (*zedek*); justice (*mishpat*); steadfast love/goodness (*hesed*); mercy/compassion (*rahamim*); faithfulness (*emunah*); and knowledge of/devotion to God (*da'at elohim*) (see Newsome, 40–41). The image of Israel being ever God's people, in unbreakable relationship, would be taken up by Jeremiah in the "new covenant" section (Jer 31:31–34) and latterly by Ezekiel in his "heart" passages (Ez 11:19–20; 36:26–28; see Harold Louis Ginsberg, "Hosea," *Encyclopedia Judaica*, 1011–1012; James Luther Mays, *Hosea, A Commentary*, 14ff).

4. Divisions and Symbolism

Hosea can be divided into two main sections: chapters 1–3 and 4–14. The first three chapters are biographical and autobiographical; the remaining eleven are pronouncements and prophecies. It seems fairly clear that an editor's hand has been at work, and this may explain why there is both biographical and autobiographical material and the "Judahite" additions (Sandmel, *The Hebrew Scriptures*, 71 n.1; see also Wolff, *Hosea: A Commentary on the Book of Hosea*, xxxiif).

Hosea was a poet of extraordinary ability. He suggested a variety of images both for God and for Israel. The metaphor of God-as-husband dominates the book. We also find examples drawn from the world of nature: flora (cypress tree 14:8 [14:9 H]); fauna (lion and leopard 13:7; bear 13:8); and natural occurrences (rain 6:3; dawn 6:3 and dew 14:5 [14:6 H]). A fuller list is suggested by Wolff (*Hosea*, xxiv). To Wolff's list can be added the image of a sentinel (9:8), a wild ass (8:9) and birds (11:11).

Hosea's characterization of God as husband and Israel as wanton wife/adulteress/prostitute fills the first three chapters. Following the biographical information about the name of the prophet and the period of his prophecy comes Hosea's "commission" to obtain a prostitute as a wife, for the land itself has been unfaithful to God (1:2).

> Promiscuity and idolatry are interchangeable terms, as the fo-
> cus shifts back and forth between the contamination of domestic
> family life and the same failure in the public sphere of worship
> and diplomacy (Francis I. Anderson and David Noel Freedman,
> *Hosea: A New Translation*, Anchor Bible, 47–48).

In the second chapter the image of God/husband and Israel/faithless wife continues. In mid-chapter is the wonderful play on words that at the future time of the eternal covenant, Israel will call God "my husband" (*Ishi*) and no longer "my master" (*Baali*). The word *Baali* has a double connotation. It can be literally the phrase my "master," that is to say, the owner of the prostitute, and at the same time it can mean "my [god is] Baal" (2:16) [2:18 H].

This image of adulterous Israel is found in later chapters as well (6:10; 7:4; 9:1 et al.). As Heschel explains, at "times Hosea employed the term "harlot" in a figurative sense, in the sense of political promiscuity" (1.41).

5. Hosea in the Christian Scriptures

The primary "proof texts" from Hosea come in Matthew. In one case the gospel writer seeks to explain why Joseph and Mary go specifically to Egypt to avoid Herod (Mt 2:14–15). This reference to an Egyptian sojourn is found only in Matthew. It is there to substantiate the prophetic words in Hosea 11:1, "When Israel was a child . . . out of Egypt I called my son." Later in Matthew Jesus quotes (from Hosea 6:6) the words that God desires "mercy, not sacrifice." This is an occasion when Jesus disputes with the Pharisees (Mt 9:13; 12:7). In Romans (9:25–26) Hosea is specifically mentioned by name when Paul speaks of the symbolic names of the prophet's children, "Lo-ammi" — "not my people," and "Lo-ruhamah" — "not beloved" (see Hos 1:10; 2:1, 23 [2:1, 3, 25 H]; 1:6, 2:23 [2:25 H]). Paul here applies the names of Hosea's children to *Gentile* Christians who experience spiritual restoration like the restoration promised Hosea's children. Finally Hosea 13:14 is paraphrased in the well-known lines in the Christian Scriptures: "Where, O death, is your victory? Where, O death, is your sting?" (1 Cor 15:55).

6. Hosea and Jewish Sources

The famous "betrothal" verses of 2:19–20 [2:21–22 H] are a major section of the weekday ritual for putting on *tefillin* (phylacteries). As the strap is wound around the middle finger, these verses are recited. Coincidentally, it is these same phylacteries that are mentioned in Deuteronomy 6:8 ("Bind them as a sign on your hand, fix them as an emblem on your forehead") as well as in the gospel of Matthew (23:5; see also Marvin R. Wilson's statements in *Our Father Abraham: Jewish Roots of the Christian Faith*, 117).

The rabbis explain God's anger with Israel in human terms. A royal couple have an altercation, and one makes a threat about divorce. Sometime later that selfsame person is seen ordering a present for the spouse. Clearly the anger was but momentary. The same midrash suggests a similar idea with a ruler first chastising his child for playing instead of studying, and then being reconciled — though specifically this latter reference uses as its proof-text verses in Isaiah 1 (*Midrash Numbers Rabbah* 2.15).

The rabbis in another passage get very angry with Hosea for *not* debating with God, for *not* defending Israel. God tells Hosea, "Your children have sinned." Hosea *should* have said: They are *your children*, the descendants of Abraham, Isaac and Jacob. Apparently Hosea did not argue but rather said to God: The whole world is yours; exchange them for someone else. Consequently God decides to see what Hosea would do under similar circumstances. Hosea is ordered to marry a prostitute and have children. Then God tells Hosea to send them away. God says: If he does so, then I shall send Israel away. Hosea explains, however, that he cannot bear to send them away. God then "teaches" Hosea: If you cannot bear to send them away and you do not even know if they are your own, how could I bear to separate myself from Israel, the children of Abraham, Isaac and Jacob? Hosea then prays and asks for forgiveness. God replies: Pray for Israel, seeing that because of you I have decreed three decrees against them. Hosea prayed, and the three decrees were annulled (Babylonian Talmud *Pesachim* 87 a–b).

The medieval commentator Rashi goes on to explain that the three decrees were associated with Hosea's children and the verses in chapter 2 cancel the punishment of chapter 1 (see Montefiore and Loewe, *Rabbinic Anthology*, 244, n. 1; Rashi to Hosea 2:2, 24, 25 and similar thoughts in *Pesikta Rabbati* 44.2).

> *Hos 1:11* [2:2 H] "gathering Judah and Israel" annuls the (secondary) meaning of Jezreel (*Zera-el* — lit. God sows, but metaphorically God "scatters" seed; Jezreel is the first child; see Hos 1:4).

> *Hos 2:23* [2:25 H] The "pity" (*rihamti*) cancels the negative quality of *Lo-ruhamah* ("Not pitied," the second child) and "You are my people" [*ammi atah*] cancels out the punishment of (the third child) *Lo-ammi*, "You are not my people" (see Hos 1:6, 9).

Though Judaism through its liturgy continues today to speak of the concept of *zechut avot* — "merit of the ancestors" (see the first blessing in the "Amidah" ["Tefilah"] prayer in the daily services) — according to one Talmudic source (Rav), the "merit of the ancestors" ceased at the time of Hosea with the words in chapter 2:10 [2:12 H], "none shall rescue her out of my hand" (Babylonian Talmud *Shabbat* 55a). In light of the previously mentioned rabbinic statements, this negative viewpoint reflects only a minority opinion.

Finally, in the synagogue, Hosea 14:1–9 [14:2–10 H] is the major haftorah (prophetical reading) along with Micah 7:18–20 and Joel 2:15–17 on the sabbath of repentance, between Rosh Hashana and Yom Kippur.

7. Text Study

Suggested reading: Hos 2:2-6, 13-20 [2:4-8, 15-22 H]

Vs 2 [4 H] "Plead with your mother." Compare this to "Rebuke your mother" (*TANAKH* and New International Version); "Argue with your mother" (Anderson, Freedman); "Accuse your mother" (Wolff, *Hosea*). The children are addressed here. God is speaking and appears as the "plaintiff against his unfaithful wife" (Wolff, *Hosea*, 33). The word "rebuke" (Hebrew: *riv* — argue, accuse) reflects clearly an angry quarrel, such as in a law court.

"She is not my wife, and I am not her husband. . . ." This statement will be reconciled at vs 16 [18 H], but here God rejects unfaithful Israel. The putting away from face and breasts probably refers to some kind of objects, marks or emblems indicating harlotry (see Gen 38:15 with Tamar and Judah; Jer 4:30; Ez 23:40).

Vss 4-5 [Vss 6-7 H] The children are mentioned here as also guilty, but the primary accusation clearly is at the wife.

Vs 6 [Vs 8] To "hedge up her way" and "build a wall against her. . . ." It is difficult to know what these terms mean. Perhaps the husband is keeping her "penned in, so that she cannot find the way to her lovers? Or is she locked out, so that she cannot find her way home?" (Anderson, Freedman, 236).
    Israel is the adulterous wife, a figure even worse than the paid prostitute, for she seeks amorous affairs.

Vs 13 [Vs 15 H] "Baals" or "Baalim." Here for the first time Hosea specifically links up Baal worship with Israel.

Vss 14-15 [Vss 16-17 H] There is an echo here of the exodus (wilderness) and specific mention of Egypt. Hosea in a few sentences recalls the long covenantal relationship between God and Israel. I will "speak tenderly" (literally "on her heart"). The "heart" (i.e. mind) is an important image in Hebrew thought, and as mentioned earlier, Jeremiah and Ezekiel both speak of new hearts/new relationships.

Vs 16 [Vs 18 H] *Ishi/Baali;* Husband/Master: dealt with above.

Vs 18 [Vs 20 H] The animals mentioned here are reminiscent of Genesis 1. This is a time of total peace, in field, sky and sea. This, presumably, is only in Israel, not the whole world. Note the pattern of three animals and three weapons, perhaps corresponding to the three children — Jezreel, Lo-ruhamah and Lo-ammi (Anderson, Freedman, 280). There also is a balance between God's creations (the animals), humankind's destructive creations (weapons), and humankind's peaceful creations (children) — who will "lie down in safety." This also is a poetic "threefold" introduction to the three "espousals" in vss 19-20 [21-22 H].

Vss 19-20 [2:21-22 H] According to some Jewish customs the bride will encircle the groom three times during the wedding ceremony. Abraham Block (33) links this to these three expressions of betrothal.

MICAH

1. Geo-Political Background

Micah lives and prophesies in the last half of the eighth century BCE, c. 750–700. The dominant power was Assyria, as cruel and tyrannical an empire as would exist in the ancient Near East. Fear of their inhuman torture of those who opposed them was a conscious part of Assyria's foreign and military policy.

> Assyria's imperial strength, its military might, its practices of enslaving the vanquished, and its policy of calculated cruelty which included such atrocities as ripping up pregnant women to destroy the recalcitrants' unborn next generation ... [produced an] unprecedented fear (Hans Walter Wolff, *Micah the Prophet*, 3).

Micah was a younger contemporary of First Isaiah. Both saw Judah and Jerusalem, and by extension Israel the northern kingdom, governed by people who, too often and in too many ways, were not God-fearing. These monarchs were self-centered, morally corrupt and corrupting others as well. His period of prophecy comes somewhere about the time of the destruction of the northern kingdom (722/721) or just thereafter.

2. Micah's Theology and Social Concerns

Micah has been a favorite for people who are involved with areas of social justice. Micah is very concerned with the poor and the exploited. He is ever ready to speak up in protest, and his words have been quoted in many a sermon and demonstration. Examples include the denunciation of those who misuse power:

> Alas for those who devise wickedness and evil on their beds! When the morning dawns they perform it, because it is in their power. They covet fields, and seize them; houses, and take them away; they oppress householders and house, people and their inheritance (2:1–2).

This sounds like the ancient equivalent of multi-national conglomerates which use and misuse power to swallow up the innocent or unwary, which offer cheap loans and foreclose at the first opportunity.

Likewise Micah attacks the general mood of amorality that is so pervasive. Justice is perverted and will be sold to the highest bidder:

The faithful have disappeared from the land, and there is no one left who is upright; they all lie in wait for blood, and they hunt each other with nets. Their hands are skilled to do evil; the official and the judge ask for a bribe, and the powerful dictate what they desire; thus they pervert justice (7:2–3).

These men and women who cheat the poor and deny justice are more than merely immoral in a secular sense. Their crimes have a societal dimension to be sure, but Micah does not divide his life into aspects of religion and aspects of government, for those divisions of "church/state" are a relatively new concept in the history of western civilization. For Micah, to be unjust in society is just another way of turning one's back on God, for God demands the highest morality as well as making cultic demands.

The judges who judge for a fee, who capitulate to the rich merely because of their wealth (7:3), are at total variance with God's laws as enunciated in Leviticus 19:15: "You shall not render an unjust judgment; you shall not be partial to the poor or defer to the great: with justice you shall judge your neighbor." These laws for magistrates are just as binding as other laws in that same section which deals with robbery, illicit carnal relations, and the prohibition against divination.

Micah's world is made up of six elements. On one side are God, the prophet, and the common people. On the other side of the equation are the three sources of power in society: the other prophets, those in authority including civil servants, magistrates and others in authority, and, finally, the ruler.

These six elements can be then effectively "paired" off into three doublets. While God is the supreme ruler of rulers, creator and judge of the world, and the one who will bring punishment upon the corrupt for their wickedness, God's human counterpart is the king as ruler of the people. Nowhere in Micah is the king or is the Davidic dynasty attacked. Indeed Micah says clearly that from Bethlehem will come the ruler of Israel (5:2 [5:1 H]), and eventually Zion will be the source of God's instruction (4:1ff).

In the second doublet are the prophet himself and the common people whom he defends. Micah has a sure sense of his self. " . . . I am filled with power, with the spirit of the Lord, and with justice and might, to declare to Jacob his transgression and to Israel his sin" (3:8). "What a testimony to fearless self-assurance! Nothing in the other prophets comes close to it!" (Wolff, *Micah the Prophet*, 5). Micah is bristling with indignation of how "they," the power brokers and city-dwellers, have exploited the common country-folk.

The third doublet are the targets of the prophet's anger: the civil servants/magistrates/rulers, and, secondly, Micah's fellow prophets. Micah's attack on this third group is threefold: 1. They have coveted what belongs to others. 2. They have perverted justice. 3. Their religiosity is hypocritical (Wolff, *Micah the Prophet*, 8ff; see Heschel, 1.98–99).

The civil servants/magistrates/rulers have sought what was not theirs. Earlier mention was made of the seizing of fields, houses and homes (2:2). They hold the reins of power and wickedly trample justice and figuratively devour the flesh of the people and break their bones (3:1–3). These magistrates "abhor justice and pervert all equity ... build Zion with blood ... give judgment for a bribe ..." (3:9–11).

The prophets are no better. They lead the people astray, they speak words of comfort as long as their stomachs are full, but "declare a war against those who put nothing into their mouths" (3:5). These selfsame prophets say that God is with them, and that no calamity will befall them, but in fact all they do is "give oracles" for money (3:11).

Micah is swift in his rebuke to his fellow prophets and tells them that their punishment will fit their crimes. Their covetousness, rapacity and lawlessness will result in their being overturned. Jerusalem shall become "a heap of ruins" (3:12). They will sow but reap nothing, plant but harvest naught. They will become an object of horror and mockery (6:15–16). As for the prophets, those who have not listened to God's real word, they will be in the dark and there will be no response from God (3:6–7).

3. Micah and Isaiah

Micah and First Isaiah prophesied in a similar time and place. It is not surprising, therefore, that there are some parallels in concepts. They often shared metaphorical language. For example:

the fidelity of the Lord endures despite his "wrath" (Micah 7:9; Isa. 9:11, 16); He remains the light of the faithful (Micah 7:8; Isa. 10:17); He is King of Israel (Micah 4:7; Isa. 6:1); and He has chosen the Davidide dynasty for the salvation of the people (Micah 5:1; Isa. 7:1–9; 9:6) (Henri Cazelles, "Micah," *Encyclopedia Judaica*, [*EJ*] 1483).

The common call of swords into plowshares in Isaiah 2:2–4 and Micah 4:1–3 is well known.

4. Micah in the Christian Scriptures

The early Church community saw Micah's statement of the new ruler coming from Bethlehem in 5:2–4 [5:1–3 H] "as an oracle concerning Christ, Matthew 2:6 quoting most of verse 2 as evidence that it was to be in Bethlehem that the Christ child would be born" (Newsome, 50).

The reference to Bethlehem as the special birthplace is also found in John 7:42. In addition, the familial unrest and discord of Micah 7:6 is echoed in Matthew 10:21, 35–36 and parallel passages in Mark (13:12) and Luke (12:53).

5. Micah and Jewish Sources

In Jeremiah (26:18) we find an important reference to the prophet Micah. This is part of the famous episode when Jeremiah is challenged by the prophets and priests and accused of preaching sedition bordering on blasphemy, namely that Jerusalem and the temple will fall! The people hearken back to Micah [called in the Hebrew, Micaiah] who some one hundred and fifty years previously had also spoken such words. As Micah was not considered culpable of a capital crime, neither should Jeremiah. The reference is important, for it indicates just how strong an impression Micah's prophecy made.

Though there are several references to Micah in Jewish legends (see Louis Ginzberg, *The Legends of the Jews*, 7.310–311) one of the most prominent post-biblical notes comes in the Talmud where Micah's statement in 6:8 "It has been told to you …" is regarded as a sterling example of summarizing God's demands for a correct covenantal relationship in terms of both rite and right (Babylonian Talmud *Makkot* 24a).

6. Text Study

Suggested reading: Mic 2:6–11

This is an important passage, though difficult to translate. It offers us a glimpse of the heated reaction that Micah found when he preached prophecies against the civil servants/magistrates/rulers and his fellow prophets. The first five lines are probably a dialogue, or the reporting of a dialogue, and the last line would appear to be Micah's aside to himself or to a disciple.

Vss 6–7a (7b) These verses begin with the reaction of those who have been the recipients of Micah's pronouncements, especially at the beginning of the chapter. They do not like his words and tell him so! They feel they are secure, and that God will deal with them in a patient manner. Neither harangue us nor speak such doom, they shout. Verse 7b either can be understood as the crowd of civil servants and their cohorts hypocritically defending their actions by saying "Do not my words do good to one who walks uprightly?" or can be read as Micah saying on God's behalf "Do not my words do good to one who walks uprightly?" which then leads naturally into the accusation of vs 8 (see James Luther Mays, *Micah, A Commentary*, 70; Wolff, *Micah the Prophet*, 49; Allen, 292–293).

Vss 8-9 Micah calls the wealthy civil servants/magistrates/rulers "enemies" of the common people, for they literally and figuratively strip the poor of their clothes, drive women out of their homes and deprive the coming generation of their rights.

Vs 10 This can be read in several ways. It could be the civil servants and others telling Micah he is not to rest, that is, he is to move along and preach elsewhere (or preferably not to speak at all). It could be that the "Arise and go" is a statement sending the women and children from their homes; or it could be Micah telling his audience that before long they shall be exiled because of their rapaciousness and greed.

Vs 11 This seems to be an aside or a comment to a disciple that, in Micah's evaluation, a prophet prophesying platitudes and the easy life is just what they would like to hear. This verse has also been understood as Micah's sarcastic and bitter concluding remark to his audience. They would prefer a man who "would lie. His preaching would intoxicate them in a drunkenness that freed them from facing reality" (Mays, *Micah, A Commentary*, 72).

Suggested reading: Mic 4:1-5

This is probably one of the most widely read passages in the Bible. It has been called the idyllic view of "A City Set on a Hill" (Mays, *Micah, A Commentary*, 93ff). It is lovely poetry with a series of internal parallels found in verse following verse.

Vs 1 The Lord's house shall be established in the mountains/raised above the hills.

Vss 1-2 Peoples shall stream to it/nations shall come.

Vs 2 Mountain of the Lord/house of the God of Jacob; instruction from Zion/word of the Lord from Jerusalem ...

Vs 3 Swords/spears and plowshares/pruninghooks.

In addition the joyous images of this section are the counterpart to the terrible and terrifying prophecies and condemnations of chapters 2 and 3. At the end of the previous chapter, Zion was to be plowed up and Jerusalem would become a heap of ruins (3:12). Here we see Zion/Jerusalem flourishing. Likewise in chapter 2, fields and homes were taken away (2:2, 9), and in this chapter people sit under vine and fig tree with none to disturb them (4:4).

Chapter 9

ZEPHANIAH, NAHUM, HABAKKUK AND OBADIAH

ZEPHANIAH

1. Introduction

With Zephaniah and likewise with many of the remaining books of the Hebrew prophets, a number of problems emerge. In several cases there is scant material which can definitively indicate the time of the prophecy. In other cases there is the clear hand of an editor or collector who has pieced together various fragments attributed to the given prophet. Finally, not all of the material found in the remaining prophets reflects exalted religious teaching; much of it is interesting, but it is not of equal value.

Zephaniah is placed during the period of the popular and reform-minded seventh century ruler, King Josiah. He probably spoke during a period of years *prior* to the seminal date of 622/621 BCE, the time of the "discovery" of the scroll of the teaching (Deuteronomy). This would make Zephaniah a contemporary of, or perhaps even a bit older than, Jeremiah.

Zephaniah is horrified by the corruption he sees in the society around him. The legacy of the four decade reign of King Manasseh (687–642) brought an abundance of pagan worship and a repudiation of God's laws for a moral life. The depravity of Manasseh's reign is spelled out in 2 Kings 21 (vss 1–11): child sacrifice, divination, various kinds of pagan worship, the death of the innocent. In the eyes of the editor of Kings, Manasseh typified an evil king. It has been literally years since someone of the stature of the prophet Zephaniah has spoken. Now the

137

silence "is shattered by the forceful and articulate voice of Zephaniah" (Ivan Jay Ball, "Zephaniah," *Encyclopedia Judaica* [*EJ*], 994).

Zephaniah calls for nothing less than a complete rejection of these idolatrous practices and all that they imply. God has called for the total destruction of Jerusalem and Judah. "I will stretch out my hand against Judah, and against all the inhabitants of Jerusalem; and I will cut off from this place every remnant of Baal ..." (Zeph 1:4).

Zephaniah is zealous with righteous fury. Not only is God offended at the depravity of the citizenry, Zephaniah himself seems to project his own personal anger as well.

As a Hebrew prophet Zephaniah's major concern is Judah and Jerusalem, yet he also has words for Judah's neighbors, both near and far. The Philistine city-states of Gaza, Ashkelon, Ashdod and Ekron will be made desolate; they shall be wasteland. Moab and Ammon will be places of nettles and salt pits not different from Sodom and Gomorrah. Further afield, Ethiopia and Assyria shall fall, Nineveh shall be deserted (2:4, 8–9, 12–13). As for Nineveh, "the owl shall hoot at the window, the raven croak on the threshold; ... [it will be] a lair for wild animals!" (2:14–15).

The book of Zephaniah has been criticized as offering "neither exalted religion nor exalted literature" (Sandmel, *The Hebrew Scriptures*, 107). Certainly there is a relentlessness to Zephaniah which can be distressing, but nonetheless the mind of the poet is visible in his words.

Zephaniah is the "literary father of Hebrew eschatology" (Sandmel, *The Hebrew Scriptures*, 110). In his view of such a complete destruction, the prophet sees literally the end of days. Indeed Zephaniah warns early on in his prophecy: "Be silent before the Lord God! For the day of the Lord is at hand ..." (1:7).

This term "day of the Lord" does not originate with Zephaniah. Amos some one hundred years earlier had used that phrase (Am 5:18–20). For Zephaniah, however, it takes on a more violent and destructive force. The closing lines of his first chapter clearly were the basis for the "Dies Irae," a medieval poem that was incorporated into the Roman Catholic Mass of the Dead. These verses shall be analyzed below in the "Text Study" section.

Zephaniah demonstrates a familiarity with Jerusalem. There are references to sections within the city and also to priests, merchants, tradesmen, judges and prophets (1:4, 10–11; 3:3–4). With these allusions we see that Zephaniah is "steeped in the cultic and literary traditions of his people" (Ball, 994).

Chapter 3 presents both a change of heart in relation to the rest of the book, and its own set of problems. From vs 9 onward a new tone is struck: despite the preceding chapters, filled with death and destruction, a remnant shall remain. "I will leave in the midst of you a people humble and lowly. They shall seek refuge in the name of the Lord — the remnant of Israel; they shall do no wrong, and utter no lies..." (3:12–13). In exchange for disgrace they shall know fame and renown; their fortunes shall be restored (3:19–20). Were these words added on by a later editor to offer a balance against the darkness of Zephaniah's prophecies? Alternately, did Zephaniah hold out hope for a saving remnant? Clearly those two, among other possibilities, do exist.

2. Zephaniah in the Christian Scriptures

The Christian Scriptures are well familiar with the eschatological notion of the coming day of the Lord. Paul speaks of it not infrequently, associating it with the "parousia" — the imminent return of Jesus as the Christ (1 Thes 5:2; 2 Thes 2:2; 1 Cor 1:8; 5:5; et al., and see also E. Jenni, "Day of the Lord" and J. W. Bowman, "Eschatology of the NT" in the *Interpreter's Dictionary of the Bible* [*IDB*]). The writers of the Christian Scriptures, however, do *not* ever *directly* quote from Zephaniah, but rather merely echo his thoughts in a vague way in Revelation where there are statements about the coming day of the Lord (Rev 6:17; see Zeph 1:14) and that this will be a day when the "wrath of God" will be poured "out on the earth" (Rev 16:1; see Zeph 3:8). The Christian Scriptures' use of Joel is a more direct connection for the day of the Lord (Jl 2:28–32 [3:1–5 H]; Acts 2:17–21).

3. Zephaniah and Jewish Sources

The future hope expressed by Zephaniah (in 3:9) that in some future undetermined time God will "change the speech of the peoples [the non-Jewish nations] to a pure speech, that all of them may call on the name of the Lord and serve him with one accord," was interpreted by the rabbis in two ways. In one instance this was understood to mean that while people convert to Judaism through the efforts of the righteous, in the "world to come" God will "convert" the nations to the divine presence (*Midrash Tanhuma, Genesis, Noah*, Buber Edition to Gen 21:1ff, Part IX [slightly modified]). Alternately it was suggested that while the nations of the world were originally divided at the occasion of the tower of Babel because of their evil ways, in the "world to come" God will make the peoples (the nations of the world) "one pure speech so that they all invoke the Lord by name and serve Him with one accord" (*Midrash Tanhuma, Genesis, Noah*, Buber Edition to Gen 11:1ff, Part VII end [slightly modified]).

4. Text Study

Suggested reading: Zeph 1:7, 12-17; 2:3

This is the famous Zephaniah "day of the Lord — yom YHWH" section. It begins and ends on the selfsame note: a specific mention of that day and at the same time caution in the beginning and muted hope at the conclusion. At the center is vs 15, the day of wrath and trouble — "*Dies irae, dies illa.*" Like his predecessor Amos who first spoke of this awesome day, Zephaniah pictures this as a most distressful time (see Am 5:18).

> Zephaniah is as harsh as Amos in preaching the imminent coming of the Day of Yahweh, and he leaves the people with no illusions concerning its serious character. His preaching is intended to shock, in order to make the people, especially its leaders, mend their ways and turn to Yahweh in humility and with eagerness to do his will. But unlike Amos he surely did not expect any repentance from the people, and when he depicted the Day of Yahweh in strong colours he seems to have had no doubt it would come — and come soon (Arvid S. Kapelrud, *The Message of the Prophet Zephaniah*, 67).

Vs 7 "Be silent ... for the day of the Lord is at hand ..." This opening line has echoes of Isaiah 13:6 where that prophet likewise suggested due concern. The phrase "for the day of the Lord is at hand" in Hebrew is literally, word for word, the same in both passages (*kee karov yom YHWH*). Isaiah counsels "Wail" and Zephaniah "Be silent" but their effect is similar. Obadiah (vs 15) and Joel (1:15) will use the same phrase, and Ezekiel (7:7; 30:3) will express a similar thought.

Vss 14–16 Once again in vs 14 Zephaniah states that the "day of the Lord is near." In these three verses (1:14–16) he will repeat, repeat and repeat the word "day." It is featured nine times, a half dozen occasions in vs 15 alone.

Zephaniah's description of this terrible and terrifying day is dramatic, but not because he offers a new, and unheard of, vision. Indeed his "pictorial words ... were known from other prophets' descriptions of the coming catastrophe" (Kapelrud, 62). He calls the day "gloom/darkness" (*afelah*), and that same word, gloom or darkness, periodically is used in the Torah, Prophets and Writings (Ex 10:22; Deut 28:29; Is 8:22;

58:10; 59:9; Jer 23:12; Jl 2:2; and Prov 4:19; 7:9). The day also is called "cloudy" and of "thick darkness" (*anan v'arafel*), words "frequently used in the narrating of the Sinai revelation," where God's presence is described as surrounded by clouds and thick darkness (Kapelrud, 63; see Ex 16:10; 19:16; 20:21 [18 H]; Num 9:15–22; Deut 4:11).

Zephaniah's description is so terrible and terrifying because it is short, pungent and dramatic in its repetition of the word "day." His calling it a day of "trumpet blast and battle cry" (*yom shofar u-teruah*) echoes both the Sinaitic revelation and the horn blast/shofar's call for war (Ex 19:16; Jos 6:5ff).

Vs 2:3 "you humble of the land." These humble, good people, who have fulfilled God's law and are righteous, may be able to survive the awesome day. They seem to be contrasted with the officials and nobility and others of the power elite of 1:8–9.

NAHUM

1. Introduction

In the article on Nahum in the *Interpreter's Dictionary of the Bible* [*IDB*] Elmer A. Leslie writes of the "poetic genius" of the prophet, whose poetry "ranks with the highest in the Hebrew Bible." He also indicates that Nahum "is animated by an intense faith in Yahweh" ("Nahum, Book of," 499). These favorable comments are refreshing to read because a fair number of scholars seem to have great disdain for this, probable late seventh century, prophet of God. Samuel Sandmel described Nahum's works as "a hymn of hate," even if his judgments were justified by the events of his day (Sandmel, *The Hebrew Scriptures*, 116). Likewise another scholar, Edward Lipinski, writes that the "absence of distinctly religious motifs [in Nahum] is remarkable" (in the *Encyclopedia Judaica* [*EJ*], "Nahum," 794).

Nahum's first chapter is a psalm, which is written as a form of an acrostic where each verse contains within it succeeding letters of the Hebrew alphabet, A(lef), B(et), etc. Unfortunately the chapter seems incomplete, for only the first half of this psalm is found (see "Text Study" below).

Nahum is dated in the seventh century at the period of the decline and fall of Nineveh for the simple reason that Nineveh is the subject of his prophecy. The general parameters are as early as c. 663, the fall of Thebes, and the actual fall of Nineveh in 612 (Childs, 441). (Note: in Nahum 3:8 NRSV uses the term "Thebes" while the Hebrew actually says "No-Amon." Amon was the tutelary deity of the city of No, which was another name for Thebes.) A majority of scholars probably follow the later Nineveh dating. Unlike many of his prophetic colleagues Nahum does not provide any autobiographical details. Without any hard information it is difficult to speak cogently about Nahum's life, but the references in the book to Judah's being free to celebrate her festivals and fulfill her vows (1:15 [2:1 H]) now that Nineveh has fallen shows the prophet's interest in this area of religious activity. It is probably for this reason that he was labeled a "temple prophet" (Leslie, "Nahum, Book of," 498).

The fall of Nineveh meant the collapse of the Assyrian empire. As has been explained in earlier chapters ["What Is a Prophet?" and "Micah"] Assyria was the most hated nation of the ancient Near East, for it conspicuously and consciously used cruel and unusual torture as well as mutilation as a part of its foreign policy and warfare. It sought to, and succeeded in, creating a climate of fear among its real and potential adversaries, as well as its vassals. Nineveh's fall certainly resulted in rejoicing, not only in Judah and Jerusalem, but throughout the ancient world.

There are no direct references from Nahum in the Christian Scriptures. Romans 10:15 nonetheless echoes a thought expressed in Nahum 1:15 [2:1 H] and Isaiah 52:7. The notion that God will destroy human evil is certainly a theme in the Christian Scriptures, but that idea is not exclusive to Nahum's prophecy (see Rev 18, 19).

2. Nahum in Jewish Sources

The rabbis were able to take a line from Nahum to explain the nature of God. In Nahum it states: "The Lord is good [to those who hope in God], a stronghold in a day of trouble; he protects those who take refuge in him" (1:7). This line of reasoning is not unique to Nahum, but it provided a homily which suggested that a human ruler would send a legion against an area and kill good and bad alike, regardless of any personal loyalty among the citizenry. Not so with God, the homily on Noah explains, for even if an entire generation were wicked and rebellious, if there were even one righteous person, God would save that person. The "proof-text" is then the line from Nahum 1:7 (*Midrash Tanhuma, Genesis, Noah* to Gen 8:1ff, Part IV).

3. Text Study

Suggested reading: Nah 1:2-4; 3:1-4

Vss 1:2-4 In the opening verses of chapter 1, it is possible to see the alphabetical acrostic:

1:2a (Aleph) [*Ayl kano...*] A jealous and avenging God is the Lord...

1:3b (Bet)   [*B'sufo u'visara...*] His way is in whirlwind and storm...

1:4a (Gimel) [*Go-ayr bayam...*] He rebukes the sea...

Vss 3:1-4 The vivid imagery of the opening lines of chapter 3 are as intense as any description of a fiercely fought battle, replete with flashing swords, chariots and horsemen, hand to hand combat and heaps of mutilated and dying, corpses and carnage near beyond description. There is a vivid sense of detail that rivals a painting by Goya.

HABAKKUK

1. Introduction

The fall of Nineveh inspired Nahum to write/speak a passionate picture of God's (eventual) destruction of the wicked. After the shouting and celebration at the fall of a hated enemy, a certain somber mood sets in. How can it be that the righteous suffer so? Who, ultimately, should accept blame for these conditions? At this point a younger contemporary of Nahum, the prophet Habakkuk, comes forward. A line in chapter 1 of Habakkuk refers to the Chaldeans. It is generally assumed that this refers to the Neo-Babylonians who defeated Nineveh. Habakkuk, therefore, is set at the very final decade of the seventh century, perhaps writing his prophecy in the light of the near-universal lament over the untimely death of popular King Josiah at Megiddo, as the monarch fought in battle against Pharaoh Neco. This is an intriguing notion, but there are certain internal problems which are still in debate. For example: "Who are the wicked of v. 4 who threaten justice and evoke the prophetic complaint?" "[T]he coming of the Babylonians in vv. 5–6 is predicted as something new, but in vv. 7–11 their activity is already fully known" (Childs, 448–449).

For all the problems concerning the "when" of Habakkuk, there is some clear consensus of the divisions within the book itself.

"1. The first cycle: 1:2–11
   a. The prophet's complaint: 1:2–4
   b. Yahweh's response: 1:5–11
2. The second cycle: 1:12–2:5
   a. The prophet's complaint: 1:12–2:1
   b. Yahweh's response: 2:2–5" (West, 354).

These cycles are then followed by a series of "Alas" or "Woe" oracles in the rest of chapter 2 of Habakkuk (2:6–20), and then a concluding psalm in chapter 3 of this prophet.

One scholar has offered an intriguing suggestion that there are close ties between Nahum and Habakkuk at the very least in the way in which the two books have been molded and possibly rearranged by a later editor's hand. In both cases there is a psalm. In Nahum it introduces the rest of the material, in Habakkuk it serves as a conclusion. In both books the psalm is used as a "framework by which to refocus" the other chapters. In Nahum the psalm is theocentric and then secondarily derives the meaning of human events from the divine purpose. "In Habakkuk the order is reversed. The reader begins with the problems of human history and only subsequently are they resolved in the light of a divine oracle." In Nahum the very specific and particular destruction of Nineveh is used to illustrate God's plan, while in Habakkuk "the historical sequence is replaced by a new theological pattern of redemptive history" which is consciously much more vague and blurs any real historical connection (Childs, 454).

Habakkuk's prophecy is unique in that we find in the first two cycles a direct dialogue with God. Like his (probable) contemporary Jeremiah, Habakkuk wants to know why it is that the wicked prosper (see Jer 12:1–2). Later in the Bible, the author of Job (21:7) wants to know this answer as well, but it is only here that such a direct response is offered. The prophet offers several answers to the problem of evil in the world:

1. History has meaning when viewed from a long perspective and with the filter of faith.
2. Individuals and nations need to be righteous.
3. The righteous live by their faith.
4. Wealth is temporary and ruthlessness is eventually punished.
5. God can overturn an evil nation.
6. Evil shall fail; not might but right.
7. Trust in God, rejoice in your faith and your communication with God (developed from E. A. Leslie, "Habakkuk," *IDB*, 505).

2. Habakkuk in the Christian Scriptures

The writers of the Christian Scriptures quote directly from Habakkuk in two instances and indicate familiarity in other places as well. The direct links are Habakkuk 1:5 and Acts 13:41, and Habakkuk 2:4 and Romans 1:17 (see Gal 3:11; Heb 10:38–39; Phil 3:9). The more important connection is the verse in Romans, for there Paul illustrates his central theme of the *justification by faith, and faith alone*. What is also of note is that Paul subtly changes the meaning found in Habakkuk. When comparing these verses this becomes clear. Examples are presented from NRSV, the *New English Bible* (NEB), and *The Holy Bible — New International Version* (NIV).

New Revised Standard Version (NRSV)
Look at the proud! Their spirit is not right in them, but the righteous live by their faith (Hab 2:4).

For I am not ashamed of the gospel; it is the power of God for salvation to everyone who has faith, to the Jew first and also to the Greek. For in it the righteousness of God is revealed through faith for faith; as it is written, "The one who is righteous will live by faith" (Rom 1:16–17).

The New English Bible (NEB)
The reckless will be unsure of himself, while the righteous man will live by being faithful [or "by his faithfulness"] (Hab 2:4).

For I am not ashamed of the Gospel. It is the saving power of God for everyone who has faith — the Jew first, but the Greek also — because here is revealed God's way of righting wrong, a way that starts from faith and ends in faith; as Scripture says, "he shall gain life who is justified through faith" (Rom 1:16–17).

New International Version (NIV)
See, he is puffed up; his desires are not upright — but the righteous will live by his faith [or "faithfulness"] (Hab 2:4).

I am not ashamed of the gospel, because it is the power of God for the salvation of everyone who believes; first for the Jew, and then for the Gentile. For in the gospel a righteousness from God is revealed, a righteousness that is by faith from first to last [or

"is from faith to faith"], just as it is written: "the righteous will
live by faith" (Rom 1:16–17).

Paul changes the prophecy of Habakkuk in a most significant way
(Howard Thurman, "Habakkuk," *Interpreter's Bible* [*IB*], 989; see also
Martin A. Sweeney, "Habakkuk, Book of," in *Anchor Bible Dictionary*,
5). Paul says that *if* you trust in God, *then* you shall attain righteousness
and life. Habakkuk begins with the person who is righteous, who *lives*
by being faithful; therefore that person trusts in God. Habakkuk begins
with the faithful life; for Paul, faithfulness is the means to an end.

In his book *A Jewish Understanding of the New Testament,* Samuel
Sandmel writes about Paul's understanding about the centrality of "faith."

> … Paul's explanation … is that … the power of faith … replaces
> the Law.
>   Paul begins first with the assertion that the Gospel which
> he preaches is a living power of God to bring man to salvation.
> One receives this salvation through believing in it; faith, in-
> deed, is the only way to righteousness and salvation. Gentile
> and Jew alike have pursued the wrong way, the Gentile pursu-
> ing "wisdom," and the Jew the Law of Moses.
>   … Salvation comes apart from the Law, in the gift of the
> Christ. And man, whether Jew or Gentile, believing in the
> Christ, attains salvation (91–92).

The hymn found in chapter 3 of Habakkuk is found in the liturgy of
many Christian churches.

3. Habakkuk and Jewish Sources

Habakkuk 3 also has a Jewish liturgical role. It is the prophetical
reading for the second day of the festival of early summer, *Shavuot* (Weeks,
Pentecost). The rabbis of the Talmudic period were well aware of the
sublime notion articulated in Habakkuk that the righteous person is
sustained by faith. In one famous and often quoted homily, they suggest
that all of God's laws can be condensed into a single dictum, and their two
possible choices for this were Amos' statement "Seek me and live" — Am
5:4, or Habakkuk's "The righteous live by their faith" — Hab 2:4 (Babylonian Talmud *Makkot* 24a).

The rabbis also derived other lessons from Habakkuk. They noted
that in the first chapter Habakkuk likens humankind to the fish of the sea

created by God, but without anyone to rule them properly (Hab 1:14). The rabbis then explained that were it not for human government setting down laws and statutes and being willing to enforce them fairly, like the fish of the sea, might not right would rule. Rabbi Hanina explained: "Pray for the welfare of the government, for were it not for fear of the government, human beings would swallow up their neighbors alive" (Babylonian Talmud *Avodah Zara* 4a).

It is probably Habakkuk 2:1 which provided the basis for another midrash about this prophet. In this instance, Habakkuk, like the later figure of the Tanna Honi (Onias) the circle-drawer (first century BCE), drew the figure of a circle, stepped in it and refused to move until God answered him (*The Midrash on Psalms* 77.1; see Babylonian Talmud *Taanit* 23a–b).

Habakkuk appears in rabbinic legend in a number of instances. He joins his "contemporaries" Isaiah, Micah and Joel in escaping Jerusalem during the villainous days of King Manasseh (*Seder Olam* 20, quoted in Ginzberg, *Legends of the Jews*, 4.278). According to the Apocrypha, he also was there to free Daniel while he was in the lions' den. Habakkuk had been residing in Jerusalem, but was ordered to go to feed Daniel. Habakkuk demurred, saying he had never been to Babylon and further that he did not know where the lion pit was located. Such excuses never work. An angel took him and, carrying the prophet by his hair, flew him to Babylon where he fed Daniel, and he then was returned to Jerusalem by the same method (*Bel and the Dragon*, 33ff; see Jossipon 3.8b–8c, quoted in Ginzberg, 4.348).

4. Text Study

Suggested reading: Hab 1:12–2:5

As explained above, this section, which is the second dialogue cycle, features two divisions: 1:12–2:1, the complaint of the prophet, and then God's reply: 2:2–5.

Vss 1:12–13 The section begins, appropriately, with the prophet praising God, acknowledging God's eternality. Yet even in this praise there is a barb, for God is said also to have placed "them" — an unspecified group — in power to judge others, and clearly those in power are devouring the innocent. God is portrayed as too pure to look upon evil, but nonetheless evil exists. It is then suggested that God is ultimately responsible! The "question fundamentally concerns not so much the

world as God himself. Why is God this kind of a God?" It has been suggested that this is "one of the most important steps in the history of Jewish speculation" (Charles L. Taylor, "Habakkuk," *The Interpreter's Bible*
[*IB*], 985).

Vss 1:14-17 The image of those in the wrong who are also in power
continues with the specific metaphor of someone fishing who draws in
the catch. This negative "fisher of [innocent] people" will be turned on
its head in the Christian Scriptures with the figure of the disciples who
will be called ones who "fish for people" in a positive way (Mt 4:19; Mk
1:17; Lk 5:10; see Jer 16:16). (A rabbinic interpretation of Habakkuk 1:14 was
noted above.)

Vss 2:1 This opening verse provides a bridge between 1:12-17 and
2:2-5. While it is likely that chapter 2 of Habakkuk followed directly upon
chapter 1, it is possible that some time has passed and in frustration
Habakkuk took his "stand." Habakkuk indicates that he is going to wait
to see if and what God will say. Is this a physical tower? An ivory tower?
In any case, it is interesting that the same verb root (*Ttzadi-Fey-Hey*)
for "I will keep watch [I will wait]" in 2:1 in Habakkuk will be used by
God in telling Ezekiel to be a "sentinel" for people in his day (see Ez 3:17;
33:7).

Vss 2:2-3 Habakkuk is told to inscribe the reply — on tablets — so
that they can be clearly read. The word for tablets (*luchot*) is the same
word used in Exodus for the tablets on which Moses inscribed the ten
commandments. Perhaps this answer is seen as just as seminal a teaching. Habakkuk is also told that though the response may not come as
quickly as he would like, he should be patient; even if "it seems to tarry,
wait for it; it will surely come, it will not delay" (2:3).

Vs 2:4 The message Habakkuk is to inscribe is found in vs 4 (see
above for NRSV, NEB, NIV). The standard Jewish translation reads: "Lo,
his spirit within him is puffed up, not upright, but the righteous man is
rewarded with life for his fidelity" (*TANAKH*). In the *Interpreter's Bible*,
it is noted that what Habakkuk means is that the righteous person will
live "if he maintains his integrity." It likens this thought to Isaiah's statement to King Ahaz during the Syro-Ephraimitic war, where Isaiah says
that if you do not believe, you cannot be trusted (Is 7:10-13). The "fidelity"
or "faith" or "faithfulness" (and it is this last word which is preferred by
the *Interpreter's Bible:* "*faithfulness* is a more accurate translation than
faith" — Taylor, "Habakkuk," 989).

Abraham Joshua Heschel explains that this "is an answer, again not in terms of thought, but in terms of existence. Prophetic faith is trust in Him, in Whose presence stillness is a form of understanding" (1.143).

Vs 2:5 This is a difficult verse to translate. The sense of it, however, is that in contrast to the righteous man who lives by his fidelity/faith/faithfulness, the arrogant/proud/wicked person (of vss 2:4a and 2:5) will be punished. (The word *yayin* is not "wine" which makes no sense, but rather "arrogant," "defiant," or "wicked"; see *TANAKH* note on this verse.)

OBADIAH

1. Introduction

Despite the fact that Obadiah is less than two dozen verses in total length, it has stirred up a fair amount of controversy and very little agreement. Critics are divided on the time of its historical setting and whether it is made up of one piece or several (Childs, 412–413). Though some set it at the year 400 BCE, others place the composition closer to the destruction of the temple in 586 BCE (Peter Ackroyd, "Obadiah, Book of," in *Anchor Bible Dictionary*, 4). This latter reading, which calls for an early exilic dating for Obadiah, makes a great deal of sense when set next to the specificity of Psalm 137. Psalm 137 is a lament by those men and women taken into exile. They mourn Jerusalem; they feel dazed and dejected. They also, in the humanness of their pain, seek angry revenge on Babylon and Edom who have caused so much hurt. Obadiah's words could have been spoken in Jerusalem or in Babylon.

There are two basic sections to Obadiah: vss 1–14, which are primarily aimed at Edom, and then a broader statement directed at the nations (but including Edom, understanding Edom and Esau as parallel and the same), which is framed within a "day of the Lord" prophecy.

2. Historical Background

When the Babylonians razed Jerusalem, burning the temple and destroying the city, most of the people were taken northeast to Babylon. Others fled, and were attacked by their neighbors the Edomites (ancient Edom is present-day southwestern Jordan–northwestern Saudi Arabia). In the years following, the Edomites moved westward and settled in and around the area of Hebron, south of Jerusalem. In the late biblical and then in the Roman period this would be known as Idumea (note the similarity in names: Edom/Idumea). The tensions with Edom had been ongoing for centuries. The Edomites were the descendants of Esau, and since the days of the Jacob-Esau controversy there had been bad feeling between Judah/Israel and Edom (see Gen 27:41; 36:1ff; Num 20:14-21; 2 Sam 8:13-14; 1 Kgs 11:15-17). The Edomite treachery following Jerusalem's fall is also mentioned by Ezekiel (25:12; 35:1-9) and Lamentations (4:21f).

The anger of Obadiah (vss 10-14) seems to be fresh, and this lends authority to its being spoken early in the exile. Furthermore there are close parallels between verses in Obadiah and chapter 49 of (his older contemporary?) Jeremiah. "(Obad. 1b-4 // Jer. 49:14-16; v. 5 // 49:9; v.6 // 49:10a)" (Childs, 412).

In the Christian Scriptures, the parallels between vs 21 and Revelation 11:15 are vague and perfunctory.

3. Obadiah and Jewish Sources

Obadiah is the Sephardic alternative prophetical reading for Genesis 32:4-36:43 (*Vayishlach*). Having said this, however, Obadiah did not fare too well in the minds of the rabbis. In one statement Isaiah is spoken of as the greatest of the prophets and Obadiah as the least important (*Aggadat Bereshit* 14:32, quoted in Ginzberg, *Legends of the Jews*, 5.195 n. 72). Nonetheless Obadiah's anti-Edomite prophecies had a certain appeal for the rabbis, for Edom was associated with hated Rome and the cruelties of the Roman oppression. Since to speak openly against Rome was sedition, the rabbis spoke against Edom instead and used this as "code language." In this way the fall of Rome is predicted in *Midrash Leviticus Rabbah* 29.2 An anti-Roman interpretation may also be the gist of *Pirke de Rabbi Eliezer*, chapter 37 end).

4. Text Study

Suggested reading: Ob vss 12-14, 15-21

Vss 12-14 These verses conclude the anti-Edomite opening section. They are powerful rhetoric outlining the cruelty of the Edomites who showed no compassion on the Judean refugees.

Vs 15 This verse serves as a crucial link between the specificity of the opening and the broader terms of "all the nations" in the rest of the chapter. The "day of the Lord" is specifically mentioned, and this day seems to be clearly one of judgment and destruction. This verse also serves as a literary balance point between the first and second sections.

Vss 16-18 "Whereas 2-15 begins with Edom and ends with an eschatological judgment on all the nations, 16-18 begins with the nations and ends with the utter destruction of Edom. Thus, Edom and the nations are not to be separated into different prophetic oracles, but represent different aspects of the same event within the divine judgment" (Childs, 414-415).

Vss 17-21 There is a strong eschatological sense to these verses. The day of God will result in the redemption of Israel. God will triumph, and a remnant shall once again possess the land. There are some general parallels between the thinking and prophecies of Obadiah and those of Zephaniah and Joel.

Chapter 10

HAGGAI, FIRST ZECHARIAH
AND MALACHI

HAGGAI

The prophecies of Haggai and his colleague First Zechariah are set late in the sixth century, about the year 520 BCE. Their activity is attested to not only by their own books, but by the "outside" source of Ezra (5:1 and 6:14). In the chronicles of Ezra the two men seem to be working side by side, supporting and encouraging Zerubbabel and Joshua in their rebuilding of the temple. What is somewhat curious is that Haggai does not mention Zechariah, and Zechariah does not mention Haggai. This is not a great problem, for it could be that their concern was to speak God's word and not of each other. Alternately it might be it was so obvious that they were working in concert that it would have seemed superfluous to mention each other's name. Personal tensions or differences in approach between the two men and/or their disciples may provide another answer.

1. Geo-Political Background

Haggai and Zechariah lived within a real world that had valid concerns and problems. In no way did they minimize the task before them. Living some two thousand five hundred years later the reader can sympathize with their plight of starting anew in the old land. A real difficulty that colors a modern understanding, however, is how little is known about this whole period. When Cyrus the Persian (558?–529 BCE) defeated the Neo-Babylonians in 539 BCE the whole face of the Near East changed. What had been the vast holdings of the Neo-Babylonian empire now was Cyrus', including Syria and Judea. Only Egypt was out-

152

side of his direct grasp. In clear contradistinction to the rule and foreign policy of Assyria and latterly Neo-Babylon, Cyrus' Persian policy was to encourage the local populace to rule themselves as long as they retained loyalty to him. In a conscious effort to instill allegiance Cyrus returned captive peoples to their homes and financially aided them not only to rebuild, but more specifically to rebuild their sanctuaries.

On a clay cylinder that dates from his reign one can read exactly what Cyrus did:

> I returned to [these] sacred cities... the sanctuaries of which have been ruins for a long time ... and established for them permanent sanctuaries. I (also) gathered all their (former) inhabitants and returned (to them) their habitations (James B. Pritchard, *Ancient Near Eastern Texts*, 208).

Among the captive peoples who were allowed to return were the Jews. Though a copy of the decree in Persian has still to be uncovered, the king's words are preserved in the book of Ezra (1:2–4; 6:3–5). *Yet not all who could return chose to do so.* Many people decided to remain in Babylon. Their reasons were manifold: they had made a new life; the return was fraught with danger; the success of the venture was unknown; a full generation had grown up in Babylon and were unwilling to return to what was probably a less sophisticated, and certainly more difficult life in Judah (see Josephus, *The Antiquities*, 11.1).

Those who did return faced a land territorially much smaller than the one which they had left. The Edomites had moved into southern Judah and there were tensions with them. There also were tensions between those who did return. Under the leadership of Sheshbazzar some work was begun c. 538, but the difficulties they faced were nearly too much for them. The wondrous promises of Second Isaiah and Ezekiel had inspired them, but the reality was considerably more grim. About fifteen to twenty years later a second effort was begun under the leadership of Zerubbabel, a grandson of exiled King Jehoiachin. Among his followers was Joshua ben Jehozadak, a priest of the Zadokite lineage. Zerubbabel served as the official governor with his authority from the Persian ruler, and Joshua served as high priest (see Ezr 1:8; 3:2ff; Hag 1:12; B. T. Dahlberg, "Sheshbazzar," "Zerubbabel," in *Interpreter's Dictionary of the Bible* [*IDB*]).

Zerubbabel and Joshua the high priest held commissions under Cyrus' successors Cambyses (530/529–522) and Darius (522–486 BCE).

There was local opposition to the rebuilding of the sanctuary as recorded in Ezra 4:1–5 (see also Ezra 5:2–6:15). The work went on for several years and a small structure was finally completed about 515 BCE, yet the "fate of Zerubbabel remains one of the unsolved mysteries of post-Exilic history" (West, 410). From c. 515 to 445 BCE, some seventy years remain shrouded in mist, but in 444 BCE we get first the arrival of Nehemiah and then in 428 BCE came Ezra. (For details and the problems of dating Nehemiah/Ezra see John Bright, *A History of Israel*, 391ff.)

2. Haggai's Message

Haggai was very determined. He had set his mind on the temple's restoration and nothing was going to prevent the realization of this goal. His work has been described as being "marked by singleness of purpose" (West, 419). Called a "political activist," it is true that "Haggai, perhaps more than any other prophet, was committed to a political programme, namely the restoration of the temple" (Childs, 470).

Haggai is composed of four prophecies. They take place over a mere four months, late in the year of 520 BCE. Each of the oracles is introduced by a date formula:

"1. The summons to rebuild the temple: 1:1–15a
   (Aug.–Sept., 520 B.C.)
2. The future splendor of the temple: 1:15b–2:9
   (Sept.–Oct., 520 B.C.)
3. Holiness and uncleanness: 2:10–19
   (Nov.–Dec., 520 B.C.)
4. God's word to Zerubbabel: 2:20–23
   (Nov.–Dec., 520 B.C.)" (West, 417–418).

The final two prophecies came on the same day.

Like his prophetical predecessors Haggai sees God's activity in history. The first prophecy explains that the drought that the people are experiencing in Jerusalem and its environs is a punishment because they have placed their own comforts before the building of the temple. The people dwell in paneled houses while God's house lies in ruins (1:4–14).

In the second prophecy, reflecting his organizational skills, Haggai appears to be working among the people, encouraging them. Do not be upset, he counsels; the temple may not have its former physical glory, but God is with us and in time "The latter splendor of this house shall be greater than the former ..." (2:9).

He then goes on to deal with certain cultic matters in the third oracle. Some scholars feel that this section may actually be composed of two prophecies (see West, 418; Childs, 465ff). Finally Haggai presents God's optimistic and apocalyptic message to the governor Zerubbabel. This shall be analyzed presently in the "Text Study" section.

Haggai has been criticized for being one-dimensional in his concerns. James Newsome writes that what "is distinctive about Haggai ... is that his understanding of righteousness and sin is basically cultic in nature.... There is no mention of *mishpat* [justice], *tsedhaqah* [righteousness/good deeds], or any other lofty moral principle so important to Amos, Hosea, and others" (162). Newsome is correct, but needlessly critical. The standard moral considerations of many of the other prophets do not arise here. Their absence, however, need not mean that Haggai was unconcerned about these issues. His contemporary (and co-worker) Zechariah certainly addresses moral issues (as shall be explained below; see Zech 7:8–10; 8:16–17). Then, Haggai had ordered (or had been ordered in) his priorities. First God's house is to be built. When the ritual aspect is in place and the people have a focal point, then one can speak of the parallel teachings of morality. The building of the temple is not an end in itself, it is a means to bring God's glory and God's teachings to the world.

Haggai's teachings do not seem to have been a great influence on the thinking of the Christian Scriptures. Only one image is replicated — Haggai's statement that God will "shake the heavens and the earth and the sea and the dry land" (2:6; see 21) which is mentioned in Hebrews 12:26–27.

3. Haggai and Jewish Sources

Haggai and Zechariah are often linked with Malachi. In rabbinic thought these three were not only the latest but also the last representatives of the prophets. When they died, said the rabbis, prophecy came to an end (Babylonian Talmud *Yoma* 9b, *Sotah* 48b). Those three are also credited with passing on the traditions to the leaders of the great synagogue (*Avot de Rabbi Natan*, chapter 1).

A number of psalms are attributed to Haggai and Zechariah in the LXX, Vulg., and Peshitta (e.g., Pss. 138; 146–149); this may account for the Christian, as opposed to the Jewish, tradition that the prophet was of priestly descent (William Neil, "Haggai," *IDB*, 509).

4. Text Study

Suggested reading: Hag 1:4–6; 2:20–23

Vs 1:4 "Is it a time for you yourselves to live in your paneled houses, while this [i.e. God's] house lies in ruins?" Haggai is asking a rhetorical question, but there is an echo here of an earlier questioner and his question. In 2 Samuel 7:2 David bemoans the fact that he is sitting in a house of cedarwood while God's house *should* be built. Not only is Haggai pointing to David's enthusiasm to build as an object lesson for the people, but Haggai accomplishes several other goals as well: (a) as David seeks advice from Nathan the *prophet,* so will this *prophet* Haggai give advice; (b) doubly more so Haggai will give advice specifically on building the temple, as did Nathan; (c) Zerubbabel is a descendant of the Davidic line; (d) thus as his physical forebear he should listen to Haggai, and (e) build the temple.

Vss 1:5–6 Because the people are not building God's house they are not faring well. Haggai here is subtly but effectively recalling the Deuteronomic tradition regarding the following of God's commandments. Deuteronomy 14:22–26 speaks of coming to the place where God will establish the divine name, and tells the people to feast there and be satisfied. They will rejoice because they honor the Lord. Likewise Leviticus 26:3ff speaks of God favoring the people in all aspects of their lives as long as they follow God's laws and commandments. Haggai's thinly veiled statement is clear: Build God's house and you will prosper too! A reasonable amount of self-interest is usually a strong motivating factor for most people. Haggai is a pragmatist.

Vss 2:20–23 This final oracle begins with a "dating" as in all the other prophecies. There is not only a strong sense of the apocalyptic here, but other messages are being conveyed. The overthrowing of chariots and drivers, the fall of horses and riders, echoes God's earlier "miracle" at the Sea of Reeds in Exodus 15, where likewise mention was made of horse, chariot and rider. As that captivity led to the epiphany at Sinai, so does Haggai suggest that a brilliant future awaits his audience and specifically Zerubbabel.

In addition, in a lovely turn of phrase and image, Haggai tells Zerubbabel that he will become a "signet ring" for God. This is redressing a balance for the fact that two generations earlier God had told Zerubbabel's grandfather Jehoiachin that were he a signet ring on God's hand he would be torn off and rejected (Jer 22:24ff). The exact same phrase ("signet ring") is featured in both cases and is purposeful.

FIRST ZECHARIAH

The book of Zechariah, like that of Isaiah, is made up of the writings of at least two and possibly three authors. Chapters 1–8 form the work of one person, and 9–14 are either taken as one unit or are further subdivided (Newsome, 201ff; Sandmel, *The Hebrew Scriptures*, 221ff). We shall return to this in further detail in chapter 11.

Though they were contemporaries, Haggai and Zechariah were men of very different temperaments. Their messages overlapped, and they both were vitally concerned with the rebuilding of the temple and the well-being of their "congregation." Each, however, had his own particular interests and style. Haggai was a pragmatic prophet who favored direct action; Zechariah was primarily a visionary.

1. Introduction

The initial oracle in Zechariah is dated Oct.–Nov. 520 BCE, some two months after Zerubbabel began work on the temple and a month prior to Haggai's final prophecy (Zech 1:1ff). It is a call to repentance. Zechariah hearkens back to his prophetic predecessors, without mentioning any specifically by name, yet he reminds his audience that the prophets' warnings overtook their ancestors, and they had to admit that God "dealt with us according to our ways and deeds ..." (1:4–6).

Having set up his framework, and by extension his own credentials, there then follows in the rest of chapter 1 and through chapter 6 a series of eight visions which take place over a two month period, Jan.–Feb. 519 BCE. In these visions, which are strange and full of colorful images and figures, Zechariah demonstrates that he is a spiritual descendant of the great exilic prophet Ezekiel. These visions take place at night. They are filled with some fantastic figures and also with angels who communicate with Zechariah. Zechariah's visions are very different from prior instances of prophetic sight. In Isaiah 6:1ff, the prophet himself explained his own vision. When Amos (7:8) or Jeremiah (1:13–14) had a vision, God directly gave the explanation and not an angel. Here God is more distant, more removed, and an intermediary is (apparently) necessary.

Among the figures that the prophet sees are:

Vision one: 1:8–17 — four horses of different colors, with riders who are roaming or patrolling the earth.

Vision two: 1:18–21 [2:1–4 H] — four horns representing the (unnamed) nations that oppressed Judah, Israel and Jerusalem.

Vision three: 2:1–5 [2:5–9 H] — a man with a measuring line, measuring Jerusalem. Zechariah is told that Jerusalem shall be so large that it will be measureless.

Vision four: 3:1–10 — Joshua the high priest with a figure accusing him before the angel of the Lord. Among the terms used for the figure are: *Satan* (alternately Accuser, Adversary) NRSV; the *Accuser* (alternately Satan) *TANAKH; the Adversary* (alternately Satan) *New English Bible; Satan* (with a note that Satan "means accuser") New International Version. This shall be analyzed further below in the "Text Study."

Vision five: 4:1–6 (and 10b–14) — features a lampstand of gold with a bowl, and two olive trees signifying two consecrated figures — presumably, but not explicitly stated, Zerubbabel and Joshua the high priest.

Vision six: 5:1–4 — a very large flying scroll, some 30 feet by 15 feet (20 cubits by 10 cubits, using one cubit = 18 inches) wherein names of wrongdoers are inscribed.

Vision seven: 5:5–11 — a floating basket with a woman representing wickedness in it, and then two other winged women who will take the tub to Babylonia (Shinar — see Gen 10:10; 11:2, 9).

Vision eight: 6:1–8 — four chariots with different colored horses going out to the four directions of the compass.

Zechariah's central message is not so very different from that of many of his prophetic predecessors. In chapters 7 (vss 8–10) and 8 (vss 16–17) he suggests standards of morality that are very familiar: render true judgment; show kindness and mercy; do not oppress the widow, the orphan, the stranger or the poor; do not plan evil in secret; do not utter false oaths. Likewise in chapter 5 in the vision of the flying scroll he speaks of the ills of theft and false oaths. Earlier still (in 3:6) he spoke of walking in God's paths and keeping God's charge.

Like his predecessors, Zechariah predicts God's return to Zion and that Jerusalem shall be "the faithful city" (8:1–3). In these thoughts, though he does not mention them by name, he effectively acknowledges his debt to Zephaniah (3:14ff), Micah (4:1ff) and Second Isaiah (40:1ff), for in effect he paraphrases some of their thoughts.

Zechariah, in addition, places the rank of the high priest on a much more important level than had been seen in the past. In the vision of the lampstand with branches (chapter 4) he speaks convincingly of the dual roles of religion and state working in close harmony. That all these visions add up to a divinely appointed messianic figure is fairly certain. Nonetheless the two figures anointed or consecrated at the end of chapter 4 (4:14) are called *b'nai hayitzhar* (lit. sons of oil, from *Tzadi-Hey-Resh*) and not *b'nai mashiach*, appointed/anointed/messiah as in the Hebrew for the word messiah (*Mem-Shin-Het*). The connection between anointed and "oil" is that rulers were anointed with oil (see 1 Sam 10:1 — Saul; 1 Sam 16:13 — David).

Something else that is unique in Zechariah is that apparently he feels that he does not receive messages from God directly. Rather Zechariah learns the meaning of his visions through the figure of an angel who acts as an intermediary between the deity and the prophet.

2. Zechariah in the Christian Scriptures

The later chapters of Zechariah provide a number of examples of "messianic" predictions for the authors of the Christian Scriptures as we shall see in chapter 11 below (i.e. Zech 9:9 — the king riding on a donkey to Jerusalem will be taken up in Matthew 21:5, John 12:15 and many other verses from Zechariah as well). Nonetheless these earlier chapters of First Zechariah would also be important. Without being exhaustive, we can note several connections between this Zechariah and the book of Revelation. The measuring of Jerusalem (2:1f [2:5f H]) is connected to the verse in Revelation 21:15. The four horses and then the four chariots with horses and their colors (1:8ff; 6:2ff) are reflected in Revelation 6:2ff, as the olive trees (4:3, 11–14) are seen in Revelation 11:4. The accuser-adversary-Satan figure (of 3:1–2) may be connected with a similar figure in Revelation 12:9 and Revelation 20:2. It is possible that Jude 9 and 23 may echo images in Zechariah 3:2f.

3. Zechariah and Jewish Sources

In the weekly lectionary of synagogue readings, Zechariah 2:10–4:7 [2:14–4:7 H] is featured as the prophetical portion to complement Numbers 8:1–12:16 (*Behalotecha*), and the same portion in Zechariah is read on the first sabbath in Chanukah.

As was noted earlier in this chapter, in rabbinic literature Zechariah is often in the company of Haggai and Malachi. Further, according to rabbinic legend along with Malachi and Haggai he accompanied the exiles from Babylon (Babylonian Talmud *Zevachim* 62a); those three also helped Jonathan ben Uzziel to translate the Targum, the Aramaic translation of the prophets (Babylonian Talmud *Megillah* 3a), and it is probable that the references to earlier prophets in Zechariah 1:4 provided the tradition that Zechariah, along with Haggai and Malachi, had received the tradition from those prophets who preceded them (*Avot de Rabbi Natan*, chapter 1).

The rabbis quoted Zechariah in a number of instances. As was mentioned in the chapter on "Jeremiah," in the early part of the second century in the Common Era, some years after Rome's destruction of the temple, a group of rabbis were bemoaning the fall of Jerusalem when one reminded them that though Zion's downfall had been prophesied, so had its being rebuilt. As the one prophecy was realized, so will Zechariah's prophecy also come about in time: "Old men and old women shall again sit in the streets of Jerusalem ... the city shall be full of boys and girls playing..." (Zech 8:4–5) (*Midrash Lamentations Rabbah* to Lamentations 5:18; see also Babylonian Talmud *Makkot* 24b end [though there seems to be some confusion between Uriah and Micah the Morashite]).

Rabbi Simeon ben Gamliel (mid-second century CE) had a favorite saying: The world is established on three things: justice, truth and peace. All three, he noted, were found in a line in Zechariah 8:16: "Speak the truth to one another, render in your gates judgments that are true and make for peace." Rabbi Simeon then went on to say "The three are, in fact, one. For when justice is exercised, truth is attained, and peace is achieved" (*Pesikta de Rav Kahana, Piska* 19.6; see also *Mishna Avot* 1.18).

That same line in Zechariah, however, was used for a very different and contemporary relevant conclusion: whenever possible, settle litigation out of court. When there is a judgment in court, if there is strict truth then there will *not* be a peaceful judgment. Hence settle out of court is the preferred advice, for "wherever there is strict truth there cannot be peaceful judgment; whenever there is peaceful judgment, there cannot be strict truth. How can one combine both? Only by an equitable [compromise] settlement, satisfying both parties" [This is what Zechariah meant in his verse, explained one rabbi] (*Talmud Jerusalem Sanhedrin* I.1. See also see Montefiore and Loewe, 392).

4. Text Study

Suggested reading: Zech 3:1-5; 4:1-6, 11-14

Vs 3:1 The word that the Hebrew uses in this passage is *Satan.* As seen in the passage, the role of this figure is merely to serve as an "accuser" or "adversary" against Joshua the high priest. He does not even have a verbal part. In fact the accuser is the one accused, by no less a figure than the Lord. Alternately, and what seems even more likely, is that it is an "angel of the Lord" who does the accusing of the accuser because the angel does all the rest in this passage and is so prominent throughout these chapters.

The figure of Satan has none of the demonic power that is featured in the Christian Scriptures, nor is he even so powerful or visible as he will be found in the early chapters of Job (see also 1 Chr 21:1). In the *New Oxford Annotated Bible* [*NRSV*], the editor writes: "In the Old Testament *Satan* (literally, 'the Adversary') is not the incarnation of evil but a functionary of the heavenly court who accuses man of wrong" (note to Zech 3:1-10). In a similar reference in Job, the editor writes that Satan "is not yet the demonic personification of later Judaism (compare 1 Chr. 21.1) and Christianity" (note to Job 1:6-8). In the (Roman Catholic) *Jerusalem Bible* a note defines the accuser as "a malevolent angel, Satan (lit. 'the *satan*,' i.e. 'the accuser')" (note to Zech 3:1).

Vs 3:4 The filthy clothes that Joshua is wearing seem to be associated with guilt of some sort which is then replaced by ritually pure garments. The word in Hebrew for pure garments or "festal apparel" (*Mahalatzot*) is used only twice in the Bible (see Is 3:22) and the context here seems to require a statement about ritual purity to serve as a balance to the impure/filthy/guilty clothes Joshua wore prior to this.

Vs 4:6 "Not by might, nor by power, but by my spirit, says the Lord of hosts." This line spoken to Zerubbabel indicates that "Zerubbabel will succeed by means of spiritual gifts conferred upon him by the Lord, cf. Isa 11.2 ff" (*TANAKH* note on Zech 4:6).

Vs 4:13 The fact that Zechariah is puzzled by these strange phenomena is a rhetorical device which allows the angel to give an explanation. In some ways it also suggests an echo of Ezekiel, for at the episode of the Valley of Dry Bones the prophet is asked "can these bones live?" and Ezekiel has to admit that the answer is beyond his human ken; only God knows (Ez 37:3).

Vs 4:14 The "anointed" figures are *not specifically* designated as Zerubbabel and Joshua (as the representatives of government and religion) but this is the thrust of the passage. To this extent, and when coupled with the statement in Zechariah 3:8, these are clearly "messianic" longings being expressed by Zechariah.

MALACHI

1. Introduction

While the book of Malachi is placed as the last of the Hebrew prophets, it was not the latest book that was written. A consensus of biblical scholars place it in that *post-exilic* period of the seventy-five years between Haggai–Zechariah and Ezra–Nehemiah (Childs, 489), perhaps the year 500 or between 500–450 BCE. Malachi can be translated literally as "my messenger." Whether the author of the book was named Malachi or it requires this translation, the prophet's "real name" is a matter of debate.

In the Masoretic or traditional Hebrew text there are three chapters, as is the case in the Vulgate (and Roman Catholic) translations, while in Protestant translations of the Bible, there are four chapters. The Protestant translations start a new chapter with the Masoretic text's 3:19 (i.e. 3:19–24 — 4:1–6).

The book is a set of six oracles or prophecies. The divisions are "introduced by a statement of the Lord or by the prophet, which is then challenged by the people or the priests, and defended by the Lord Himself in words of reproach and doom" (Edward Lipinski, "Malachi," *Encyclopedia Judaica* [*EJ*], 812). The sections are:

   a. 1:2–5   God's love for Israel/disdain for Edom.
   b. 1:6–2:9   Denunciation of improper priestly behavior.
   c. 2:10–16   Denunciation of mixed marriages and callous divorce.
   d. 2:17–3:5 God will bring justice.
   e. 3:6–12   A call for proper tithes.

f. 3:13–4:3 [3:13–21 H] Vindication for the righteous, punishment for the wicked.

These sections are then followed by a conclusionary passage (4:4–6 [3:22–24 H]), which indicates that Elijah will be bringing a new message to the people.

By the time Malachi prophesied, the temple had been rebuilt. This is attested to in the book itself, for people are bringing sacrifices (1:10; 3:1, 10) even if they are not very zealous about it. A governor is ruling over the land (1:8), so there seems to be a set secular order. Clearly the priests are in place at the temple.

Some of the major concerns of Malachi as a prophet are the facts that the priesthood has degenerated (1:6–2:9), there have been marriages to foreign women (2:11), and the people are remiss in their payment of their tithes (3:8). The problem of intermarriage and a laxness in proper payments are also mentioned prominently in the statements found in the books of Ezra and Nehemiah — Ezr 9:1f; 10:2f, 16–44; Neh 10:30 [31 H], 32–39 [33–40 H]; 13:10–14, 23–29 (Lipinski "Malachi," 813–814).

Though Malachi was very concerned with matters of cult and sacrifice it is not clear by what set of laws the people were operating. Some years later in Nehemiah (8:1ff) Ezra is featured reading the "book of the law of Moses" ("scroll of the Teaching of Moses" — *TANAKH*). Ezra is assisted by the Levites (Neh 8:1–2, 7–8) who explain the teaching to the people. The people, it would appear, are not familiar with these Levitical-explained teachings. One theory is that Ezra brought the Priestly Code from Babylon, and that consequently Malachi was working with an earlier code, that of Deuteronomy (Robert Pfeiffer, *Introduction to the Old Testament*, 614; and Robert Dentan, *Interpreter's Bible*, "Malachi," 1117–1118). Support for this comes from several sources within Malachi:

> his contempt for the offering of blemished victims (1:8) rests on Deut. 15:21 ("lame or blind"); 17:1; his demand for the full payment of "tithe and heave offering [*teru-mah*]" (3:8–10) corresponds to the law of Deut. 14:22–29 (tithe and *terumah* are mentioned together elsewhere only in Deut. 12:6, 11, 17; the priests are called "sons of Levi" (3:3; cf. 2:4, 8), as in Deuteronomy (21:5), where Levite and priest are synonymous terms, and not . . . "sons of Aaron" (as in the Priestly Code) (Pfeiffer, 614).

Like his predecessors Haggai and Zechariah, Malachi deals with a congregation that is despondent and apathetic. They had expected a return of Israel's former glory, if not actually the messianic kingdom

promised/prophesied by Zechariah. Life was difficult and the temptation to assimilate into the wider community must have been fairly strong.

2. Malachi in the Christian Scriptures

The book of Malachi has a special place in the Christian Scriptures
because the final verses of this book were understood by Matthew, Mark
and Luke to refer to John the Baptist. In Luke 1:17 the verses from the end
of Malachi are reflected, specifically referring to Elijah's coming to "turn
the hearts of parents to the children . . ." (see Mal 4:6 [3:23 H]). Indeed
Jesus (in Matthew 17:10–13) indicates that "Elijah has already come" but
was not recognized by the people, and Mark's gospel also reflects the
idea that John the Baptist is Elijah (Mk 6:14–17).

There are parallels between Malachi and Elijah as shall be detailed
at the conclusion of this chapter. Earlier we noted parallels between
Elijah and Moses (see chapter on "The Former Prophets"). Consequently it is not surprising that the early Church saw Malachi's Elijah (or
Malachi-as-Elijah) as a pivotal figure linking Moses and Jesus. It could
be argued that when Elijah (or read John the Baptist-as-Elijah) was rec-
onciling the parents with their children (Mal 4:6 [3:24 H]), he was medi-
ating between Moses and Jesus, or the older and newer generations, or
older and newer teaching. The transfiguration episode certainly places
all three, Moses, Elijah and Jesus, visibly and unambiguously together
in open communication (Mt 17:1–8; Mk 9:2–8; Lk 9:28–36).

Malachi's more general statement about sending a "messenger to
prepare the way before" the Lord (Mal 3:1) in Matthew 11:10 stands by
itself. In Mark 1:2 Malachi's statement is blended with a statement from
Isaiah 40:3 ("the voice of one crying out in the wilderness: 'prepare the
way of the Lord, make his paths straight . . .'"). Paul quotes from Malachi
1:2–3 in Romans 9:13 to demonstrate a point of God making choices.

The difference in the positioning of Malachi in the Christian Bible
and the Hebrew Bible is of great significance. In both Bibles Malachi is
the final of the book of the twelve, the minor prophets ("minor" in their
length of chapters). In the Hebrew Bible, however, the Prophets (Nevi'im)
are followed by the Writings (Ketuvim) Psalms, Proverbs, Job, Song of
Songs . . . [see the chapter titled "What Is a Prophet?"] which end with
the four historical books of Ezra, Nehemiah and 1 and 2 Chronicles. In a
Christian Bible, Protestant or Roman Catholic, Malachi is followed
directly by the gospel writers. (N.B. Mark's gospel is the oldest, and it is
surely no coincidence that he quotes Malachi already in 1:2. It may have
been that at one point Mark's gospel preceded that of Matthew's in the
early church.)

3. Malachi and Jewish Sources

Malachi is often linked with Haggai and Zechariah. They were the last of the prophets according to rabbinic tradition, and when they died prophecy came to an end (Babylonian Talmud *Yoma* 9b; *Sotah* 48 b). They were all three associated with the setting up of the great synagogue (*Avot de Rabbi Natan,* chapter 1). In one rabbinic text it is also suggested that along with his other prophetic colleagues, Malachi was there at Sinai receiving God's prophecy (*Tanhuma, Yitro,* para. 11, f. 124a–124b, quoted in Montefiore and Loewe, 158).

The rabbis also found statements in Malachi that offered examples of Jewish/rabbinic values. These values addressed relationships between human beings and relationships between humans and God. In one teaching in the Mishna, people are exhorted to be like the students of the high priest Aaron who made peace and pursued peace (*Mishna Avot* 1.12). Taking up a line in Malachi 2:6 "he held the many back from iniquity" it was suggested that this referred to Aaron himself who through his own force of personality moderated people's behavior, influencing them toward peaceful action (*Avot de Rabbi Natan,* chapter 12 beginning). Similarly, using a proof-text from Malachi 2:7, the rabbis suggest that there are responsibilities associated with priestly leadership. If you speak the truth, you are one of God's representatives, but when you abuse your position your words are worthless (*Sifre Numbers Korach,* para. 119, f. 39b, quoted in Montefiore and Loewe, 154).

In Malachi we find the famous line "Return to me and I will return to you, says the Lord of hosts" (3:7). How great is repentance, taught the rabbis. If a person sins and repents, God forgives (this is a reference to Ezekiel 18:22), but if one does not return God warns several times. Only then if the person does not change does God exact punishment (*Midrash Tanhuma Genesis, Wayyera* to Gen 19:24ff, Part I [referred to earlier in the chapter on Ezekiel]). Malachi's reference to Moses, "Remember the teaching of my servant Moses" (4:4 [3:22 H]), elicited a wonderful anecdote. The rabbis asked themselves: How can Malachi say this is Moses' teaching? Surely it is God's teaching. In response the following tale was told.

When Moses came down from Sinai [carrying the teaching], the Adversary [Satan] approached God and inquired, "Where is the Torah?" God replied, "I have given it to the earth." The Adversary then went to the earth and said, "Where is the Torah?" The earth replied [quoting Job 28:23], "God … knows its place." Satan then went to the sea and the deep and asked and each said [again

quoting Job (28:14)], "it is not with me." The Adversary returned
to God and complained that he had asked all over and had not
found it. God said, Go to Moses and ask, which the Adversary did.
Moses then replied, "What am I that God should have given
me the Torah?" God then turned to him and said, "Moses, are
you a liar?" Moses then turns to God and says, "This lovely and
hidden thing in which You, God, took so much pleasure, should
I take credit for it?" Then God said, "Because you have been
modest therefore shall it be called by your name, as it says [in
Mal 3:22]: "Remember the teaching of My servant, Moses" (Babylonian Talmud *Shabbat* 89a).

4. Text Study

Suggested reading: Mal 3:1-5, 10-12; 4:5-6 [3:23-24 H]

Vss 3:1-5 This is in the midst of the fourth prophecy that deals
with theodicy: the question of God's justice (see 2:17–3:5). The Christian
Church understood the anonymous "messenger" to be Elijah-as-John the
Baptist, but the prophet himself certainly does not make this designation
even though the sense is eschatological in character. This emissary appears as the "messenger of the covenant" (3:1 — in Hebrew "messenger"
and "angel" are the same word: *mal'ach*). This messenger/angel is going
to sift out the priesthood ("descendants of Levi") to distinguish between
the righteous (committed) and the merely perfunctory. The image that
Malachi presents is fairly drastic. The priests will have been put through,
if not a "baptism of fire," then certainly a smelting of fire. Malachi's list
of wrongdoing is well within the prophetic tradition which reflected
social concerns alongside matters of worshiping God.

Vss 3:10-12 Here Malachi reflects clear Deuteronomic thought
when he links God with a cause-effect relationship to proper ritual and
the blessings of nature. Malachi's mention of rain/blessing and banish-
ment of insects/prosperity in the fields is essentially a restatement of
Deuteronomy 11:13–15 which states that if the people are faithful, then
rain will be granted so that the field will prosper.

Vss 4:5-6 [3:23-24 H] In Jewish tradition a prophet's words do not
end on a pessimistic note, so line 4:5 [3:23 H] is repeated after the final
verse.

*   *   *

Malachi did not specifically associate Elijah with the anonymous "messenger" of 3:1. A later editor, however, did make the connection (Willard Sperry, *Interpreter's Bible*, "Malachi," 1143–1144; Childs, 495–496). In the post-biblical era of the Mishna, Elijah took on, or, better, he was given the role of announcing the coming day of the Lord, the coming of the Messiah; he would help bring about resurrection of the dead, and he would also settle certain disputes that had proved enigmatic for the rabbis (see these Mishna passages: *Sotah* 9.15; *Shekalim* 2.5; *Baba Metzia* 1.8; *Eduyot* 8.7).

If it was an editor who added the final verses of Malachi linking Elijah with the anonymous messenger, this connection was not without some degree of a reasonable basis. Indeed Malachi the prophet, whose name can be translated as "my messenger," Malachi the prophet-with-a-message, became on some level the medium and the message combined. Elijah's whereabouts *were* in question. He had not died, but rather was taken to heaven in a fiery chariot (2 Kings 2). Now, perhaps, he was God's messenger. There are some fascinating parallels between Elijah and Malachi's prophecy. (These Elijah/Malachi connections are developed from Childs, 495–496.)

a. Both prophets give a message for "all Israel": 1 Kgs 18:20; Mal 1:1.
b. Attention is drawn by both prophets to those who revere God and those who take a different path: 1 Kgs 18:21; Mal 3:15–18.
c. In each case the land of Israel is suffering (and needs the blessing of rain): 1 Kgs 18:1; Mal 3:9–12. [See also Jas. 5:17–18]
d. The people are challenged to make a decision in both cases: 1 Kgs 18:21; Mal 3:18.
e. An offering is involved: 1 Kgs 18:32ff; Mal 3:3.
f. Fire from heaven is involved: 1 Kgs 18:38; Mal 3:2; 4:1 [3:19 H].
g. The wicked are punished: 1 Kgs 18:40; Mal 4:3 [3:21 H].

On another level, not only is Malachi connected to an Elijah, he also is a latter-day Moses figure. Moses is specifically mentioned in Malachi 4:4 [3:22 H]. Then much the same rubrics as were found with Elijah-Malachi can be found with Moses and Malachi. Indeed a fair number of these parallels are found in the Korah rebellion, where Korah and his followers are called "Levites," and these same words (in the Hebrew, *b'nai Levi*) are used in Malachi (Num 16:8; Mal 3:3).

a. Message for all Israel: Num 16:19; Mal 1:1.
b. Division within the community: Num 16:1ff; Mal 3:15–18.

   c. Land suffering/need for water: Num 16:13; Mal 3:9–11.
   d. People challenged to decide: Num 16:4ff; Mal 3:18.
   e. An offering involved: Num 16:18; Mal 3:3.
   f. Fire from heaven: Num 16:35; Mal 3:2; 4:1 [3:19 H].
   g. Wicked punished: Num 16:31ff; Mal 4:3 [3:21 H].

Chapter 11

JOEL, SECOND AND THIRD ZECHARIAH

JOEL

1. Introduction

A. Divisions Within the Book

Short of the fact that Joel is listed as the son of Pethuel (Jl 1:1) little is known about the life of this prophet. The general consensus of scholarship places him about the years 400–350 BCE (but some still hold out for a date in the seventh century; see Childs, 387; Pfeiffer, 350; Bright, 431; Joel A. Thompson, *Interpreter's Bible* [*IB*], "Joel," 732; *Jerusalem Bible*, 1140; Theodore Hiebert, "Joel, Book of," in *Anchor Bible Dictionary*, 878).

Depending on which translation of the Bible you consult, there will be some differences in chapters and verses. (The traditional Hebrew text [Masoretic text] like the Latin Vulgate has four chapters in the book of Joel. The Roman Catholic translation of the Bible follows the Vulgate tradition, while the standard Protestant translation has only three chapters. Chapter 1 of Joel is the same. Chapter 2 of Joel begins the same way but chapter 3 in the Masoretic/Vulgate is 2:28–32 in the Protestant version. Likewise chapter 4 in the Masoretic/Vulgate is chapter 3 in the Protestant version.) The book falls into two sections, chapters 1:1–2:27 and 2:28–3:21 [chapters 1–2 and 3–4 H]. The first section is set in the present and is dominated by an image of devouring locusts which are accompanied by a devastating drought. The second section is set in the future. The spirit of the Lord has come in abundance, and with it the day of the Lord. Judgment is taking place, but also great relief from the former calamities.

Joel's literary ability is without question. He uses vivid, concrete examples with similes and metaphors as well. Assuming a fourth century date, Joel shows familiarity with his prophetic predecessors, Amos, Zephaniah, Ezekiel, Second Isaiah and Obadiah. He appears to mimic a phrase from the Hebrew of Obadiah 1:17 in 2:32 [3:5 H]. He consciously intertwines many past prophetic images into his own oracles. (For a detailed description of parallels see Thompson, 731–732.)

The first section is dominated by the relentless onslaught of the ravaging juggernaut of locusts and their fellow insects. Chapter 1 indicates that what little the first wave has left has been wiped clean by those that succeeded them. Its "teeth are lions' teeth, and it has the fangs of a lioness. It has laid waste my vines, and splintered my fig trees; it has stripped off their bark and thrown it down…" (1:6–7). The harvest is non-existent and the priests cry out that the day of the Lord is coming (1:15). In the second chapter the tension mounts. The locusts have now entered the cities. No place is safe from them. They climb the walls and enter the windows like thieves, they dash about all over the city. The very sun and moon seem darkened by their ubiquitous presence (2:8–10). Only at this point does the Lord actively give counsel: "… return back to me with all your heart, with fasting, with weeping, and with mourning…" (2:12). The people respond and do repent, followed by God's promise of future reward.

The second section begins with a tremendous outburst of energy (2:28–29 [3:1–2 H]). God is "pouring" the divine spirit onto the people, young and old, sons and daughters, whatever one's social position. All this preceded what is determined to be a time of great physical changes in the world of nature: "blood, fire, columns of smoke"; there shall be a solar eclipse and the moon shall turn blood-red (2:30–31 [3:3–4 H]). Those who call on God's name shall be saved.

The second section continues (3:1ff [4:1ff H]) with God punishing the enemies all about Judah and Jerusalem: Tyre, Sidon and Philistia. Likewise the Greeks are mentioned. All of these areas are directly to the west of Judah, either northwest or southwest. This predominant westward view is unique among the prophets, for so many had focused on Aram, Assyria, Babylonia, Edom, and so on. The nations will march against Zion, but they will not succeed. God will stand in judgment, God will shelter the people and at the end shall dwell in Zion. In the closing verse Joel nods briefly at Egypt and Edom, two of the traditional enemies, and notes that they will be a desolate wasteland (3:19 [4:19]).

Though some would argue that the two sections reflect different authors or different periods (see Driver, 34ff), a great deal can be said for a literary unity within the book.

> The lament (1.4–20) parallels the promise (2.21–27), the announcement of a catastrophe (2.1–11) matches the promise of better days (4.1–3, 9–17), and the summons to repentance (2.12–17) is set over against the promise of the spirit (3.1 ff.). Such obvious paralleled expressions in 2.27 and 4.17 (EVV 3.17) speaks against sharply separating the first two chapters from the last (Childs [acknowledging the work of H.W. Wolff, *Die Botschaft des Joel*], 389).

We could likewise point to the imagery of sun and moon being darkened in 2:10 and similar images in 2:31 (3:4 H) and 3:15 (4:15 H).

B. The Locusts

The locusts have provoked a great deal of discussion. What do they mean? Was this a real phenomenon or is it purely metaphoric? In his commentary S.R. Driver features a ten-page, closely printed "Excursus on Locusts" which features illustrations as well (Driver, 84–93). The early Church fathers favored an allegorical interpretation as "powers of darkness which threaten the Church." Other explanations included suggestions as to specific empires which had threatened Israel: Egypt, Assyria, Babylon and Greece. Still other possibilities were offered: Babylon, Persia, Greece and Rome (William Neil, "Joel, Book of," *Interpreter's Dictionary of the Bible* [*IDB*], 927). Not content to find explanations in the world of humankind a still more imaginative level is sometimes offered: the locusts are "supernatural apocalyptic creatures" (Thompson, 733; see Pfeiffer, 574).

Certainly the simple and straightforward explanation that these are indeed real locusts has a great deal of support among scholars, for it reflects a scientific observation of the unquestioned devastation that a horde of such insects can bring to an agricultural community.

Assuming that these are actual insects, what do they represent in the prophet's mind? This plague of locusts, like all natural phenomena, stems from God. Since God has brought them, they must be part of God's punishment. Certainly when chapters 1 and 2 of Joel are read together it appears as if God's voice is there before the terrible and terrifying host. "The Lord utters his voice.... Yet even now, says the Lord, return to me with all your heart, with fasting, with weeping ..." (2:11–12). Certainly Joel was steeped in the prophetic tradition of his people; his use of previous prophetic utterances attests to this. In the same fashion Joel may have seen this latest curse upon the land (which included a drought, see 1:20) as a latter day linear descendant of the God-caused drought which was finally concluded following the denouement between Elijah and the priests of Baal (1 Kgs 18). Alternately there are echoes of the locusts that appeared in Egypt as a sign to motivate the Pharaoh to act at the time of Moses, in accordance with God's demands. One of the words that Joel uses for locust is *arbeh* (1:4) which has been defined as "the adult, flying locust" (Thompson, 737; see also Brown, Driver, Briggs, *A Hebrew and English Lexicon of the Old Testament* [Resh-Bet-Hey], 916), and this same word *arbeh* is used in Ex 10:4, 12–19). This Torah connection is strengthened by Joel's quote from later in the book of Exodus when the prophet suggests that the Lord may forgive, for God is "gracious and merciful, slow to anger, and abounding in steadfast love . . ." (2:13) a direct echo of Exodus 34:6.

To suggest that the locusts are a punishment does not, however, tell us about the wrongdoing. Joel would appear to be mute on this point, or perhaps just not specific. It may be that he detects a general malaise in the land. It is not that the people have committed specific wrongdoing. Joel does not speak of profaning the sanctuary, of syncretism, of the oppression of the poor, orphan or widow. Joel's condemnation seems to be on the one hand less specific, and on the other more widespread. The call to repentance involves all Israel, literally old, young and in between; from babies nursing on the breast to the elders, to the bride and bridegroom at their home (2:16). The ubiquity of those who need to repent is the natural corollary to the ubiquity of the presence of the locusts. Set against this broadly based need for repentance involving all sectors of society is the "reward" of the outpouring of God's spirit. As described in chapter 2:28–29 (3:1–2 H) it will touch male and female alike, young and old, free and slave.

C. Joel as Apocalyptic Writing

It has been suggested that Joel's importance for biblical theology is "as a harbinger of the apocalyptic school" (Neil, "Book of Joel," 928; see Pfeiffer, 574).

Apocalypticism is a kind of religious thought that has its roots in the Persian period and more specifically in the Persian religion, Zoroastrianism. It is dualistic in nature and involves two cosmic forces, God and some kind of adversary; furthermore it involves two distinct ages, the present which is irretrievably dominated by the forces of evil which suppress the righteous and then latterly the eschatological future which will be an eternal age where God will rule and the righteous will know eternal blessing (Martin Rist, "Apocalypticism," *IDB*, 157).

When apocalypticism is defined very broadly, it can encompass elements from Joel, but it is clear that there exist major problems. The locusts as a sign (or punishment) from God: they are *neither* a cosmic force of evil that opposes God, nor do the locusts suppress the righteous for an extended period of time, for, as explained above, the people are called upon to repent, and it presupposed that they will do so (2:12ff).

In Judaism, God is always in control. Any force or forces in opposition to God and God's will are clearly *inferior*. Likewise, though in Christianity the Satan figure is considerably more powerful, and is a tempter and oppressor of humankind, Satan (devil) is still not equal to God's power.

> Apocalypticism, then, may be readily differentiated from prophetism, messianism, and the expectation of the kingdom of God; for these are not dualistic, cosmic in scope, and eschatological, as is the apocalyptic hope. Instead, they are based on the belief that God is in control of this age, not Satan, and that this age will not come to an end, but is improvable. A hope of the resurrection was in time added to this belief, but even so the basic position of apocalypticism is quite different (Rist, 158).

Apocalyptic-like elements, however, are echoed in Joel. The prophet's vision of the future time, complete with outpouring of the spirit, the battles with the nations, the valley of decision and the day of the Lord (3:14 [4:14 H]), as well as the image found toward the end of the final chapter with the mountains dripping with wine and the hills flowing with milk, with Judah's watercourses full and a spring issuing from the temple (3:18 [4:18 H]), all contain a sense of the apocalyptic and eschatological.

To acknowledge that Joel contains elements that are similar to the apocalyptic is a far cry from saying that Joel is part of apocalyptic literature. But Sandmel nevertheless writes: "Joel's prediction of a judgment that is to befall a vague group of nations at a vague time is an apocalypse" (*The Hebrew Scriptures*, 218).

D. Outpouring of Spirit ... Prophesying ... Visions

Joel's prediction of the sons and daughters prophesying [*ve-nib'u*] and young men seeing visions [*hezyonot*] in 2:28 [3:1 H] is not the first example of group prophecy. There is an earlier instance recorded in Numbers 11:26–27, the story of Eldad and Medad. There Moses says, "Would that all the Lord's people were prophets..." (Num 11:29). In both

Numbers and Joel the word used for "spirit" (*ru-ach*) and prophecy (from the root letters *Nun-Bet-Aleph*) is the same. "Visions" (*hezyonot*) is another form of prophecy (see Ob 1:1; Nah 1:1; also see Chapter 1, "What Is a Prophet?").

2. Joel in the Christian Scriptures

The most direct uses of Joel are to be found in Acts (2:17–21; see Jl 2:28–32 [3:1–5 H]) and Rom 10:13; see Jl 2:32 [3:5 H]). Nonetheless, having said this, there can be no doubt that Joel was an influence on the final book of the Christian Scriptures, Revelation, which is also known as the Apocalypse.

In Revelation 9:7–8 locusts are found; they are "like horses equipped for battle ... and their teeth [are] like lions' teeth ..." These images are found in Joel (1:4, 6; 2:4). On the terrible day of the Lord, Joel asks rhetorically how can one endure it (2:11), and a similar question is asked in Revelation (6:17). The sun eclipsed and the moon blood red (Jl 2:31 [3:4 H]) are the bases for the same images in the Christian Scriptures (Rev 6:12); Joel's sickle (3:13 [4:13 H]) is repeated there as well (Rev 14:15, 18; see Mk 4:29); and finally the life-giving water issuing from the temple (Jl 3:18 [4:18 H]) is also repeated (Rev 22:1).

The images of Joel were certainly taken a considerable step further than when first uttered four or five hundred years prior to the writing of Revelation. Joel's words of the outpouring of spirit (in 2:28–32 [3:1–5 H]) were also understood in a different fashion. Acts 2, perhaps written by Luke (see *The New Oxford Annotated Bible, NRSV*, introduction to Acts), mentions a description of the Jewish festival of Shavuot (Weeks, Pentecost) when in Jewish tradition God gave the Torah to Moses on Mount Sinai. The twelve apostles are in Jerusalem when suddenly during the morning they are "filled with the Holy Spirit" and speak in a variety of foreign tongues. When those who see them are amazed, Peter comes forward and explains that this is what was spoken of by Joel when he said, "I will pour out my Spirit," and then Peter essentially (but not exactly) quotes Joel's words.

In Romans (10:13) Paul draws from Joel (2:32 [3:5 H]) to re-emphasize his notion that salvation is a matter of faith. "For one believes with the heart and so is justified, and one confesses with the mouth and so is saved ... there is no distinction between Jew and Greek; the same Lord is Lord of all and is generous to all who call on him ..." (Rom 10:10, 12). This teaching by Paul is then followed by Joel's line that anyone who invokes God's name shall be saved.

Paul actually goes considerably beyond Joel's words. He implies that Joel had only been addressing the Jews, and now the new teaching is for all humankind. In fact, Joel's statement is very general and does not single out any faith or ethnic group. In reply to those who suggest that Judaism is only particularistic and Christianity is universalistic, a "more prudent judgement is that Judaism and Christianity are both marked by motifs of universalism and particularism" (Sandmel, *The Hebrew Scriptures*, 221).

3. Joel and Jewish Sources

The famous lines suggesting that God would "pour his spirit" onto old and young alike were understood by the rabbis as referring to the world to come. In this world there are slanderers and in one fashion or other people are motivated by the evil inclination (*Yetzer hara*). Hence God has withdrawn the divine presence from among the people. This will be different in the next world, for having given the people a new heart (Ez 36:26) God would restore the divine presence among the people. "Then afterward I will pour out my spirit on all flesh..." (Jl 2:28 [3:1 H]). This lovely homily then closes with the words from Isaiah 54:13: "All your children shall be taught by the Lord, and great shall be the prosperity of your children" (*Midrash Deuteronomy Rabbah* 6.14). A similar suggestion for the future is offered elsewhere which suggests that in this world only a few people have prophesied, but in the world to come "all Israel will be made prophets" (and then comes the line from Joel 2:28 [3:1 H]: "Then afterward I will pour..." (*Midrash Numbers Rabbah* 15.25).

Joel 3:18 [4:18 H] contains the promise that in the eschatological day of the Lord, when Israel is dwelling safely in Zion, "the mountains shall drip with sweet wine, the hills flow with milk..." The rabbis explained that this is Israel's reward for maintaining its relationship with God by preserving its ethnicity. In the words of the midrash "Israel performed the will of God when in exile, for it refused to mix with the nations and so kept the covenant with God" (*Midrash Numbers Rabbah* 13.2).

4. Text Study

Suggested reading: Jl 2:1-14

In these fourteen verses are found several examples of the strikingly strong images that Joel uses so very effectively. Whether the marauders of this chapter are a continuation of chapter 1 or are to be understood as "supernatural creatures" is a matter of scholarly debate (see Pfeiffer, 574; Thompson, 733–734).

Vs 1 The "day of the Lord is coming, it is near ..." Other prophets have used the phrase, or words very close to it (Ez 30:3; Zeph 1:7, 14; Am 5:18, 20), and Joel himself uses the words "day of the Lord" again and again (1:15; 2:1, 11, 31 [3:4 H]; 3:14 [4:14 H].

Vs 2 The darkness/gloom/cloud imagery was discussed in the chapter on Zephaniah (1:15). In chapter 2 Joel echoes and answers a thought first expressed in chapter 1:

1:2: [Joel asks] "Has such a thing happened in your days, or in the days of your ancestors?"

2:2: [Joel answers that] "their like has never been from of old, nor will be again after them in ages to come."

Vs 3 The locusts front and rear appear as *fire* and *flame* which shall be appropriately quenched in the eastern sea (Salt Sea) and the western sea (Mediterranean Sea) respectively in vs 20.

Joel further suggests that before these marauders the land was like the garden of Eden, and following them it was desolate. Here the prophet consciously reverses a positive image that had been spoken by Ezekiel (36:35) and Isaiah (51:3) where desolation had been followed by Eden-like lushness. Coincidentally in 3:10 [4:10 H] Joel would also reverse the positive image of swords into plowshares/spears into pruning hooks (Is 2:4; Mic 4:3) and turn farm implements into weapons of war.

Vss 4–5 The marauders are horses/steeds; they charge/leap; they rumble as chariots; they create a noise; they are a powerful army, underscoring that same phrase ("powerful army") in vs 2. (In the Hebrew it reads: [vs 2] *'am rav v'atzum;* [vs 4] *k'am 'atzum.*)

Vss 7–9 The military metaphors and similes spill over; they build up, one on another, not dissimilarly from the way that the attackers spill over, build up their assault upon the city one on another. In these three verses they are portrayed as: warriors/soldiers/chargers. They are seen as: charging/scaling/keeping their course/not swerving/not jostling/climbing/entering. The object of their attack is also described: the city/the walls/the houses/the windows.

Vs 10 Not only does the earth physically quake or shake with their onslaught, but the heavens above metaphorically tremble and the dust stirred up by their pounding literally obscures sun, moon and stars.

Not since Zephaniah's day of trouble and distress (*Dies irae, dies illa,* Zeph 1:14–16) with its repetition of the word "day" has there been such a powerful example of image piled on image.

Vs 13 Rending heart/not clothing. This inward image of repentance is not only powerful, but it also reflects the biblical custom of rending one's garment as a sign of mourning or great distress (see Gen 37:29, 34). A torn garment (*keriya*) continues to be a sign of Jewish mourning.

The image of the heart as indicative of the whole person is a familiar concept in biblical thought (see Deut 6:5; Jer 31:33; Ez 36:26; Ps 16:9; Lam 2:19 et al.; see also Brown, Driver, Briggs [Lamed-Bet-Bet] 523). In *Midrash Ecclesiastes Rabbah* 1.16.1 *numerous* references to the heart are listed.

SECOND AND THIRD ZECHARIAH

1. Introduction

The last six chapters of the book of Zechariah are considered by many to belong to a different hand (or hands) than the earlier eight chapters. This separation from Zechariah 1–8 is based on literary, linguistic and stylistic grounds. It is supported by differences in theological outlook and historical reference.

The problem is not "if" Zechariah 9–14 is separate from Zechariah 1–8, but to determine when they were written. To further complicate matters, the chapters are further subdivided into two sets of three chapters each, 9–10–11, and 12–13–14. These are sometimes called Second Zechariah and Third Zechariah (Deutero-Zechariah and Trito-Zechariah).

The range in speculation for the date of the writing of the final six Zechariah chapters ranges from the period of Alexander the Great c. 333 BCE and after, to the time of the Maccabees, c. 165 BCE and after, close to a two hundred year period. In any case these chapters provide some valuable insights into the mind of Jewish thinkers of the Hellenistic period in the land of Judah (see William Neil, "Zechariah, Book of," *IDB*, 947; Robert Dentan, "Zechariah," *Interpreter's Bible*, 1089f).

The late date reasoning is based on the reference made to Greece (*Yavan* in Hebrew) in 9:13:

the juxtaposition of the houses of David and Levi (12:12–13); the apparent conflict between Judah and Jerusalem (12:2, 5, 7; 14:14);

and the appearance of dispersion (10:8–10). However, the names of "house of Joseph" and "house of Ephraim," as well as "Assyria" which appear to reflect situations contemporary to the prophet" present great problems (Yehoshua M. Grintz, "Zechariah," *Encyclopedia Judaica* [*EJ*], 957).

The six chapters present a variety of problems because no one knows the real meaning of the references and there are a number of allegories which defy clear interpretation. There seems to be little consensus on how to subdivide the prophecies, once the initial break of chapters 9–11 and 12–14 have been made. Sandmel (*The Hebrew Scriptures*, 221) suggests five sections; Newsome (202) offers six sections; the article in the *Interpreter's Bible* (Dentan, "Zechariah"), ten (1091); and according to the article in the *IDB* (W. Neil), "Zechariah, Book of," (946) some scholars suggest four independent oracles in chapter 9 by itself!

We can briefly summarize these chapters. Chapter 9 begins with a condemnation of Israel's neighbors, Syria, Phoenicia and Philistia (9:1–8), and then has a prophecy of redemption for Israel (9:9–17).

Chapter 10 of Zechariah begins with a praise of God who brings the natural blessing of rain (10:1). It goes on to speak of false diviners and God's anger at these leaders (10:2–3). The chapter continues with God's victories for Judah and Ephraim, and how the people will be gathered from distant lands (10:4–12).

Chapter 11 of this prophet sees an angry God. Filled with allegory and unknown allusions, the dominant images are shepherds, flocks, and two staves which in turn will be broken (11:7, 10, 14).

Chapter 12, like chapter 9, begins with the word Massa [*Mem-Sin-Aleph*] — "an oracle," "a pronouncement," or possibly "a burden." It pictures a major attack on Jerusalem by the nations of the world, but they shall fail.

Chapter 13 brings both purification and denunciation. Prophecy (or perhaps false prophecy) will end. The wicked will be punished and the virtuous will be purged of any past wrongdoing.

Chapter 14 is not only the last chapter; it is also the longest and perhaps the most enigmatic of these final six chapters. It begins with the siege and defeat of Jerusalem, including plunder, rape, and an exile for a part of its population (14:1–2). Immediately thereafter God makes war on the nations, the Mount of Olives is split in two, and other similar earthquake-like events take place (14:3–5). This is followed by a miraculous revelation, Jerusalem rebuilt and God's universal rule; and all the surviving nations shall either recognize God and be rewarded or reject God and be in turn rejected (14:6–21).

To summarize the chapters is easier than explaining what these many oracles actually mean. There are numerous interpretations and, as shall be shown subsequently, the writers of the Christian Scriptures saw a great deal of prophetic foreshadowing in Second and Third Zechariah.

Assuming that the material is written in the period of the fourth to second centuries, there seems to be a pervading sense of disappointment. Not only have the bright prophecies of Ezekiel and Second Isaiah not been realized, but the terrible days of Malachi and Joel are *not* followed by the hopeful and hoped-for glorious rebuilding of the land. If anything Judah, now smaller than for hundreds of years, is feeling neglected by God and at the same time is suffering at the hands of her neighbors. There is a sense of both despair and anger that strongly permeates the messages of chapters 9–14. There certainly are *apocalyptic-like* elements in the chapters, *but* (as explained in the comments on Joel) true apocalypticism has an opposite and equal force allied against God, a real and present dualism which just is not present in the Hebrew prophets, or for that matter in the Hebrew Scriptures (see Rist's article on "Apocalypticism" in *IDB*). The term "Satan" (adversary/accuser) that was seen earlier in Zechariah 3:1–2 does not appear at all in Second or Third Zechariah, and though there are examples of evil people or nations, they in no way can stand up to the power of God (Zech 9:1–8; 12:2–6; 14:3).

Certainly there is a sense of having been wronged, and the nations around Judah's borders have caused ongoing troubles for her citizenry. Syria, Phoenicia and Philistia shall not only be uprooted, but those lands shall be annexed to Judah (9:1–17). The nations will be conquered (9:15) and the rotting away of their corpses is vividly described (14:12).

Not only has there been trouble from without, but the local leadership likewise seems to have failed the people. The allegory of dealing with the worthless shepherds (or shepherd) and likewise worthless sheep has had many interpretations (11:4–14). It "has been dated variously from the fall of Samaria [722/721] to the Maccabean period" (Neil, "Zechariah, Book of," 946). The image of uncaring shepherds was seen before (in Jer 50:6–7; Ez 34; Is 56:11) as was the image of people turning on each other (Jer 19:9). The staffs labeled "Favor" and "Unity" (Zech 11:7) which shall be broken are an ironic echo of the two pieces of wood in Ezekiel's hand (Ez 37:16ff) where they are a positive image. The dismissive contempt of vs 9 is extremely, even brutally powerful:

So I said, "I will not be your shepherd. What is to die, let it die; what is to be destroyed, let it be destroyed; and let these that are left devour the flesh of one another" (Zech 11:9).

On a far more pleasant note, the eventual disposition of Jerusalem is a time and place of delight. The weather will be temperate, with plenty of warm sunshine; fresh water will be abundant, summer and winter; and best of all, on that day the Lord alone shall be worshiped — "on that day the Lord will be one and his name will be one" (Zech 14:6–9; see note to 14:9 in *TANAKH*).

2. Later Zechariah(s) and the Christian Scriptures

The final six chapters in Zechariah provided a fair amount of material for the writers of the Christian Scriptures. Matthew and the author of Revelation drew the most heavily from these verses, though each of the gospel writers is represented. Certainly the dominant image is the king riding into Jerusalem on a donkey, as depicted in Zechariah 9:9. Victorious, glorious, but ever humble, this figure is highlighted by Matthew as Jesus enters the city by the Mount of Olives (see Zech 14:4) and is greeted by the crowds (Mt 21:4ff). John presents a similar image, and Mark and Luke echo the episode, but with less detail (Jn 12:12ff; Mk 11:1ff; Lk 19:28ff).

The "thirty shekels [pieces] of silver," which are paid out to the shepherd in 11:12–13, are echoed in the same sum paid to Judas who betrays Jesus (Mt 26:15; 27:9). What this figure means is very unclear. Thirty pieces of silver was the worth of a Hebrew slave, as recorded in Exodus (21:32), but the sense in Zechariah is that the sum is a paltry one (see Eli Cashdan on 11:12 in "Zechariah," *The Twelve Prophets*, 316; "The *Lordly price* [in 11:13] is ironic," explain the editors in *The New Oxford Annotated Bible* in their note to 11:12–13; Robert Dentan, "Zechariah," *Interpreter's Bible* [*IB*], 1104, suggests, however, that it is not an inconsiderable amount). In any case, coincidentally or not, Matthew appears to refer to this incident in Zechariah, but he mentions Jeremiah as the author. He then garbles the text in any case, so that Matthew's meaning is not only obscure, but is a blend between Exodus and Zechariah.

The worthless shepherd (Zech 11:17) seems to be hinted at by John (10:12–13), and in Revelation, though there are not direct quotations, there are hints of Zechariah passages (Rev 1:7; see Zech 12:10, "pierced" man; Rev 22:1, 17, see Zech 14:8 [also Ez 47:1–12], "the water of life"; Rev 22:3, see Zech 14:11, "Jerusalem secure").

3. Zechariah and Jewish Sources

Liturgically, Zechariah 14:1–21 is the prophetical reading for the first day of the biblically ordained autumn harvest festival Succot, connected through the "Succot" [festival of "Booths"] reference in 14:16. Zechariah is often linked by the rabbis with Haggai and Malachi as the three prophets who accompanied the exiles back from Babylon (Babylonian Talmud *Zevachim* 62a) and who together formed the final voices of prophecy in Israel (Babylonian Talmud *Yoma* 9b). Zechariah, along with Haggai and Malachi, also was credited with helping Jonathan ben Uzziel write the Targum for the prophets (Babylonian Talmud *Megillah* 3a). (See the chapter on "First Zechariah," above.)

The rabbis also turned to Zechariah to preach and teach. In some cases they found answers in Zechariah's statements, and in other cases the prophecies of this unknown prophet (these unknown prophets) provided a springboard for the rabbis to inculcate certain moral or ethical values.

For example, the rabbis understood the famous line in Zechariah 9:9 "your king comes to you; triumphant and victorious is he, humble and riding on a donkey ..." as referring to the future messianic ruler. In this interpretation, the rabbis and the gospel writers were of the same opinion. In this passage which speaks of the coming of the messiah, it goes on to mention the "thirty pieces of silver," and here a very different view is presented than that in the Christian Scriptures. In the time of the messiah, Israel will not require the teaching of the messiah (and a support text from Isaiah 11:10 is quoted, i.e. for Israel will be taught directly from God), but the messiah will give the nations thirty precepts (and then comes the support line from Zechariah 11:12) which the nations will undertake to follow in the new kingdom (*Midrash Genesis Rabbah* 98.9; see notes in Montefiore and Loewe, 669 note 28). In a later midrashic work, the line from Zechariah 9:9 where the messiah is pictured as glorious and triumphant is bound together with some of the more traditional Christian notions of the suffering of the Messiah (*Pesikta Rabbati* 34.1–2; Montefiore and Loewe, 584–586, and accompanying notes).

The rabbis saw the Bible as a whole, a work which was not only divine, but which was also closely interconnected. The verse in Zechariah 9:14 referring to the Lord's being manifest by the sounding of the trumpet (*shofar*, or ram's horn) was seen as the future counterpart to the ram caught by its horn in the binding of Isaac episode in Genesis 22. Just as a ram was present when Isaac's life was saved, so will future Israel know its salvation in the same way, for the Lord will sound a ram's horn (*Midrash Genesis Rabbah* 56.9 and *Midrash Leviticus Rabbah* 29.10). The Christian Scriptures also refer to God's trumpet at the end of days (1 Cor 15:52; 1 Thess 4:16).

When Jacob was blessed by Isaac, part of the promise for the future was an abundance of new grain and wine. What was this? the rabbis wondered. They then found the answer in Zechariah where it explains that in the future time the young men will be "like new grain and young women like new wine" — Jacob will have many descendants (*Midrash Genesis Rabbah* 66.3 on Gen 27:28 and Zech 9:17).

In the mind of the rabbis, the Bible provided answers not only for the context in which it was written, but for later times as well. The rabbis saw a clear warning in Zechariah pointing to the period of Persian influence with its religious teaching of theistic dualism. The rabbis taught, "Do not associate with those who teach that there are two deities in the world, for in Zechariah it infers that those 'two' shall perish and die; that means whoever speaks of the deities shall perish" (*Midrash Numbers Rabbah* 15.14 and *Midrash Deuteronomy Rabbah* 2.33, basing their interpretation on a combination of Proverbs 24:21 and Zechariah 13:8). Considering that some of the apocalyptic-like elements of Second and Third Zechariah were probably influenced by Persian thought, this rabbinic teaching is particularly appropriate.

Persian dualism and apocalypticism is also seen in the Christian Scriptures. Gog and Magog were merely a person and place in Ezekiel 38–39, but in the Christian Scriptures they take on a much larger role (Rev 20:8 — the battle of Armageddon). The rabbis also taught of the Gog/Magog terror, but explained that nonetheless God would triumph gloriously. The rabbis' "proof texts" included Zechariah's words: "the Lord will go forth and fight against those nations" and then "the Lord shall become king over all the earth" (*Midrash Leviticus Rabbah* 27.11 and *Midrash Esther Rabbah* 7.23 quoting Ps 2:2, Is 42:13 and Zech 14:3, 9; the Esther passage also quotes 1 Sam 7:10 and has a slightly different order of quotations).

4. Text Study

Suggested reading: Zech 14:6–21

These verses are clearly eschatological, dealing with the last days. They tell of the ultimate triumph of God as ruler of the world and who will be centered in Jerusalem.

The later verses (16ff) speak of an international recognition of God's power, and there is a sense of universalism that the bounty of God's goodness is open to all who would choose to receive it. The festival of Booths, Succot, in Judaism celebrates the autumn harvest. There are clusters of concepts associated with the image of Succot. There is a sense of the movement of time; dormant winter, virile spring and powerful summer have passed, and now comes the maturity of the autumn of our years. In the Jewish calendar, Rosh Hashana and Yom Kippur (the New Year and Day of Atonement) which are a period of reflection, prayer and repentance have just passed. A new beginning is possible. Once again, and in a new way, people in the Jewish community take charge of their own lives. All these concepts and images are present in that mention of Succot/ Booths in vs 16.

Earlier it was noted that chapters 9–11 and 12–14 were not by the same hand as the author of chapters 1–8. In a cogently argued case, Brevard S. Childs suggests why those latter chapters were appended to the former ones. When taken together, a commonality of themes complement each other. In this sense the whole is made greater by the combination of its parts. While the connections between the two (three) sections of Zechariah should not be over-stressed, there are parallels in content.

> 2:5ff (9:8 and 14:11) — Jerusalem with divine protection
> 8:12 (14:6ff) an image of paradise
> 5:3 (14:11) a curse sent out and then removed
> 1:18ff [2:1ff H] (14:17) a curse on the nations
> 2:11 [2:15 H], 8:20ff (14:16) ultimate conversion of nations/
> worship of God
> 8:18ff (14:20) cultic rites
> 3:8; 4:6 [14] and (9:9ff) — the messianic figure (482–483 [with
> some small verse misprints in the Childs' text])

This concluding chapter of a prophet very late in the biblical period provided answers for a number of questions that concerned the rabbis of old, and many others as well. For example, in 1 Samuel 8 the people sought an earthly ruler and in a sense they were rejecting the rulership of God. Then, after the debacle of Zedekiah and the fall of the first temple, the people saw the errors of their ways and said: Now we desire our first ruler. According to the rabbis, God then consented and said: Once again I will rule over the earth (*Midrash Deuteronomy Rabbah* 5.11, quoting Is 33:22 and Zech 14:9).

Then, what of all those many prophets who are mentioned in Samuel, Kings, Jeremiah and elsewhere of which we know their existence, but nothing of their prophecies (see 1 Sam 19:20; 2 Kgs 2:3; Jer 29:1, et al.)? In the future time God will resurrect them and will publish their prophecies (*Midrash Song of Songs Rabbah* 4.11.1; *Midrash Ruth Rabbah*

[Proem] 2 quoting Zech 14:5). The rabbis further explained that there also were prophets in Israel who were not so specified, and they too will be associated with God in the future time (*Midrash Ecclesiastes Rabbah* 1.11.1, again quoting Zech 14:5).

Finally, in reference to the festival of Succot, it is the only day that the nations will be expected to observe in the messianic era.

Chapter 12

JONAH

1. Introduction

A. *In a Class by Itself*

Biblical Jonah presents problems and possibilities. Commissioned by God, he runs away. Told to go east, he heads west. Sent overland to Nineveh, his intention is to go by sea to Tarshish. His plans for escape notwithstanding, Jonah soon finds himself caught up with God's power. A storm breaks upon his ship with unremitting force. He owns up to his guilt only when confronted. Thrown overboard and imprisoned within the belly of a great fish, Jonah ponders his fate and finally prays. After three days he is spewed out. Recommissioned, he sets out for Nineveh, and once there Jonah, chastened, carries out his call. Yet he does so with diffidence: he delivers his prophetic message sparingly. Resenting their repentance, he is insolent in his replies to God. Jonah raises prophetic reluctance to a new level.

Though each of the fifteen of the books of the literary prophets was special and different in its own right, the book of Jonah is in a class by itself. Jonah could be linked back to the time of the former prophets, for some think that this Jonah is the same Jonah mentioned in 2 Kings 14:25 in the eighth century BCE. Using another set of criteria it could be set in the post-exilic period (Jonathan Magonet, "Jonah, Book of," *Anchor Bible Dictionary*, 941). Jonah is delightful and enigmatic. It is a book of intrigue and innocence, of anger, humor and fantasy. To combine all those myriad qualities is quite a feat. To do so and also contain a psalm is amazing. Then, most important of all, to be accepted into the sacred prophetic literature alongside such giants as the Isaiahs, Jeremiah, Ezekiel and Amos, Hosea and Micah, is surely a wonder.

Putting the matter differently, the inclusion of the book of Jonah

185

into the prophetic canon is startling because in the whole four chapters, totaling some forty-eight verses, less than half a verse, some eight words in English (and five in Hebrew), is the sum total of Jonah's direct prophecy to the people of Nineveh. Furthermore, those words are not even particularly poetic; they say simply: "Forty days more, and Nineveh shall be overthrown!" (3:4). Though neither the word "Israel" nor "prophet" appears in Jonah or any other synonym for prophet or prophecy, the formulaic "*devar YHVH*-word of the Lord" appears twice: 1:1; 3:1.

B. Prophecy? Parable? Allegory? History?

Given the brevity of Jonah's actual prophecy, shorter by far than the one chapter of Obadiah, a number of questions present themselves. Furthermore, the recipient of that prophecy is first of all a people outside of the land of Israel; and then, second, it is directed at Israel's enemies: the citizenry of the capital of the cruelest nation of the ancient Near East, Assyria.

Is Jonah prophecy at all? The answer is clearly in the affirmative. Not only is there specific prophecy within Jonah (3:4), but the book was regarded as true prophecy by the compilers of the Hebrew Bible, and hence included within that section and not in the writings. The prophetic message of Jonah is presented in a different way than most other books, but that does not make it any less prophetic. Furthermore, for over two thousand two hundred years, the book has been regarded by others as prophecy, and therefore it has, if for no other reason, been legitimized by these processes.

Is Jonah a parable, an allegory? The parable as a form in the Bible has a venerable history. The word *parable* means "to be similar" or to be "comparable." In many cases it involves a brief narrative which is used in order to teach a lesson. Without question, as a didactic form, while it is not absent from the Hebrew Bible (see Jgs 9:7–15; 2 Sam 12:1–4), it is found far more frequently in the Christian Scriptures (Matthew uses the term parable "seventeen times, Mark thirteen times, and Luke eighteen times and the author of Hebrews uses it twice" (M. Lucetta Mowry, "Parable," *Interpreter's Dictionary of the Bible* [*IDB*], 649). The parable and the *allegory*, a tradition where "one ignores its literal meaning and discovers new, hidden meanings in each term," both use metaphors and similes (M. Lucetta Mowry, "Allegory," *IDB*, 82). Certainly Jonah has been treated at times as a parable, and the "great fish" (*dag gadol*, lit. "great fish," not "whale" — 2:1) has been understood in allegorical terms. That Jonah has been taken as a parable or an allegory, however, does not make it one or the other.

Is Jonah a history? There are those who defend Jonah as history by pointing to the mention of a man by the same name in 2 Kings 14:25 (there also Jonah ben Amittai). All we know of this former-day Jonah is that he was called a prophet, came from Gath-hepher, and prophesied correctly that Jeroboam II (c. 785 BCE) would expand his territory. The historicity of Jonah presents great problems. Was there really a storm that raged so severely, and the next moment abated as Jonah entered the deep? Was there a plant that grew overnight to such proportions, and then withered as quickly? Was Nineveh sixty miles across (a figure based on a person walking twenty miles in one day, for it is recorded that Nineveh was "three days' walk across" [3:3])? If the one hundred and twenty thousand population of Nineveh did repent overnight, would it not be written elsewhere? Yet aside from Jonah, there is neither biblical nor extra-biblical confirmation of this strange occurrence.

The most likely answer is that the book of Jonah was understood and can continue to be understood as prophecy and that the prophecy has strong parable-like qualities.

C. Jonah as Part of a Prophetic Tradition

Jonah was probably set down somewhere in the two hundred year period between c. 400–200 BCE. There are a number of words and technical phrases such as the use of the "*sheh*" for "*asher*" [that, which] in the first and last chapters (1:7, 12; 4:10b) which indicate late Hebrew language structure, and the influence of Aramaic. Furthermore

> [the] influence of Isa. 40–66 upon the author, inspiring him with his vision of a world upon which God might yet have compassion through Israel's ministry, points to a date in the fifth century or later. It could not have been later than the third century B.C., since Jonah's name has been included by Jesus ben Sirach as one of the twelve (Ecclus. 49:10). The narrowness of the nation's sympathies as reflected in Jonah suggests a time when the exclusiveness engendered by Ezra in 444 B.C. had long been at work in the community. The closest therefore that we can fix the date is somewhere between 400 and 200 B.C. (James D. Smart, "Jonah," *Interpreter's Bible* [*IB*], 873).

Though a late book in the prophetic tradition, Jonah reflects certain qualities of its predecessors. Like the primarily action-oriented lives of and narratives about Samuel, Elijah, and Elisha, there is considerably more narrative and movement in this book in relation to either spoken prophecy or even dialogue than in any other book among the literary prophets.

Like Jeremiah and Ezekiel (and the midrashic legend about Habakkuk — see Chapter 9) Jonah is a reluctant prophet. Admittedly he takes his reluctance a bit further than was seen before, and his reticence is based on different grounds, but there are precedents for his feelings. Like the prophet Amos (assuming Amos' home in Tekoa is located in Judah, not Israel) Jonah is commanded to prophesy in a land different from his own.

There are other parallels. Jonah sits under a plant, and complains, as does Elijah (Jon 4:6–9; 1 Kgs 19:4); the book of Jonah speaks of God changing a decision, and a similar prophecy is found in Jeremiah (Jon 3:8–10 and Jer 18:7–8). The Ninevites remark that perhaps God will take note of their repentance and a similar question is raised in Joel (Jon 3:9 and Jl 2:14). Finally both Jonah and Joel echo the descriptive words of God's attributes as first spoken in Exodus: gracious, compassionate, slow to anger, abounding in kindness, renouncing punishment (Jon 4:2; Jl 2:13; Ex 34:6–7). N.B. The words in Jonah and Joel have slight differences (Gabriel H. Cohn, "Book of Jonah," *Encyclopedia Judaica* [*EJ*], 173).

D. Major Ideas

The outline of Jonah is fairly simple. It divides neatly into two major sections. Chapters 1 and 2 are Jonah's commission and unsuccessful flight, while chapters 3 and 4 center on his experiences in Nineveh. That the book is the work of one hand has been ably demonstrated (Jonathan Magonet, *Form and Meaning;* Childs, 419).

The purposes of the book are manifold, for numerous lessons are taught. Among them are: i) God is omnipresent, the God of Israel and the nations as well. ii) God is omnipotent. iii) Repentance is always possible. iv) Knowledge brings responsibilities.

Jonathan Magonet offers another way to view Jonah, as four "polarities" at work: a) Knowledge of God/Disobedience of God; b) Particularism/Universalism; c) Traditional Teaching/New Experience; d) The Power of God/The Freedom of Man (*Form and Meaning*, 90).

i. God Is Omnipresent: the God of Israel and the Nations as Well

Earlier reference was made to the notion that Jonah was written in the two hundred year period following Ezra/Nehemiah. The period in question, c. 400–200, is difficult to evaluate properly, for there is so little material available. Reading the literal words of Haggai, Joel and the later chapters of Zechariah, as well as Ezra/Nehemiah (and trying accurately to read between the lines), we can speculate on what life was like at that time. The land of Judah has suffered a great deal. The nations around her have been cruel. Her former glory is no more. While a Haggai would say "The latter splendor of this house shall be greater than the former..." (Hag 2:9) this did not seem to come about. A "spirit of bitterness and vengefulness toward other lands" permeated the people. "The nation had endured so much at the hands of enemies" (Smart, "Jonah," 872). The famous turnabout of the Isaiah-Micah call for peace, Joel's ironic suggestion "Beat your plowshares into swords, and your pruning hooks into spears..." (Jl 3:10 [4:10 H]) to attack the enemy nations, is representative of the feelings of the people. Zechariah's statement that the Lord was going to fight the nations (Zech 14:3), if not theologically and morally uplifting, is nonetheless an understandable call. These people are angry and depressed. It is not unlike the anger of the author of Thessalonians and Timothy when he writes about the power of wickedness (2 Thes 1:6–9; 2:3–12; 2 Tim 3:1–9).

It is to this very understandable mood of isolationism, of particularism, that the author of Jonah offers his prophecy. The message of Jonah presupposes that the majority of the people of Judah either have forgotten or have rejected the notion put forward by Second Isaiah, namely that Israel has a role to be a beacon to the world at large, a "light unto the nations" (Is 42:6; 49:6; see 51:4).

Jonah underscores God's rulership of the nations *and the nations' recognition of God's rulership.* The mere fact that Jonah is sent to a distant land to prophesy is a strong statement in its own right. Jonah is to be a light to the nations, or at least to one foreign country (and this was a people which was evil incarnate, a state that had made torture an instrument of its foreign policy). Nineveh's evil is never in question; it is spoken of directly (1:1–2; see 3:1–2). The Ninevites openly acknowledge their immorality (3:8).

Not only do the Ninevites come to recognize God's power by positively responding to Jonah's prophecy, but even earlier the final view we have of the pagan sailors is that they are now God-fearers who offer proper prayers to the Lord (3:5–9; 1:16).

The pagan sailors are paragons of virtue. Though they learn from his own mouth that Jonah is the "cause" for the storm, they try valiantly to row toward the shore. It is with great sorrow and regret that they heave him into the sea (1:10–15).

Jonah himself acknowledges that he *knew* that were he to go to Nineveh, the people would listen; that is why he sought to escape his commission (4:2). Jonah accepts the truth of Isaiah 42:6; he just did not want to act on it!

ii. God Is Omnipotent

The author of Psalm 139 summarized the issue succinctly. Jonah would have saved a great deal of time and effort if he had stopped to read it. "Where [God] can I go from your spirit? or where can I flee from your presence? ... If I take wings at the morning and settle at the furthest limit of the sea, even there your hand shall lead me ..." (Ps 139:7, 9–10).

In the Jonah narrative, through a variety of phenomena, God's power in the world is ably demonstrated. The wind blows up a mighty storm (1:4). The sea itself grows tempestuous, and then when Jonah is jettisoned it ceases its raging (1:11, 13, 15). A huge fish plays its part, first swallowing, then retaining and finally spewing Jonah onto dry land (1:17; 2:10 [2:1, 11 H]). Finally a plant's speedy growth, a worm's destruction, a hot wind's heat, and a searing sun's rays all demonstrate that all nature is at God's command (4:6–8).

iii. Repentance Is Possible

Some two hundred (or more) years earlier (in c. 590/580) the prophet Ezekiel had spoken God's prophecy with the words: "For I have no pleasure in the death of anyone, says the Lord God. Turn, then, and live" (Ez 18:32). Ezekiel did not indicate that only the house of Israel should repent. Indeed in speaking those words, probably in Mesopotamia, not so far from Nineveh, the message of Ezekiel may have been on the mind of Jonah's author. Nineveh was but a symbol of "the nations" at large. Repentance was open to all who chose to do so, and they could repent in their own land. Unlike the author of Third Zechariah, the Jonah narrative does not indicate that the foreign nations must come to Jerusalem to acknowledge God's power. Indeed as the word Israel is not found in Jonah, neither is the word Jerusalem. In the second chapter on two occasions there is mention of God's "holy temple" (2:4, 7 [2:5, 8 H]) but at no point is it indicated that the nations need to either acknowledge its existence or go there (see Zech 14:16–19).

Another aspect of repentance is shown. God will go several steps to offer someone chances to repent. Certainly God gives Jonah a second "opportunity" to go to Nineveh, and when there God provides Jonah with several possibilities to admit his wrongful attempt to flee the divine demand.

iv. Knowledge Brings Responsibility

The lines from Second Isaiah, that the people of Israel had a responsibility to the nations, is reflected in Jonah.

It is too light a thing that you should be my servant, to raise up the tribes of Jacob and restore the survivors of Israel; I will also make you a light to the nations, that my salvation may reach to the end of the earth (Is 49:6).

With knowledge comes responsibility. Humankind is free to question God, even to challenge God, as Jonah does with seeming impunity (4:1ff). Nonetheless, in reply to questions there come answers. When the answer is given, whether or not it is in the form of a rhetorical question as it is at the conclusion of Jonah, the person is compelled to act. Mere faith in God's power or faith in God's attributes may fit for some occasions, but at other times direct action is required (see *Midrash Exodus Rabbah* 4.3).

The message that "Knowledge brings responsibility" is directed at all people. The captain of the ship and the ruler of Nineveh both act responsibly. Their deeds reflect an acknowledgement of the one true God.

2. Jonah in the Christian Scriptures

The most prominent use of the book of Jonah comes in Matthew where Jesus likens (in 12:39) his own coming entombment for three days to the days that Jonah spent in the midst of the "belly of the sea monster" — NRSV; "sea-monster's belly" — NEB; "belly of a huge fish" — NIV. A parallel but far from exact account is found in Luke. In this latter case no mention is made of either the three days or the fish; rather it is merely said that as Jonah was a sign for the Ninevites, so likewise would the Son of Man be a sign for the present, evil generation (Mt 12:39–41; Lk 11:29–30). It has been suggested that the extra details of the Matthean account is an "interpolation" by that gospel writer, for one of Matthew's characteristics is to use texts from the Hebrew Bible to "prove" his point. Jesus' reference to Jonah is considered by many scholars as "an illustration based on a popular story." It is "not a pronouncement on the historicity of either event" (William Neil, "Book of Jonah," *IDB*, 966).

3. Jonah and Jewish Sources

The rabbis had a field day with Jonah. They were far from blind to his disobedience, but they sought to find a reasonable explanation for his flight. They therefore suggested that in an earlier episode in his life Jonah had predicted the destruction of Jerusalem. When this did not come about he was labeled as a "false prophet." This was particularly galling since his patronym, Amittai, can mean "truthful one" (from the Hebrew word "Emet — truth" (see Brown, Driver, Briggs [derivative of Alef-Mem-Nun], 54). When Jonah was then commissioned to go to Nineveh he initially rejected this role for two reasons. On one level he had a presentiment that the Ninevites would in fact repent. As a loyal Israelite, with no particular love for the nations, he was concerned with what God would do to Israel if God saw a pagan nation so readily repent, and Israel was so very stubborn (*Mekilta: Pisha* 1.100ff; see also *Midrash Lamentations Rabbah* Proems 31, where God takes up that very point. His suppression of prophecy brings strong condemnation in the rabbinic literature. In early texts, namely the *Sifre* to Deuteronomy as well as the *Mekilta de Rabbi Ishmael,* both of which are compiled by the end of the second century CE, Jonah is severely criticized for his actions. The line taken in the *Mekilta* is that the prophet purposely withheld honor due to God while seeking honor for himself. For this transgression, God limits the prophetic message of Jonah (see *Sifre: A Tannaitic Commentary to the Book of Deuteronomy Piska* 177; *Mekilta, Pisha* 1.100–103; *Mishna Sanhedrin* 11.5; Babylonian Talmud *Sanhedrin* 89a). Jonah was further concerned that, on a more personal level, if/when the Ninevites did repent, once again he would be labeled a "false prophet" (*Pirke de Rabbi Eliezer,* chapter 10 and elsewhere; see Ginzberg, 6.349, note 27).

The rabbis were also conscious of the three days in the great fish, and how it was utilized by Christianity. Consequently they pointed out that the initial mention of a rescue after three days came in Genesis (with the "rescue" of Isaac on the mountain, Gen 22:4) and that there were other similar salvific events after three days (Gen 42:17–18; Ex 19:16ff; Jos 2:16; Est 5:1; Ezr 8:32), most notably in Hosea 6:2 where it says "After two days [God] will revive us; on the third day [God] will raise us up...." The rabbis saw this as a statement about resurrection, something very far from Hosea's mind, but it supported their contention of the importance of the third day (*Midrash Genesis Rabbah* 56.1; *Midrash Esther Rabbah* 9.2).

The rabbis, as did many later Christian religious leaders, speculated on the meaning and the size of the great fish. Among other explanations, they suggested that this was one of the special miracles God ordained at the beginning of creation, and that at a future time this particular fish would go against its regular nature and spew out Jonah (*Midrash Genesis Rabbah* 5.5; see also Ginzberg, 1.51; 4.249ff; Gaster, 2.654–655). In the midrashic literature this larger-than-life creature is compared to a huge synagogue. The fish's eyes were great windows so the prophet could see outside. A pearl which sends out light is suspended within its belly. The light of this pearl is as bright as sunlight at noon, and the proof-text is from Psalm 97, "light dawns for the righteous" (*Pirke de Rabbi Eliezer*, chapter 10).

A series of special locales are visited while Jonah is in the fish. All of these places have a unique relationship with Israel (*Pirke de Rabbi Eliezer*, chapter 10). This is done very cleverly. Each of these sites is linked to a verse in the second chapter of Jonah where one finds Jonah's prayer of supplication. The fish shows Jonah where the Israelites crossed the Sea of Reeds (the word "reeds" [*suf*] is found in Jon 2:5 [2:6 H]). He also is shown Sheol and Gehinnom (Sheol is mentioned by name in Jon 2:2 [2:3 H]). In addition Jonah is taken to the exact place below God's temple in Jerusalem where the legendary "foundation stone" of the world is located. There Jonah meets up with the "B'nai Korah" who are praying at this foundation stone. The Korahites inform Jonah that since this spot is located directly under the temple in Jerusalem, if he prays he will be answered. Jonah 2:7 [2:8 H] reads: "As my life was ebbing away, I remembered the Lord; and my prayer came to you in your holy temple." The image of the B'nai Korah standing and praying itself contains multiple messages. There is a negative sense, for the very name Korah reminds God of the rebellion of Korah against Moses (Numbers 16) where it is stated that the earth opened its mouth and swallowed up Korah and his company, and that they went down to Sheol alive. Still, they are praying, a very appropriate activity in any case, and especially relevant to Jewish activity since the book of Jonah is read in the synagogue in the afternoon service of Yom Kippur, the Day of Atonement). On a more positive note, the phrase "B'nai Korah" also refers to a Levitical group of singers (1 Chr 6:22; 2 Chr 20:19) at the Jerusalem temple, and that term also appears as a superscription among a dozen of the Psalms (42, 44–49 et al.). Their ties to the temple in Jerusalem underscore a certain piety on the part of the Jewish people. A kind of *zechut avot* (merit of the ancestors) plays in here.

That Jonah was able to make himself heard so quickly in such a large city as Nineveh was due to his sonorous voice (Ginzberg, 4.250).

The rabbis, however, were less sanguine about the ultimate fate of Nineveh. Unlike the suggested conclusion of Jonah, where the Assyrian capital becomes a model of piety, the rabbis suggested that Nineveh after forty days, or possibly forty years, returned to their evil ways. Then they were more sinful than ever. Consequently the punishment that Jonah had prophesied came about and the earth swallowed them up (*Pirke de Rabbi Eliezer*, chapter 43; see Ginzberg, 4.253; 6.351 note 37).

4. Text Study

Suggested reading: The whole book (48 verses)

The significance of the three days in the large fish has been noted above. What is also significant, and which speaks to the unity of this book, is how often the number three appears, and in addition how often three and four items or events, or combinations of threes and fours, appear in Jonah.

a) *Three* days, *three* nights; Nineveh is *three* days' walk (2:1; 3:3).

b) Chapter 1 features the "lots" *three* times, all in one verse (1:7).

c) Chapter 1 features the word "Tarshish" *three* times, all in one verse (1:3). It will also appear once more in chapter 4 and therefore can be part of the "four" pattern (4:2).

d) The "fish" appears *three* times in a row (1:17; 2:1 [2:1–2 H]) and as with Tarshish will appear once again at the end of that particular episode (2:10 [2:11 H]).

e) In the third chapter, following the Ninevites' repentance, in one verse God has *three* reactions: God "saw what they did . . . renounced the punishment . . . and did not carry it out" (3:10).

f) In the final chapter God "provides" *three* items: a plant, a worm, an east wind (4:6, 7, 8).

g) In the final chapter Jonah and God "dialogue" *three* times:

      Jonah 4:2–3   God 4:4
      Jonah 4:8   God 4:9
      Jonah 4:9   God 4:10–11

h) Dry land (*yabasha*) is mentioned *three* times (1:9, 13; 2:10 [2:11 H]).

i) Nineveh is mentioned *nine* (3 × 3) times: 1:2; 3:2, 3, 3, 4, 5, 6, 7; 4:11.

j) In Nineveh, depending on one's interpretation, there are *three* or *four* designations: small, great, king (and nobles): 3:5, 6 and 7. There are also four designations: man, beast, flock, herd: 3:7.

k) The "ship" (*onia*) is mentioned *three* times (1:3, 4, 5) and a synonym for ship, "vessel" (*s'finah*), appears once (1:5), for a group total of *four*.

l) In Hebrew, the word "sea" is mentioned *twelve* times (3 × 4): 1:4, 4, 5, 9, 11, 11, 12, 12, 13, 5, 15; 2:3 [2:4 H]. (N.B. In *TANAKH yam* is twice translated as "overboard" and in 2:4 it is in a plural form, *yamim*.)

m) There are *120,000* inhabitants in Nineveh (3 × 4 × 10,000) (4:11).

n) Jonah's *three* narrative chapters, plus the psalm chapter, is *four*.

o) In the Hebrew text, Jonah is mentioned *eighteen* times (3 × 3 +
    3 × 3): 1:1, 3, 5, 7, 15; 1:17, 17 [2:1, 1 H]; 2:1 [2:2 H]; 10 [2:11 H]; 3:1, 3, 4;
    4:1, 5, 6, 6, 8, 9.
p) In Jonah there are *forty-eight* verses (3 × 4 × 4).
q) The city will be overthrown in forty days (4 × 10).

Is there some hidden symbolism between the "threes" and the "fours,"
is there some religious reason or mystic message? I think not. Rather I
would venture that the author or editor of Jonah simply delighted in pre-
senting this book with a very tight internal structure which allowed him
or her to utilize this as part of the book's literary form. In addition, the
combination of threes and fours may have helped this story to be learned
and memorized. Further, combinations of threes and fours are part of
the prophetic tradition as found in the opening chapters of Amos.

CONCLUSION

The prophets of old were men and women who were filled with God's spirit. They ranged from sophisticated city-dwellers, such as Isaiah and Jeremiah, to people from the countryside such as Amos. They spoke as individuals, but they prophesied "the word of the Lord."

We have the records of many of them, but not all. As discussed in the chapter "What Is a Prophet?" it is difficult to know if we have their direct words or if their prophecies were edited. Though the vast majority of the prophets in the Bible were men, reference is also made to women prophets or to women prophesying (Is 8:3; Ez 13:17; Neh 6:14); most notable among these is the prophet Hulda (2 Kgs 22:14; 2 Chr 34:22) whose prophecy to the king of Judah is recorded but we have scant information of her person.

The prophetic life was often lonely. Prophecy was not a popular activity. The prophets spoke because they could not keep silent. "My heart is beating wildly; I cannot keep silent..." explains Jeremiah (Jer 4:19). "The Lord God has spoken; who can but prophesy?" says Amos (Am 3:8). Yet to speak was to endanger oneself. As Abraham Joshua Heschel wrote, "the prophet was not a *primus inter pares*, first among his peers. By his very claim, his was the voice of supreme authority. He not only rivaled the decisions of the king and the counsel of the priest, he defied and even condemned their words and deeds" (Heschel, 2.260).

Not all prophets brought words of condemnation. Second Isaiah's words are filled with prophecies of comfort and of hope. Likewise, sections of Ezekiel and even Jeremiah suggest that a better time will come.

How do we respond to the words of the prophet in our own day? As has been mentioned in the book, the prophets spoke to their time and place, but their ideas, their insights, their wisdom touch us and can guide us. The human condition remains the same. We are in need of the word, and we need to know that God is with us. Through the prophetic word spoken of old, we can come closer to God, and walk with God. As Micah explained so eloquently, has God not told us "what is good; and what the Lord requires of you but to do justice, and to love kindness, and to walk humbly with your God?" (Mic 6:8).

This book was written to introduce the reader to the prophets. We have considered the historical context in which they lived, their prophecies and literary styles, as well as how their words were interpreted in both the Christian Scriptures and in the writings of the early rabbis, the florescence of the midrashic literature. The examples taken from the midrashic sources are available in English editions. Numerous references provide opportunities for further study.

In addition to introducing the prophets in a general sense, there is another goal. This book addresses a need for both Jews and non-Jews to study the prophets and how these sacred texts were understood in the early centuries of the Common Era. Judaism and Christianity have a great deal to learn from and to teach one another.

Prior to teaching full-time at a university, I served as a congregational rabbi for twenty-one years, both in England and in America. In that time I have grown in my own understanding of and appreciation for Christianity. I am the executive director of a firm called Bridges for Understanding which promotes lectures, seminars and discussions in the interfaith arena. I have been influenced by the writings and thinking of Rabbi Leon Klenicki, the International Director of the Department of Interfaith Affairs of the Anti-Defamation League in New York.

Klenicki has written the following which bears directly on this issue: "Understanding the other is not easy for Jews and Christians because we must surmount two thousand years of prejudice and memory. ... For Christians that involves overcoming triumphalism, recognizing theological and social prejudices that have been and are still present in Christian thinking and actions.... We Jews must surmount two thousand years of memories that haunt us with images of the past, many of them referred to as legends by our parents, the memory of memories.... We [Jews] must overcome also the temptation of self-righteousness! Both Jews and Christians must rid themselves of triumphalism" ("Toward a Process of Healing" in Leon Klenicki, ed., *Toward a Theological Encounter*, 4).

Jews can benefit from the Christian experience, just as Christians can benefit from the Jewish experience. It starts with small beginnings, but as we listen and learn, we start to appreciate that the other is not only a human being with similar experiences, but that though we clearly differ on a range of issues, by the same token there is much that we share simply because we are all children of God.

In my view, only good things can result from interfaith dialogue. Let us build bridges where we can, forming alliances and friendships in the process.

Sometimes the road to understanding between Christians and Jews can begin over a meal. Sitting and "breaking bread" together is more than just a social act, it is also a symbolic act which speaks out of both of our traditions. Likewise inviting the other into our home — and it may be our religious home, the synagogue or the church — helps to cement relationships. Both places are natural venues to study about the prophets.

Some people have doubts about dialogue because they think it leads to conversion. There is nothing to indicate that Jews — or Christians — leave their faith because of dialogue. If anything, it strengthens one's faith through greater knowledge and self-appreciation.

From a Jewish viewpoint, we need to recognize Christianity for what it has to offer. As Leon Klenicki has written, "We [Jews] are not alone in the universe, [not] solitary islands of belief but peninsulas linked to the Eternal and to one another; and there is much to learn in our respective covenantal experiences of God. . . . [We Jews] have to know and experience the Christian person as chosen by God, with a specific task and a different way" (Leon Klenicki, "In Dialogue," 32). The same is true in the other direction: Christianity needs to recognize Judaism for what it has to offer. There are many paths to know God, and even as we affirm our own, so can we affirm others, recognizing that each of us has a task, and there is much work to be done.

"Thus says the Lord" was the hallmark of the prophet. Yet the prophet is much more than the person who conveys God's message. As Heschel wrote, the "prophet is not a mouthpiece, but a person; not an instrument, but a partner, an associate of God" (1.25). Without doubt a central problem is the distance in time between our present and that of the prophets. As we study, as we learn, we draw those times closer together. We can become, in our own time, partners of God.

In closing, I am reminded of a saying in the Talmud which seems very appropriate. It is the observation of a set of rabbinic scholars who lived about eighteen hundred years ago in the land of Israel. They said: We are creatures of God, and our neighbors are creatures of God. We work in the city, and they work in the country. Each of us rises early to do our work. Just as our neighbors cannot excel in our work, so we cannot excel in theirs. Will you say that we do great things, and they do lesser things?

We have learned that it does not matter whether people do much or little as long as they direct their hearts to heaven (Babylonian Talmud *Berachot* 17a). Not all of us think alike, or act alike. We do have differing approaches and vocations. We do, however, share a great deal within the religious community. May we work and learn together, even as we direct our hearts to heaven.

GLOSSARY

BCE Before the Common Era; the same time frame as BC [Before Christ] but is an inclusive term.

CE Common Era; the same time frame as AD [Anno Domini — in the Year of our Lord] but is an inclusive term.

Christian Bible, Christian Scriptures Twenty-seven books of the "New Testament" formed of the four gospels (Matthew, Mark, Luke and John), the Acts of the Apostles, the epistles of Paul and Revelation (or the Apocalypse). The Christian Scriptures tell the story of Jesus and the early development of the Christian Church.

Derasha Sermon, connected to the term midrash.

Former, Pre-Literary, Pre-Classical Prophets [Nevi'im Rishonim] The books of Joshua, Judges, 1, 2 Samuel and 1, 2 Kings. The term also refers to the specific prophets mentioned in those books, including Samuel, Nathan, Ahijah, Elijah, Micaiah and Elisha. See Chapter 2, The Former Prophets.

Gospels The first four books of the Christian Scriptures. They tell the story of the life of Jesus. The first three, Matthew, Mark and Luke, are known as the synoptic gospels because they are largely a synopsis of each other.

Hebrew Scriptures The Hebrew Bible, TANAKH. The thirty-nine books of the Jewish Bible. In Christian Bibles the Hebrew Scriptures will often precede the Christian Scriptures. See Chapter 1, What Is a Prophet?

Hozeh Hebrew for "Seer" or "Gazer." See Chapter 1, What Is a Prophet?

Jewish Bible, Jewish Scriptures See Hebrew Scriptures.

Ketuvim Hebrew for "Writings." The third part of the Hebrew Scriptures. See TANAKH and Hebrew Scriptures.

Latter, Literary, Classical Prophets [Nevi'im Aharonim] The books of Isaiah, Jeremiah, Ezekiel, Hosea, Joel, Amos, Obadiah, Jonah, Micah, Nahum, Habakkuk, Zephaniah, Haggai, Zechariah and Malachi. See Chapter 3, The Latter Prophets.

Midrash, Midrashim Midrash (plural: Midrashim) is a kind of rabbinic literature, first delivered orally, then eventually written down and set into a collection. There are a number of different midrash collections. Midrash offers an exegesis (interpretation) of a Jewish biblical text. The earliest collections come from about the second century CE, but may well reflect earlier material.

Navi Hebrew for prophet. Most common word used in the Hebrew Bible for prophet. See Chapter 1, What Is a Prophet?

Nevi'im Rishonim Hebrew for early prophets. See Early, Pre-Literary, Pre-Classical Prophets.

Nevi'im Aharonim Hebrew for latter prophets. See Latter, Literary, Classical Prophets.

Nevi'im Hebrew for prophets (plural of Navi). Second part of the Hebrew Bible. See Chapter 1, What Is a Prophet?

New Testament See Christian Scriptures, Christian Bible.

Old Testament See Jewish Bible, Jewish Scriptures.

Ro'eh Hebrew for seer. See Chapter 1, What Is a Prophet?

TANAKH Hebrew acronym for Torah [Teaching], Nevi'im [Prophets], Ketuvim [Writings]. The three parts of the Hebrew Scriptures. See Chapter 1, What Is a Prophet?

Torah Hebrew for teaching (sometimes translated as law). First part of the Hebrew Bible: Genesis–Exodus–Leviticus–Numbers–Deuteronomy. See Chapter 1, What Is a Prophet?

BIBLIOGRAPHY

Aberbach, Moses. "Elijah." In *Encyclopedia Judaica [EJ]*. New York: Macmillan; Jerusalem: Keter, 1972.

Ackroyd, Peter. "Obadiah, Book of." In *Anchor Bible Dictionary*. David Noel Freedman, ed. New York: Doubleday, 1992.

Allen, Leslie C. *The Books of Joel, Obadiah, Jonah and Micah*. Grand Rapids: William B. Eerdmans; London: Hodder and Stoughton, 1976.

Anderson, Francis I. and David Noel Freedman. *Hosea: A New Translation*, Anchor Bible. Garden City: Doubleday, 1980.

Angel, Marc. "Messiah: Jewish View." In Leon Klenicki and Geoffrey Wigoder, eds., *A Dictionary of the Jewish–Christian Dialogue*. A Stimulus Book. New York and Ramsey: Paulist, 1984.

Avot de Rabbi Natan. Published as *The Fathers According to Rabbi Nathan*. Translated by Judah Goldin. New York: Schocken, 1974.

Ball, Ivan Jay. "Zephaniah." In *Encyclopedia Judaica [EJ]*. New York: Macmillan; Jerusalem: Keter, 1972.

Bowman, John Wick. "Eschatology of the NT." In *Interpreter's Dictionary of the Bible [IDB]*. Nashville: Abingdon, 1962.

Bloch, Abraham P. *The Biblical and Historical Background of Jewish Customs and Ceremonies*. New York: Ktav, 1980.

Bright, John. *A History of Israel*, Third Edition. Philadelphia: Westminster, 1981.

———. *Jeremiah*, Anchor Bible. Garden City: Doubleday, 1965.

Brown, Francis, S. R. Driver, and Charles E. Briggs. *A Hebrew and English Lexicon of the Old Testament*. Oxford: Oxford Univ. Press, 1962.

Brunner, E. *Revelation and Reason*. Translated by Olive Wyon. London, 1947. Quoted in Kaiser, *Isaiah 1–12: A Commentary*.

Buss, M. J. "Prophecy in Ancient Israel." In *Interpreter's Dictionary of the Bible, Supplementary Volume [IDBS]*. Nashville: Abingdon, 1976.

Carley, Keith W. *The Book of Ezekiel, Cambridge Bible Commentary on the NEB*. Cambridge: Cambridge Univ. Press, 1970.

Cashdan, Eli. *Zechariah*. In *The Twelve Prophets*. London: Soncino, 1948.

Cazelles, Henri. "Micah." In *Encyclopedia Judaica [EJ]*. New York: Macmillan; Jerusalem: Keter, 1972.

Childs, Brevard S. *Introduction to the Old Testament as Scripture*. Philadelphia: Fortress, 1979.

Cleland, James T. "Zechariah." In *Interpreter's Bible [IB]*. New York and Nashville: Abingdon, 1956.

Cohen, A. *Everyman's Talmud*. London: Dent; New York: Dutton, 1949.

Cohen, M. A. "Ahijah the Prophet." In *Interpreter's Dictionary of the Bible, Supplementary Volume [IDBS]*. Nashville: Abingdon, 1976.

Cohn, Gabriel H. "Jonah." In *Encyclopedia Judaica [EJ]*. New York: Macmillan; Jerusalem: Keter, 1972.

Dahlberg, Bruce T. "Sheshbazzar"; "Zerubabbel." In *Interpreter's Dictionary of the Bible [IDB]*. Nashville: Abingdon, 1962.

Dentan, Robert "Malachi"; "Zechariah, Book of." In *Interpreter's Bible [IB]*. New York and Nashville: Abingdon, 1956.

Driver, S. R. *The Books of Joel and Amos*, Second Edition. Cambridge: Cambridge Univ. Press, 1915.

Dubnov, Simon. *History of the Jews*, Vol. 1. Translated by Moshe Spiegel. South Brunswick, London: Yoseloff, 1967.

Falk, Harvey. *Jesus the Pharisee*. New York, Mahwah: Paulist, 1985.

Forster, Brenda. "The Biblical 'Omen and Evidence for the Nurturance of Children by Hebrew Males." In *Judaism*, Volume 42, Number 3, Summer 1993.

Gaster, Theodor H. *Myth, Legend, and Custom in the Old Testament*, 2 vols. Gloucester: Peter Smith, 1981.

Ginsberg, Harold Louis. "Hosea." In *Encyclopedia Judaica [EJ]*. New York: Macmillan; Jerusalem: Keter, 1972.

Ginzberg, Louis. *The Legends of the Jews*, 7 vols. Philadelphia: Jewish Publication Society, 1967.

Graetz, Heinrich. *The History of the Jews*. Philadelphia: Jewish Publication Society, 1891.

Greenberg, Moshe. "Ezekiel." In *Encyclopedia Judaica [EJ]*. New York: Macmillan; Jerusalem: Keter, 1972.

Grintz, Yehoshua M. "Zechariah." In *Encyclopedia Judaica [EJ]*. New York: Macmillan; Jerusalem: Keter, 1972.

Haran, Menahem. "Amos." In *Encyclopedia Judaica [EJ]*. New York: Macmillan; Jerusalem: Keter, 1972.

Heaton, E. W. *The Old Testament Prophets*. Atlanta: Knox, 1977.

Heinemann, Joseph. "The Nature of the Aggadah." In Geoffrey H. Hartman and Sanford Budick, eds., *Midrash and Literature*. New Haven and London: Yale Univ. Press, 1986.

Herbert, A. S. *The Book of the Prophet Isaiah 1-39*. Cambridge: Cambridge Univ. Press, 1973.

Heschel, Abraham Joshua. *The Prophets*, 2 vols. New York: Harper Colophon, 1975.

Hiebert, Theodore. "Joel, Book of." In *Anchor Bible Dictionary*, David Noel Freedman, ed. New York: Doubleday, 1992.

Holy Bible, The. New International Version (NIV). East Brunswick: International Bible Society, 1978.

Howie, Carl G. "Ezekiel." In *Interpreter's Dictionary of the Bible [IDB]*. Nashville: Abingdon, 1962.

Hudson, Winthrop S. *Religion in America*, Fourth Edition. New York: Macmillan; London: Collier Macmillan, 1987.

Huffmon, H. B. "Prophecy in the Ancient Near East." In *Interpreter's Dictionary of the Bible, Supplementary Volume [IDBS]*. Nashville: Abingdon, 1976.

Jacobs, Louis. *A Jewish Theology*. London: Darton, Longman & Todd, 1973.

Jenni, Ernst. "Day of the Lord." In *Interpreter's Dictionary of the Bible [IDB]*. Nashville: Abingdon, 1962.

Jerusalem Bible, The. Alexander Jones, General Editor. Garden City: Doubleday, 1966.

Josephus, Flavius. *The Antiquities*. In *The Complete Works of Josephus*. Translated by William Whiston. Boston: Walker, 1823.

Kaiser, Otto. *Isaiah 1-12: A Commentary*. Translated by R. A. Wilson. Philadelphia: Westminster, 1976.

Kapelrud, Arvid S. *The Message of the Prophet Zephaniah*. Oslo: Universitetsforlaget, 1975.

Klausner, Joseph. *The Messianic Idea in Israel*. New York: Macmillan, 1955.

Klenicki, Leon. "In Dialogue" No. 1. New York: ADL, 1993.

———. "Toward a Process of Healing." In Leon Klenicki, ed., *Toward a Theological Encounter*. A Stimulus Book. New York and Mahwah: Paulist, 1991.

Klenicki, Leon and Geoffrey Wigoder, eds. *A Dictionary of the Jewish-Christian Dialogue*. A Stimulus Book. New York and Ramsey: Paulist, 1984.

Kuntz, J. Kenneth. *The People of Ancient Israel*. New York: Harper and Row, 1974.

Lacocque, Andre. "Messiah: Christian View." In Leon Klenicki and Geoffrey Wigoder, eds. *A Dictionary of the Jewish-Christian Dialogue.* A Stimulus Book. New York and Ramsey: Paulist, 1984.

Leibowitz, Nehama. "Balak." In *Studies in Bamidbar ("Numbers"),* Revised Edition. Jerusalem: World Zionist Organization, 1982.

Leslie, Elmer A. "Nahum, Book of"; "Habakkuk." In *Interpreter's Dictionary of the Bible [IDB].* Nashville: Abingdon, 1962.

Lindblom, Johannes. *Prophecy in Ancient Israel.* Philadelphia: Muhlenberg [Fortress], 1962.

Lipinski, Edward. "Nahum"; "Malachi." In *Encyclopedia Judaica [EJ].* New York: Macmillan; Jerusalem: Keter, 1972.

Mays, James Luther. *Hosea: A Commentary.* Philadelphia: Westminster, 1969.

———. *Micah: A Commentary.* Philadelphia: Westminster, 1976.

McKenzie, John L. *Second Isaiah,* Anchor Bible. Garden City: Doubleday, 1968.

Magonet, Jonathan. *Form and Meaning.* Frankfurt/Bern: Lang, 1976.

———. "Jonah, Book of." In *Anchor Bible Dictionary.* David Noel Freedman, ed. New York: Doubleday, 1992.

Mekilta de Rabbi Ishmael. Translated by Jacob Z. Lauderbach. Philadelphia: Jewish Publications Society, 1976.

Metzger, Bruce M. *The New Testament,* Second Edition. Nashville: Abingdon, 1983.

Midrash, The [Midrash Rabbah]. New York: Soncino, 1977; London: Soncino, 1939. Genesis Rabbah, Exodus Rabbah, Leviticus Rabbah, Numbers Rabbah, Deuteronomy Rabbah, Ecclesiastes Rabbah, Song of Songs Rabbah, Ruth Rabbah.

Midrash on Proverbs, The. Translated by Burton L. Visotzky. New Haven and London: Yale Univ. Press, 1992.

Midrash on Psalms, The, 2 vols. Translated by William G. Braude. New Haven and London: Yale Univ. Press, 1959.

Midrash Tanhuma, Vol. 1 Genesis. S. Buber edition. Translated by John T. Townsend. Hoboken: Ktav, 1989.

Mishna, The, 6 vols. Philip Blackman, ed. New York: Judaica, 1965.

Montefiore, Claude G. and Herbert Loewe. *A Rabbinic Anthology.* Philadelphia: Jewish Publication Society, 1960.

Mowry, M. Lucetta. "Allegory"; "Parable." In *Interpreter's Dictionary of the Bible [IDB].* Nashville: Abingdon, 1962.

Muilenberg, J. "Jeremiah the Prophet." In *Interpreter's Dictionary of the Bible [IDB].* Nashville: Abingdon, 1962.

Napier, B.D. "Prophet, Prophetism." In *Interpreter's Dictionary of the Bible [IDB].* Nashville: Abingdon, 1962.

Neil, W. "Haggai"; "Joel, Book of "; "Jonah, Book of "; "Malachi"; "Zechari-
ah, Book of." In *Interpreter's Dictionary of the Bible* [*IDB*]. Nashville:
Abingdon, 1962.
New English Bible (*NEB*). Oxford and Cambridge: Oxford Univ. Press,
Cambridge Univ. Press, 1970.
New International Version (*NIV*). See *Holy Bible, The.*
New Oxford Annotated Bible with the Apocrypha (*NRSV*), Bruce M.
Metzger and Roland E. Murphy, eds. New York: Oxford Univ. Press,
1991.
New Revised Standard Version (*NRSV*). See *New Oxford Annotated
Bible with the Apocrypha.*
Newsome, James D. *The Hebrew Prophets.* Atlanta: Knox, 1984.
North, Christopher R. "Immanuel"; "Isaiah." In *Interpreter's Diction-
ary of the Bible* [*IDB*]. Nashville: Abingdon, 1962.
Noy, Dov. "Elijah [In Jewish Folklore]." In *Encyclopedia Judaica* [*EJ*].
New York: Macmillan; Jerusalem: Keter, 1972.
Paul, Shalom M. "Prophets and Prophecy." In *Encyclopedia Judaica* [*EJ*].
New York: Macmillan; Jerusalem: Keter, 1972.
Pesikta De Rab Kahana. R. Kahana's Compilation of Discourses for Shab-
bat and Festal Dates. Translated by William G. Braude and Israel J.
Kapstein. Philadelphia: Jewish Publication Society, 1975.
Pesikta Rabbati (Discourses for Feasts, Fasts and Special Sabbaths).
Translated by William G. Braude. New Haven and London: Yale Univ.
Press, 1968.
Pfeiffer, Robert H. *Introduction to the Old Testament.* New York: Harp-
er, 1948.
Pirke de Rabbi Eliezer. Translated by Gerald Friedlander. New York:
Sepher-Hermon, 1981.
Porton, Gary G. "Midrash: The Palestinian Jews and the Hebrew Bible
in the Greco-Roman Period." In Hildegard Temporini and Wolfgang
Haase, eds., *Aufstieg und Niedergang der romischen Welt* (Berlin
and New York, 1979), II 19.2, p. 104, quoted in Jacob Neusner, *The
Way of Torah: An Introduction to Judaism,* 5th edition. Belmont:
Wadsworth, 1992.
Pritchard, James B. ed. *Ancient Near Eastern Texts.* Princeton: Prince-
ton Univ. Press, 1958.
Ramsey, A. N. "The Authority of the Bible." In *Peake's Commentary on
the Bible.* London: Nelson, 1962.
Rist, Martin. "Apocalypticism." In *Interpreter's Dictionary of the Bible*
[*IDB*]. Nashville: Abingdon, 1962.
Rosenthal, Gilbert S. "Messianism Reconsidered." In *Judaism* Volume 40,
Number 4, Fall 1991.

Sanders, J. Alvin. "Enemy." In *Interpreter's Dictionary of the Bible* [*IDB*]. Nashville: Abingdon, 1962.

Sanders, J. N. "The Word." In *Interpreter's Dictionary of the Bible* [*IDB*]. Nashville: Abingdon, 1962.

Sandmel, Samuel. *The Enjoyment of Scripture*. New York and London: Oxford Univ. Press, 1972.

———. *The Hebrew Scriptures*. New York: Knopf, 1963.

———. *A Jewish Understanding of the New Testament*. Cincinnati: Hebrew Union College Press, 1957.

Scholem, Gershom. *The Messianic Idea in Judaism*. New York: Schocken, 1971.

Scott, R. B. Y. *The Relevance of the Prophets*, Revised Edition. New York: Macmillan, London: Collier-Macmillan, 1969.

Sifre: A Tannaitic Commentary to the Book of Deuteronomy. Translated by Reuven Hammer. New Haven and London: Yale Univ. Press, 1986.

Slotki, I. W. *Isaiah*. London: Soncino, 1949.

Smart, James D. "Amos." In *Interpreter's Dictionary of the Bible* [*IDB*]. Nashville: Abingdon, 1962.

———. "Jonah." In *Interpreter's Bible* [*IB*]. New York and Nashville: Abingdon, 1956.

Sperry, Willard. "Malachi." In *Interpreter's Bible* [*IB*]. New York and Nashville: Abingdon, 1956.

Sweeney, Martin A. "Habakkuk, Book of." In *Anchor Bible Dictionary*, David Noel Freedman, ed. New York: Doubleday, 1992.

Talmud, Babylonia (Babylonian Talmud, [*Talmud Bavli*]). London: Soncino, 1935. *Berachot, Shabbat, Pesachim, Yoma, Sukkah, Taanit, Megilla, Hagiga, Sotah, Sanhedrin, Makkot, Avodah Zarah, Zevachim*.

Talmud, Jerusalem (Jerusalem Talmud [*Talmud Yerushalmi*]). *The Talmud of the Land of Israel: A Preliminary Translation and Explanation, Vol. 31, Sanhedrin and Makkot*, translation by Jacob Neusner. Chicago and London: Univ. of Chicago Press, 1984.

TANAKH [Torah, Nevi'im, Keutvim] The Holy Scriptures. Philadelphia: Jewish Publications Society, 1985.

Tanna debe Eliyyahu. Translated by William G. Braude and Israel J. Kapstein. Philadelphia: Jewish Publications Society, 1981.

Taylor, Charles L. "Habakkuk." In *Interpreter's Bible* [*IB*]. New York and Nashville: Abingdon, 1956.

Thompson, Joel A. "Joel." In *Interpreter's Bible* [*IB*]. New York and Nashville: Abingdon, 1956.

Thurman, Howard. "Habakkuk." In *Interpreter's Bible* [*IB*]. New York and Nashville: Abingdon, 1956.

Van Sickle, C. E. *A Political and Cultural History of the Ancient World*,
    Vol. 1. Boston: Houghton Mifflin, 1948.
West, James King. *Introduction to the Old Testament*, Second Edition.
    New York: Macmillan, 1981.
Westermann, Claus. *Isaiah 40-66: A Commentary*. Translated by David
    M. G. Stalker. Philadelphia: Westminster, 1969.
Wilson, Marvin R. *Our Father Abraham: Jewish Roots of the Christian
    Faith*. Grand Rapids: William B. Eerdmans; Dayton: Center for
    Judaic-Christian Studies, 1989.
Winward, Stephen. *A Guide to the Prophets*. Richmond: Knox, 1969.
Wolff, Hans Walter. *Hosea: A Commentary on the Book of Hosea*. Trans-
    lated by Gary Stansell. Philadelphia: Fortress, 1974.
———. *Micah the Prophet*. Translated by Ralph D. Gehrke. Philadel-
    phia: Fortress, 1981.
Wright, G. E. "Sinai, Mount of." In *Interpreter's Dictionary of the Bible*
    [*IDB*]. Nashville: Abingdon, 1962.
Zucker, David J. "Jesus and Jeremiah in the Matthean Tradition." In *The
    Journal of Ecumenical Studies*, 27:2, Spring 1990, 288-305.